Men in the Nursery:
Gender and Caring Work

D1052874

Men in the Nursery: Gender and Caring Work

Claire Cameron, Peter Moss
and Charlie Owen

P·C·P

Paul Chapman
Publishing Ltd

Paul Chapman Publishing Ltd
A SAGE Publications Company
6 Bonhill Street
London EC2A 4PU

SAGE Publications Inc
2455 Teller Road
Thousand Oaks, California 91320

SAGE Publications India Pvt Ltd
32, M-Block Market
Greater Kailash - I
New Delhi 110 048

British Library Cataloguing in Publication data

A catalogue record for this book is available from the British Library

ISBN 1 85396 431 X
ISBN 1 85396 388 7 (pbk)

Library of Congress catalog card number available

Typeset by Dorwyn Ltd, Rowlands Castle, Hants
Printed and bound in Great Britain

Contents

Acknowledgements

The authors would like to thank the workers and parents who took part in the study and the managers of centres who permitted us to interview staff on the premises. Without them the study would not have been possible. We would also like to thank colleagues at Thomas Coram Research Unit and readers who included Peter Aggleton, Bronwen Cohen, Chrissie Meleady and staff, children and parents at Sheffield Children's Centre, Margy Whalley, and Robin Wright. They did not all agree with all of our views and conclusions, and as authors we take responsibility for the contents of the book, including any mistakes it may contain. The authors would also like to thank Susan McQuail who conducted interviews for the study, and Caroline Bell who helped in innumerable ways. This work was undertaken at Thomas Coram Research Unit which receives support from the Department of Health and the Department for Education and Employment. The views expressed in this book are those of the authors and not necessarily those of either Department.

Prologue

When we began the work on which this book is based our starting point was what happens when men are employed in nurseries and similar early childhood services, and the traditional gender composition of childcare work was altered. As the work proceeded, and in particular as we interviewed workers and parents – both men and women – it evolved to become a study of gender and caring work. If one of our main starting questions was 'why are there so few men in childcare work?', a main question by the end was 'why are there so many women in childcare work?'.

Specific childcare institutions have a critical role in the book. We argue that a central feature of virtually every childcare institution is that it is gendered: not just because the workforce is nearly always women, but because the way the work is thought about by parents, workers, government policies, colleges who train workers, managers and policy makers and, not least, wider society, assumes childcare to be 'women's work'. Within the broad equating of caring work of all sorts with women's work, childcare is particularly equated with, and considered akin to, one form of caring – mothering. Yet despite the gendered nature of childcare work, gender is regularly ignored, a taken-for-granted assumption, so self-evident it is rendered invisible. One of the important consequences of studying the experiences of men childcare workers, and comparing them with those of women, is that it makes visible the gendered nature of the work and opens up possibilities for exploring and questioning this phenomenon.

The study on which this book is based was undertaken in 1997 and 1998. It was part of a larger investigation entitled 'Men and Women Working in Day Care' and carried out by us at Thomas Coram Research Unit at the Institute of Education University of London. The work was initially funded by the Department of Health (1996–1998), and subsequently by the Department for Education and Employment (1998–1999) as responsibility for day care services was transferred from one Department to another. The larger study was concerned with describing and analysing the characteristics of staffing of day care services for young children as we detail in Chapter 2. Because of the funding arrangements, the study took place in England. In that respect it is an English study, although some of the data sources on which we rely refer to Britain (e.g., the

Labour Force Survey) or parts of the UK or Britain (e.g., studies in Scotland). In the book we will use the convention of referring to Britain, while bearing in mind that there may be local variations in circumstance.

Our interest in gender in these services for young children stemmed in part from earlier work by the European Commission Childcare Network. This expert working group provided support to the Commission's Equal Opportunities Unit between 1986 and 1996 on the broad subject of reconciling employment with the care and upbringing of children. The European Union has long recognised the importance of men assuming more responsibility for the care of children as one condition of achieving gender equality in employment, and the childcare network made the theme of men as carers one of its priorities. This theme covered both men as fathers and as workers in services for young children and the Network produced reports investigating the implications and possibilities of employing more men in childcare services (Ghedini *et al.*, undated; Jensen, 1996).

Through this earlier work, together with visits and an international seminar undertaken as part of the study, we noted the different approaches adopted to the issue of men's employment in childcare in Britain as compared with Scandinavia. In Denmark and Norway, for example, the idea and practice of men childcare workers is widely accepted, if still not yet widely implemented. In Britain, there is much more ambivalence and caution. One of our aims was to question and understand these national differences.

This book begins by giving voice to childcare workers, through presenting the stories of six men and women working in childcare centres of various kinds. It shows them to be a heterogenous group, with differing origins and routes into childcare and education work and differing ideas about the effect of having a more mixed gender workforce. This introduces a major theme of the book – diversity, not only between men and women, but among men and women. Their working lives and their gender identity in their work, as recounted in their stories, provide a way of relating the theoretical material which follows to the substance of 'real lives'.

In the remainder of Chapter 1 we set out the literature, ideas and debates that we have found particularly relevant to our exploration of gender in childcare institutions. We use the term 'gender' to mean a socially constructed, rather than a fixed, category, that is a source of individual identity and which is constructed and makes sense in relation to others and in relation to circumstance. Various debates about the ways in which gender is analysed across the study of work, organisations, and identity have proved helpful to the present study. But two have been particularly important to our analysis and are outlined at the end of Chapter 1: the relation between mothering, fathering, the self and work; and the purpose and ethos of childcare institutions.

Chapter 2 considers matters of mapping and sourcing. It gives a brief account of early childhood services and the early childhood workforce in Britain, making some comparisons with other European countries, in part to make visible the 'taken-for-granteds' in the British set up. It outlines the current policy context for early childhood services, and the statistics on men in caring work both in Britain in some countries overseas. Chapter 2 also provides an account of the research context and process. We detail the methods adopted in the study and the various data sources drawn upon. There is a brief introduction to the centres where we interviewed workers and from which our sample of parents was drawn, and the chapter ends by noting the evolutionary processual character of our analysis.

In Chapter 3 we begin to use the experiences of our informants to document how and why men and women become workers in childcare institutions. Their educational and work backgrounds reveal many different ways into childcare. The idea of childcare as a linear career is less apparent than a series of work moves structured by opportunity and circumstance. Men workers seemed to receive less support and more ambivalence from their families and friends for their choice of work than women workers did. The critical work of the institution in valuing its workforce not just for being there, but also as a body of skills that require extension and stimulation, emerged as a central theme.

The working environment for staff as a group of adults and in their practice with children is examined in Chapter 4. It considers the job conditions of childcare work, including a comparison of salaries with the national average. Both formal and informal ways of working and being together as 'men' and 'women' are examined. We discuss various exclusionary practices by staff, which potentially cast the man worker as in a position of being on the margins of institutional life – the man worker as Other (and here it is important to note that in the minority of childcare centres which employ men workers, there are almost invariably just one or two). Issues about whether the work with children is the same or different for men and women workers are considered along with issues of difference between girls and boys. Tensions between gender difference and individuality are explored. Finally, the issue of role models, one of the most frequent justifications offered for wanting more men childcare workers, is critically questioned.

Chapter 5 analyses the interaction of the institution with the outside world, through staff practice and relations with parents. It considers both the development of an ideology of parent involvement across early years services and how the men and women workers we spoke to went about establishing their relations with parents. We elicit differences in workers' relations with mothers and fathers, and question the common assumption that men workers will encourage more involvement by fathers.

The views of mothers and fathers themselves are discussed in Chapter 6, drawing on interviews we undertook as part of the study. Again, the national picture on parental views about early childhood services is reviewed before examining findings for the light they throw on parental support for, and reservations about, the practice of employing men workers. Differences between men, and between men in varying work contexts, recur as an important theme in the parents' accounts.

Issues of risk and protection are considered in Chapter 7. A link between men workers and potential sexual abuse of children in childcare institutions is often claimed: we set out to analyse the evidence. We situate the British and North American debate in relation to Scandinavia, contrasting the different approaches adopted in policy and practice. We provide workers' perspectives on issues of physical contact with children and give an account of how allegations against workers are interpreted and managed by childcare institutions. We argue that the issues of men's employment and the issues of protection from risk of sexual abuse are both important but should be uncoupled and viewed as distinct.

The book is drawn to a close in Chapter 8. We review the evidence we presented and revisit and explore further four central themes of the book: these are caring work as mothering work; incorporating the self and gender identities; gender visibility and reflexive institutions; and gender equality and resistance to men. Finally, we reconsider the case for changing the gender composition of the childcare workforce, and suggest steps that might be taken to effect such change. The links between making gender visible and the reflexivity of the institution's practice are reiterated and considered central.

Claire Cameron
Peter Moss
Charlie Owen
Thomas Coram Research Unit,
Institute of Education University of London

1

Childcare Work and Gender – An Introduction

Jeremy

Jeremy is white, 23, cohabiting and childless. He works in a private nursery in London and holds the NNEB. Previously, he worked as a nanny and as a nursery nurse in local authority nurseries. Jeremy feels caring is rewarding work. 'You go home and you've got a sense of achievement 'cos you've seen a child write their name for the first time or you've seen them draw their first recognisable picture of them or their mum or dad.' Jeremy got the idea of working in childcare from his brother, whom he helped at a Saturday drama club for children.

After being bullied in school, Jeremy left without any formal qualifications. The childcare course at school was not open to him: the choices of a steady stream of girls took precedence. Jeremy joined a YTS programme and did a GCSE in English and a City and Guilds course in Childcare. Through his mother, he got a part-time job nannying for twin baby boys, and, concurrently, completed an NNEB course. The only other male childcare student dropped out after the first year, and this forced Jeremy to talk to the women.

As a man working in all women staff groups, Jeremy gets two perpetual questions: 'How do you cope?' and 'Why do you do it?'. Because Jeremy has got so accustomed to working with women he sees it as the norm. He knows the women don't get asked the same questions and recognises that he is unusual and parents are inquisitive. While his mother supported his choice of employment, Jeremy's father and friends joked about him getting paid to sit around playing all day. Jeremy found this frustrating because 'it's not an easy job by any means'.

In the nursery, Jeremy tries to respond to children exactly as any other member of staff would. He sees little difference between his own skills and those of a comparably trained and experienced woman. One prospective employer was interested in Jeremy for his football skills. Jeremy thought this was 'ridiculous . . . any girl could kick a football around'. 'We're all positive role models', he says. Once, while working in a nursery, Jeremy challenged a request from a deputy manager to not cuddle the children. He was very angry

1

about this, as he saw physical comfort of children as an essential part of his job, and not something only appropriate for women. When the nursery changed the ruling to mean no one should cuddle the children, Jeremy turned down the offer of an extended contract.

Jeremy believes it is the individual that makes a difference to children, not necessarily their gender. He says 'I don't think it makes a difference (to have men employed), it is nice for the children to see males working in this sort of setting', especially those who have never come into contact with men and may be wary of them. He thought of requests to chat with children of lone mothers as an added dimension to his skills, rather than defining his work.

Jeremy's experience is of prejudice against employing men childcare workers. Schools 'don't even talk to you about childcare options'; telephoning employers for jobs, when they find out you're a man, they tell you the job has gone. 'I've had that so many times', Jeremy said. Despite his experience, Jeremy would like more men to enter childcare work. He is also ambitious. He wants to become a manager, he wants to gain some more qualifications, and he wants to earn a better salary.

Sam

Sam is 32, white and divorced. He has four children he sees regularly, and now has a long-term partner who has two children of her own. He has no formal qualifications in childcare. He did begin a degree but failed to finish. When we met him, he worked part-time in a voluntary sector family centre in a town north of London. One other man worked there, in a staff group of 16. The families attending the centre are mostly referred by other agencies for specific problems. Sam planned to reduce his hours and begin the Diploma in Social Work. Sam was a full-time father for some years while his wife went to college, and then worked full time. This fathering experience, and that of part-time youth work and part-time residential care work, qualified Sam for recruitment to the family centre.

Sam previously worked in roofing, bus driving and landscape gardening. He wanted to move away from this type of employment, as he found the attitudes of his (all male) colleagues to be very 'traditional'. 'I felt out on a limb some-times', he says. Paradoxically, when Sam began working in childcare, the attitudes he came across were also deeply traditional. He found that his new colleagues had rather particular, limited, ideas about men working with chil-dren, formed, he thinks, from their experience of their own families. They expected Sam to be incompetent, at least to start with. With time, the staff have grown to trust him and they now work well as a team.

Sam sees differences between men's and women's ways of working. Men, he thinks, are more prepared to discuss a problem and do something about it: women 'moan a lot. There's a lot of unproductive talk here.' Women, he says, provide a matriarchal model that children respond to and seem to be expect-ing. 'I can't breastfeed,' Sam says, 'and that puts me in a different position.'

Men, on the other hand, are less inhibited, more spontaneous and involved in their play with children.

Sam has found, however, that he is expected to represent 'men' as a category. This is difficult as Sam feels he is different from the image of 'men' the workers, children and parents are used to. Sam finds that if he wears brightly coloured clothes, for example, his 'manliness' is routinely challenged. Boys will say to him 'boys can't wear that'. Sam prefers to see himself as an example that questions the way men have to be: 'maybe I'm rejecting the old sort of stereotypes and role models and by default that means I'm something else.' Sam says he challenges views about men constantly, and slowly, as relationships with families build, they understand him as a different sort of man. There is another dimension to being a man and a role model in family centres. Sam sees a positive value in being 'a man' when children have been abused by, and are wary of, men. For him, being a man who does not hit or shout at children enables the child to begin to rebuild trust.

Tom

Tom is 41, white and a father of a 4 year-old child. He trained as a primary teacher in the early 1970s and works as a teacher-coordinator in a local authority combined centre in London. One other man also works at the centre, a nursery nurse. The centre offers a range of early education and care services for working parents and the children who attend come from a broad range of backgrounds.

Previously, Tom taught junior age children both here and overseas. He transferred to teaching nursery age children when he worked for a multicultural support service as a peripatetic teacher. Teaching nursery age children enabled him to develop his interest in the process of young children's learning rather than subject-based teaching. Now, Tom is a member of the senior management team as well as a teacher. Tom didn't consciously set out to become a teacher, although there were plenty of teachers in his family and they supported his choices. Some friends thought his choice of age group odd, and, when he says he works in a nursery, people assume he has something to do with horticulture.

Tom thinks that the issue of gender differences between men and women workers is lent complexity by his long duration as a teacher. He says he has grown used to working with women and doesn't necessarily think of his head or deputy as 'being women as such. I think of them as being my line managers.' Similarly, he says he has grown used to his own methods of working and is unsure whether his teaching and behaviour with children is typical of how men are. The teaching team plan the curriculum to avoid giving the children examples of gender stereotyped behaviour: he says 'the women wouldn't always do the cooking and . . . I'm quite reluctant to do the woodwork'.

But despite the planning, Tom is aware that there are subtleties in adult behaviour, and individual characteristics which shape men's and women's approaches to recurrent issues in the nursery. Tom gave the example of how men and women interpret the children's behaviour as fighting, or as rough and tumble play. The women workers tend to be less tolerant of this boisterous activity and to interpret it negatively.

One area of difference between men and women workers is the behaviour of each in their close physical contact with children. Whereas people are used to women having close physical contact with children, Tom says they are not used to men so doing. Men should not be excluded from working with children but they should be more cautious. He sees a difficulty here in that both men and women are employed on the basis of an equal opportunities policy so men and women cannot have differently specified working conditions, but men workers have a responsibility to be aware of the potential for misinterpretation of their behaviour with young children.

Tom believes that the paucity of men teachers in early years work can partly be explained by the fact that the salary structure is geared to large establishments, whereas nurseries tend to be (relatively) small scale. A second reason may be the strong female ethos of the work, which means, Tom says, that men entering the work need to be fairly confident, as 'they (the women staff) can give you really quite a hard time.' In Tom's view, the work he does is neither 'women's work' nor is it predicated on a model of mothering, but the way gendered adults interpret both their task and the behaviour of girls and boys means gender remains a pervasive issue in everyday teaching life.

Angela

Angela is 34, white, cohabits and has one baby daughter. She owns and runs two Montessori nursery schools in London. Among the total staff group in the two schools, she has two men workers. The schools cater for children whose parents pay fees. Angela opened the first school when she was 21 years old. She always knew she wanted to work with children and after she left school she went to work at a private nursery school as an 'apprentice'. After a year she went to London to complete Montessori training and to train in drama. She worked as an actor while preparing to open the first of her schools. After about eight years, she opened a bigger school nearby. At the time of interview she was on maternity leave, but still kept a managerial watching brief on both schools. She says the advantage of her unconventional route into teaching was that 'I've got quite a long way in a short space of time'. Her family were completely supportive of her choice: they could see her single minded devotion to the work.

Angela recruited men teachers through having students on placement in her schools who have stayed. She can see distinct advantages to having men working in the nursery. Men are more laid back. The children love having a man teacher; 'he is just different and they respond to him differently'. She considered whether there should be any differences in the work expectations of the men and the women when she first appointed a man: she decided that equality was important for the staff and the children to witness. Having a man teacher has taught Angela that there are differences between the ways boys and girls prefer to be. She says that on the whole, boys need to have a chance to run around and develop their physicality. Girls, on the other hand, have a need to work quietly and develop their fine motor skills. Boys, in fact, lose out in settings not employing men, as they then have no one to recognise and develop their potential.

Angela views the nursery school as like a family and sees parallels between families and the gender of the workforce. By this she means that children in families have men and women looking after them and the same should be the case in their care outside the home. But rather than men and women workers modelling nurturing parenting roles, Angela believes role models are about promoting values: they should be role models of 'nice, decent people . . . adults the children want to be with.'

Angela has had positive experiences of employing men workers. She thinks moving towards a more truly mixed-gender workforce in childcare will bring only benefits to children and to the workplaces themselves. The prospect of men competing with women for jobs previously held by women she sees as possibly 'a healthy thing'. At present, Angela thinks that two factors account for the few men in the childcare profession. First, the poor wages paid to childcare workers, and second, the stigma attached to work with young children, the stigma that questions why anyone would want to work with young children.

Corinne

Corinne is 37, black and a mother of one child. NNEB qualified, she works as a deputy manager at a local authority centre for children under 3 in London. The centre takes children from the local neighbourhood, and includes some on a priority admissions basis, and some with fee paying parents. The children thus come from a wide range of backgrounds.

Originally Corinne qualified in fashion design: she worked in the fashion industry for 12 years. She left because of the stress of the work and, while unemployed, helped her sister at a playgroup. Corinne's sister suggested that childcare might provide an alternative career. Her family was supportive but her friends were somewhat surprised to see her move from the world of fashion to 'getting down on the floor' with babies and young children.

Corinne's experience of men childcare workers is that they don't necessarily take women seriously. She has had problems gaining their respect. She is unsure whether this is because she is a woman, or a black woman. 'It's always a challenge and it's almost like a battle of wills.' As a deputy, Corinne has to work with managers, some of whom are men, both inside the nursery and at a local authority level, as well as with the staff group. With management the issues are slightly different, but still, she says, 'it's been difficult at both ends of working with men'. Some parents, fathers in particular, don't take women staff seriously. 'They refuse to talk to you (and) . . . there are times where they feel that they can intimidate you because you are a woman.'

Corinne has seen differences in the ways men and women work with children. Women find it easier, and come across as better, at the physical care and cuddling of young children. While women easily pick up and cuddle children, men don't get that close. Corinne also thinks that men treat boys and girls differently from each other. Men she says 'can mess about with the boys, but the girls, you can mess about but it's kind of a gentler manner and they're treated in a slightly different way. A woman will treat boys and girls exactly the same.'

Despite occasional difficulties in working with men and fathers, Corinne views mixed-gender working as very important. To not employ men gives children the wrong messages about what men and women do. It gives the message that only women look after children. But Corinne believes there is still a long way to go, as people still tend to see childcare work as women's work, and thus not attractive to men.

Corinne has hit a 'glass ceiling' in childcare, a profession that is supposed to be 'women's work'. As a deputy she can progress no further up the career ladder in her local authority as heads of centres must have a teaching qualification, something she does not have. The restructuring of the service to combine care with education has acted against the interests of women workers like Corinne, and in favour of men, who tend to be teacher trained. Working with men has not been easy for Corinne, but in the interests of children's understandings of gender equality, she believes it is important that men are employed.

Mandy

Mandy is white, 21 and cohabits. She is an NNEB trained nursery nurse in a local authority nursery in London. Previously she worked in a school. The nursery takes children on a priority admissions basis which in effect means they are mostly children defined as 'in need'. Mandy left her previous job because she wanted more responsibility and to earn a higher wage. She first found she enjoyed working with children while on a work placement from school.

Mandy's experience of working amongst a mixed-gender staff group is limited: both in the school and in the nursery, men are employed, but not directly with her. Consequently, she has watched the men workers only from afar. In a situation where only one man is employed, Mandy sees the sole man worker as somewhat distinctive, in comparison with the women. Within the staff room setting, the man worker is 'a bit on his own'. With the children the man represents something of a novelty, and he is also 'quite loud and fun'. In her experience, men's voices are much louder and deeper than women's, and this can make the children 'more fearful' of them. For Mandy, individual personality is a more important characteristic than gender. A woman member of staff could be similarly inclined to 'jump up and down and he'll have sort of a bit of fun and (the children) like that.'

Mandy believes there are so few men because they aren't encouraged. To succeed, men 'have to have a positive image of themselves . . . because there are always little comments from friends . . . you've got to be a very positive and strong person (to) take the criticism.' Moreover, Mandy is aware that mothers who come to the nursery are sometimes 'hypersensitive', 'because you hear all the horror stories of men working with children'. Mandy's model of nurseries is of them being 'substitutes for (the children's) own homes', where the practice of employing men is 'out-of-the-ordinary'. She would like to see a mixture of men and women staff, mainly to add diversity to staff dynamics: 'a room full of women, you know, it breaks it up a bit.'

Gender and Childcare: An Analysis of Workers' Reflections

The stories we have presented above provide a vivid introduction to some of the men and women whose views and reflections form the main data source for our analysis of gender in childcare work. These childcare workers are unusual, for they are an evenly balanced group of three men and three women. As we show later, it is rare indeed for men to work with preschool aged children in childcare centres. This study uses the reflections and views of workers, and parents, to make visible the largely invisible issue of gender in childcare institutions. This is not a study of the representations of gender in the curriculum, although that is a part of it; the gender we are uncovering stems from the gender composition of the staff, the historic understandings of what childcare institutions are for, and the way men and women staff, and mothers and fathers of children, understand 'what is going on' in the centres. As we document in Chapter 2, childcare services for preschool aged children are expanding rapidly in Britain, and current government initiatives suggest that this growth should continue, primarily to meet the needs of the workforce, but also to promote educational outcomes for children (DfEE, 1998). This study is a contribution to understanding the shape, structure and character of that expansion.

We use the term 'childcare' to refer to various group settings providing daytime (and non-residential) care for children under school age, such as day nurseries, combined centres, private nursery schools and family centres. Because the original remit for our work came from the Department of Health, we have included only those services referred to as 'day care services' under the Children Act 1989, and were therefore a Department of Health responsibility when the study began. This excludes services in maintained schools, such as nursery and reception classes, which were then a responsibility of the Department for Education and Employment. Thus although we subscribe to the view that 'care' and 'education' for young children are inseparable, and would prefer to use a generic title such as 'early childhood services' for all provision for children under compulsory school age, we have used the terms 'childcare services' and 'childcare work' to emphasise that our study was conducted in a particular set of services – and although many of our conclusions may hold good for nursery schools or classes, our evidence does not allow us to generalise to these school-based settings. Where we do use the terminology of 'early childhood', it means we are referring to all forms of centre-based provision, school-based or otherwise.

We also recognise that our work does not refer, or apply, to important forms of home-based provision, such as childminding or nannies. This is not to say that gender is unimportant or irrelevant for such provision. It means that we had to limit our work, and we decided to prioritise group settings.

Our central proposition is that gender is, perhaps unwittingly, embedded within the being of childcare institutions and childcare work. All caring work, paid or unpaid with children or adults, is widely understood to be, and is actually practised as, women's work, something that women 'naturally' do. Childcare work with young children is no exception. But, we would argue, childcare work is, and has been, modelled on a particular concept of care – 'mother-care'. If most forms of caring work are strongly gendered, 'mother-care' provides an additional dimension and intensity to the general association of caring with women's work. It has consequences not only for the gender composition of the childcare workforce (almost completely composed of women), but for the way that 'childcare' work with young children is conceptualised and practised.

Leading on from this, our central question concerns the unravelling of gendered understandings of childcare work within childcare centres. Why is the work so gendered, and what are the implications of this for children, workers and parents? We understand 'gendered' to operate at two levels, the individual and the institutional. At the individual level, workers bring to their work, through their gender identity, particular meanings about the roles, tasks and ways of being 'man' or 'woman' in the particular context of childcare work. At the institutional level, historical and pedagogical understandings of why childcare exists, how it is conducted and organised, and what is gender appropriate have evolved through practice and policy, and over time. Gender, in other words, contributes to the meaning and structure of childcare work, and the term 'gendered' here refers to the fact that gender is embedded in our understandings of the work, even though it may not be visible or obvious.

The invisibility of gender is apparent when one talks to childcare workers and parents of children attending childcare centres. Mothers in our study said: 'it doesn't matter whether it's a man or a woman who I talk to about my child, so long as they are competent'. Similarly, women workers said: 'we're all equal here, we all do the same jobs'. But when one talks to men workers, acutely felt differences in the expectation of their roles emerge, from both parents and the institution itself. Men workers refer to parents who avoid talking to them, to staff room conversations from which they are excluded, and to being 'encouraged' to undertake the practical jobs around the building. Men are not just sidelined within childcare work. They are also glorified. Descriptive terms such as 'he's fun', 'he's a novelty for the children', and 'men are so much more laid back than women' all convey an image of a benevolent visitor with few responsibilities; at the very least, caring and teaching work undertaken in a different style to that adopted by the women workers.

That different style is the essence of the 'gender' we are uncovering in this book. We adopt a social constructionist perspective to understanding gender (Lorber and Farrell, 1991). Gender is built into the social order and is a major social status with significant consequences for everyday life. Gender shapes the individual's opportunities and is intertwined with other social categories, such as 'race' and ethnicity. It structures the experiences of men and women in social institutions such as law, medicine, religion and politics (*ibid.*). Gender is also embedded in structures of power and authority in work and organisations, so that men tend to be concentrated in positions of power, and women not, even in occupations and organisations where there are more women employed than men (Crompton, 1997). One's gendered identity is largely constructed by a series of individual, practical accomplishments which are cast as particular expressions of masculine and feminine 'natures' (West and Zimmerman, 1991:14). For example, both mothering and caring work have come to be defined as feminine and women's labour in these occupations is said to be 'natural' for women.

Connell (1987) developed a theory of gender that integrated the generalities of the category and individual interpretation. The generalities of gender identity are the basis in sex differences of men and women, and the structuring of advantages such as wealth and income towards one gender, men, and away from the other. Individual interpretations of gender incorporate many other features of identity such as 'race', ethnicity, sexuality, (dis)ability, employment and so forth. Taking into account these diverse sources of gender identity, Connell introduces the terms *masculinities* and *femininities*. He further describes masculinities by explicitly incorporating dimensions of power and authority, and by referring to 'hegemonic masculinities' to describe dominant ideologies of masculinity. We take the view, then, that gender not only structures individual life chances and social institutions, it is also a phenomenon of difference between men and women that is conveyed within the structures of communication or discourses[1] of everyday life.

Gender is made visible through the language used, through the ways differences for men and women workers, and for boys and girls, are thought about, discussed and acted upon. The idea of multiple gender identities may be particularly useful in analysing the reflections and views of men and women childcare workers and those of mothers and fathers. The workers' stories revealed above illustrate diversity and heterogeneity. There is a range of different levels of further and higher education, of employment backgrounds, of sources of influence in workers' choices, in experiences of, and views about, childcare work. But it is also possible to identify commonalities. One consistent theme is the issue of whether and how childcare is 'women's work'. Workers not infrequently tend to believe people 'out there' think the work is women's work, and attribute this belief as responsible for the lack of men in the profession. The men don't say they think it is women's work, for they would be writing themselves out of the script if they did. The women workers, on the other hand, tend to see the men workers they know as examples of exceptions to the general rule that childcare is work for women.

This idea of a connection between childcare work and the gender of the worker is central, because the belief that it is women's work enables the perception that men's views about the work and caring for children are essentially 'out of place'. Men have to emulate women in their childcare work, or, alternatively, they have to mould a new way of being with young children. The similarities between childcare and mother-care have been repeatedly noted by others (Singer, 1993; Penn, 1997). Workers draw on notions of close contact and nurturing to define their childcare project (Penn, 1997). This model of 'motherhood' as an underpinning philosophy for childcare work presents workers who are men with a dilemma. They cannot look to models of fatherhood for an equivalent source of caring work, for fatherhood itself is seen to be contested and inconsistent (Williams, 1998; Collier, 1995). Nor do many men workers feel comfortable with emulating the woman-mother version of caring within childcare work. What is the contribution of ideas about masculinity/ies to men workers' conceptions of themselves? They know themselves to be different; the question is, how to be?

Literature, Ideas and Debates

We will start with some broader debates before moving on to consider the literature and some ideas to frame our analysis that we have found helpful. Within Britain at least, there are two main ways in which gender has been thought about within childcare work. First, it has been debated as an issue of equality between men and women, and between girls and boys. Within educational and care settings, the issue of gender equality has evolved from an avoidance of stereotyping in the curricula offered to children, to a recognition of the importance of meeting individual and diverse needs that arise from a range of circumstances, to the potential benefits of employing a mixed gender workforce. The benefits were seen as encouraging fathers to care for their children; enabling children to experience different, gendered, ways of caring; and, on a more global scale, as contributing towards the breaking down of gender segregation within workforces.

Equality

The capacity of children's institutions to encourage or discourage the perception of gender stereotypes was recognised within early education services in the 1970s (Arnot, 1987; Yates, 1997). The aim for early childhood services was to structure play and learning so that girls' and boys' opportunities did not favour particular sets of experiences, and so predispose them to particular sets of beliefs about men and women; the dominant concern at the time being girls' underachievement in schools (MacNaughton, 1998).

By 1991, when the Children Act 1989 was implemented, the accompanying Guidance recognised the issue of diversity, although it gave emphasis to race and ethnicity, rather than gender. It said 'People working with young children should value and respect the different racial origins, religions, cultures and languages in a multi-racial society so that each child is valued as an individual without racial or gender stereotyping' (DoH, 1991: 6.10). While falling short of explicitly recommending the employment of men, the Guidance promoted practice that 'enables children to develop positive attitudes' towards 'differences of gender' (*ibid.*). Specific support for the involvement of men in the lives of children came from the European Council Recommendation on Childcare in 1992, Article Six of which committed Member States to promote and encourage, with due respect for the freedom of the individual, increased participation in the care and upbringing of children, care which included fathercare and care in childcare services.

In 1996 the left-wing think tank, IPPR, published its proposals for public policy on Men and their Children. It argued that in a period of reassessment of the purpose and roles of fathers, men's role as carers for children should be given greater visibility than in the past. The increased employment of men as carers and teachers in childcare and education services was seen as one method of achieving this (Burgess and Ruxton, 1996: 28). Deliberate and visible encouragement of men's caring would, they argued, assist in the realisation of 'equal opportunities (for both men and women) to be both breadwinners and carers' (*ibid.*: 8).

In the search for gender equality, the category of 'men' is treated fairly uncritically: men are assumed to have more to offer children (and women) than the traditional roles of breadwinner and patriarch, but the issue is how to encourage structural changes to demonstrate men's nurturing potential. Changes to the employment practices of childcare services are seen as one part of the structural changes that could be made to further gender equality. Whether it is possible to view men in relation to children as a unitary category is doubtful, however. Williams (1998) points out that the debate over fatherhood is not just about emerging roles, but also about problems of father absence from their children, and problems of father distance from caring and nurturing behaviour.

Risk

The second main way that gender/men and childcare has been thought about is to conceive of a departure from the historical norm, or the widespread entry of men workers, as a threat, or, at the very least, a risk, to the wellbeing of children and women workers. The premise of this perception of threat is based on the fact, and the tradition, of women-as-mothers caring for children, both within families and within childcare workplaces. This mothering role guides childcare work such that the gender identity of the workers comes to be seen in an essentialist way, as 'naturally' women's work, whereas men childcare workers, being 'not women', are seen as 'unnatural'. From this premise, it is but a short step to see men in general as ill-equipped, or deficient for the task of caring for young children. Further, King (1994: 12) argues that there is a common perception of men who are employed in caring work as being homosexual and effeminate, and that these associations are 'negatively loaded'.

A further negative association with men childcare workers is that an un-quantifiable minority of men pose a threat to children's wellbeing because they have a perverse sexual orientation to children. Such men are often known as paedophiles. The threat to children, then, comes from the assumption that men in general, and paedophiliac men in particular, will mistreat or sexually abuse the children with whom they are working.

There is some evidence to suggest that men with paedophilia do seek out access to groups of children and that efforts to screen recruits to childcare work are inadequate to deal with the tactics employed by some men to gain access to children (Hunt, 1994; Barker et al., 1998). This evidence poses a doubly potent threat to men workers with children: how do we know in advance which men are likely to abuse children in childcare centres? Is it better to screen out men as a category?

This begs questions of the scale of abuse, the known gender of abusers, and the range of types of abuse. If the discussion is extended it is not clear that eliminating men will eliminate allegations of abuse as women also abuse children, although to a lesser extent (Finkelhor et al., 1988). The regulation of childcare centres in Britain was updated in the Children Act 1989. This legislation included enforcement provisions to ensure that the providers of substandard childcare could be prosecuted. Elfer and Beasley's (1997) evaluation of local authority enforcement activity under the Children Act found evidence that allegations of abuse were a frequently given reason for prosecution. However, many difficulties exist in the process of prosecution, too many to rely on court activity as a reliable measure of abuse within childcare centres (Elfer and Beasley, 1997). In addition, the general abuse of children through poor standards of care has been given media coverage (e.g., Public Eye, 1996; Heart of the Matter, 1994), but the issue of gender has not been raised in connection with these.

Men childcare workers are also seen as a threat to women workers in terms of their promotion prospects. Half of the respondents to a survey of English childcare college lecturers thought a disadvantage of men childcare workers was the prospect of their adversely affecting women's career opportunities (Cameron, 1997b). There is some evidence that this may be the case. A survey of the childcare workforce in independent nurseries (Local Government Management Board (LGMB), 1999) found that while there were very few men, twice as many of them were in senior positions than junior posts. The question remains as to whether this will continue. In contrast to the large-scale public bureaucracies of education, nursing and social work, nearly all childcare work takes place in the private and voluntary sector, on a small scale, with limited opportunities for promotion for women or men (Moss *et al.*, 1995). Childcare work has high turnover rates which may be to do with generally low wages (Whitebook *et al.*, 1998), or may be to do with the workforce being female and women's pattern of use of the labour market being different to that of men (Crompton, 1997; Whelan, 1993). How men's particular career paths mesh with the characteristics of the organisation of childcare work is an unknown at present but requires a critical eye.

Finally, Pringle (1995) argued that a combination of male domination of organisations where caring work is located (such as local authority social services departments and the NHS) through their occupation of key positions, and the evidence of men's violence in domestic and public spheres, poses a threat to women and to children in welfare services in general, within which he includes childcare. Drawing together the evidence from the US and from Britain of the prevalence of sexual abuse in domestic and institutional settings, Pringle argued that 'sexual abuse of children in welfare settings may be at worrying levels' (Pringle, 1995: 182). On the question of the risk to children specifically from men, Pringle argued that it is 'clear from all the relevant research that the large majority of men working in formal childcare settings will not sexually abuse the children in their care [but there are] indications that a significant minority of men in those settings may do so' (Pringle, 1998: 323).

These two main ways of thinking about gender in childcare, as an issue of equality, and as an issue of risk, can be conceptualised as discourses. These discourses have their origins in separate sets of ideas about relations between men, women and children, and between children and institutions, but the articulation of the discourses can run in tandem and overlap. Although the discourses have distinctive origins, and map our understanding of divergent views about men and children occupying the same work space, there are limitations in pursuing the idea of competing discourses as a framework for the present study. To do so may ultimately be to polarise views about men and women working in childcare. This is not the object of our study. The issue, as noted above, is to examine what happens to childcare when the traditional gender balance of the workforce is altered, when the men are let in. In doing so we draw on these discourses, in particular we draw on the hegemonic or dominant ideologies[2] which frame these discourses, to provide a more pro-ductive account of gender and childcare.

Having introduced the two main debates about men and childcare in Britain, we will now review the limited literature addressing men workers in childcare centres. The incidence of men workers is rare and this imposes constraints on the possibilities for research. As we show in Chapter 2, men make up a small proportion of the childcare workforce in Britain, as well as elsewhere such as the USA, and even in Scandinavia, where a rather different, and potentially more positive approach to childcare staffing has led to an active recruitment campaign. The research available therefore tends to be small scale studies of men (and sometimes women) working in institutions or surveys of students (and sometimes tutors). In Britain, there has also been a steady trickle of articles in practitioner journals (e.g., Wallace, 1995, Rawstrone, 1998). Bearing in mind the limitations of available studies, what do they tell us?

About the Workforce

Men childcare workers are a more transient, and a more personally ambitious, workforce than women workers. Clyde's (1994) survey of Australian childcare students clearly showed that men were seen as more transitory workers in the field. Skelton's (1991) study of British men primary school teachers and students showed that men teaching students internalised an awareness that career ambition was expected of them by colleagues. Seifert's (1984) study of Canadian men and women early childhood teachers argued that although men and women have similar reasons for working in the field (a liking of children), men workers had more complex career goals than women, and had constructed clear future plans leading from their work and out of the classroom. The men tended to be 'enticed to work elsewhere' by informal 'advice' from friends or relatives who did not criticise but rather stressed the attractiveness of other employment (Seifert, 1984: 4). Williams' (1992) study of US men in nontraditional occupations, including elementary teaching, argued that a complex process of career 'tracking' takes place that channels men into particular specialities and positions seen as 'masculine', and these tend to coincide with their own ambitions, and, in addition, rewards them with 'better paying and more prestigious' jobs (Williams, 1992: 257).

Men workers tend to be welcomed and praised for their choice of employment in childcare. In Murray's (1996) study of men and women childcare workers in California, the men received an 'inordinate amount of positive feedback in comparison to women workers': their presence was 'highly valued' by women workers (1996: 376). In Penn and McQuail's (1996) study of women and men childcare students in London, the authors noted myriad ways in which men students were encouraged and nurtured by tutors and women students alike. For example, positive statements of welcome were constantly reinforced by tutors' praising comments such as 'I always tell them it's great to have them'. One tutor claimed the men were 'spoiled and privileged – they get looked after by the women (students)'. Women workers' welcome of men workers was also noted by Jensen (1996) in her report of an evaluation of a Swedish 'equal rights' childcare centre that employed a workforce composed of half men and half women. She said 'everybody is positive towards the male pedagogues (workers)', including the women pedagogues (Jensen, 1996: 9).

In sum, men in the childcare workforce stand out from women workers not for their motivation to do their work, but for their importation of characteristics of 'maleness' into the field of 'women's work'. Further, their very differences from women are encouraged. Penn (1998) concurs with Williams (1995) when she argued that men childcare workers, along with men in other nontraditional occupations, bring their masculinity/ies with them into their work.

What Men Can Do in Childcare

The point of employing men childcare workers can be to 'contradict sex-role conventions . . . his special contribution is not acting like a man but in disproving the idea that men need act in some special "manly" way' (Seifert, 1974: 71). But doing this may be difficult. Seifert argued that staff relations may be a cause of difficulty as women staff 'may experience discomfort reconciling a "man" and "feminine work"' (*ibid.*). The women staff may doubt his competence; he may have to be extra capable and extra interested in children (*ibid.*). One way of dealing with the 'status inconsistency' of a man childcare worker is to see him as an exceptional representative of his gender, in which case stereotypes of 'men' in general can be conserved. This may have consequences for how a man worker sees his role: if he accepts he is exceptional, Seifert argued he rescinds the opportunity to challenge sex-role stereotypes; if he does not, he may construct himself as incompetent with children, in line with the stereotype (Seifert, 1974: 72).

Smedley (1997) argued that British men primary school student teachers' version of caring is different from that of women. Whereas women teachers could rely on notions of caring derived from mothering, the men teachers did not see this as relevant for them. They saw themselves as less nurturing, and less able to be physically nurturing, due to societal suspicion about men and caring. The question of 'how should we be?' for men workers was very evident among this group. Norwegian kindergarten teachers Nilsen and Manum (1998) argued that the recruitment of men workers can help open up new ways of working with children that value exploration and 'the outdoors' more highly than in the past. These new ways of working do not exclude women, but adults who work with children should be able to balance being closely connected to 'childlike ways' and at the same time being clearly adult. They should offer 'co-experience in being creative with children' (Nilsen and Manum, 1998: 110). The authors claimed this co-experience offered a model of caring that would demonstrate the opposite of prevalent societal violence and 'destructive attitudes'. Nilsen and Manum argued that men caring for children should lead to more caring fathers in the next generation.

Men childcare workers are frequently referred to as 'role models' for children in the literature. Different interpretations of role modelling are noted. One interpretation is that male teachers will more effectively help boys understand their sex-role, and promote educational achievements, than female teachers. Gold and Reis's (1982) review of this literature suggested that although the arguments about male teacher role modelling made intuitive sense, research evidence with preschool age children provided only slight support for such measures as 'masculine sex identification', spatial aptitude and mathemathics, and attitudes and behaviour in school. Gold and Reis concluded that 'it is noteworthy that each study reported more failures to find results than significant outcomes' (Gold and Reis, 1982: 502).

A more recent interpretation of role models is that men could model new ways of being 'men'. Clyde (1989: 97) has argued that the idea that men preschool workers could model being nurturing, loving and understanding, in other words, like many women, became popular in the 1980s. Ruxton's study of men working in family centres in Britain found that 'the vast majority of staff recognised the importance of positive male role models which help to challenge stereotypical views of men as "breadwinners" alone, and to "validate" their roles as carers' (Ruxton, 1992: 25). Hill (1990) noted that a male childcare worker provided an opportunity 'of a role model who is male yet uninhibited in his caring, loving and gentle attitude' (Hill, 1990: 37).

On a more general level, Nilsen and Manum (1998) argued that 'children need role models: they need adults who act and behave in a certain way, so the child says, "That's how I'm going to be when I grow up!"' (Nilsen and Manum, 1998: 112). In addition, Murray's (1996) study of men childcare workers in the US noted that men were recruited 'because of the perceived need to have male role models for children' (Murray, 1996: 374). Finally, Christianson (1994) reported on a project to increase the number of men teachers on a US Headstart programme based on the premise that male role models were an added benefit for children.

Men workers are valued not just for being male, but also for their contribution towards the project of childcare. Jensen (1996) reported on the development of a gender pedagogy' in Denmark. This is based on the idea that childcare institutions play a role in developing a more equal society but that in order to do so it is not enough merely to offer 'the same' to both girls and boys. Rather, it is necessary to value differences between girls and boys and to provide a curriculum and sets of relationships that meet these differing needs. A mixed gender staff group, argued Jensen, is better equipped to do this, because of its inherent diversity. It is not a matter of men just offering being male, but of recognising boys' and girls' ways of doing things and how workers can offer imaginative environments to meet the children's methods. Children, she said, 'do not do what we say they should do, but they do what they see we do' (Jensen, 1996: 21).

The Relationship between Childcare Centres and their Communities

The impact of societal ideas about men as childcare workers, both in promoting gender equality and as a threat to children's safety, can be seen in the literature. Hill (1990) noted that parents of children attending a childcare centre employing a man believed that the 'children will learn to appreciate that men can be warm, caring and sensitive' and will learn to have increased expectations of men (Hill, 1990: 37). Jensen (1996) argued that the presence of men childcare workers, and their use of 'man's talk' can be 'influential in getting fathers more involved in the centre and in the daily life of the child' (Jensen, 1996: 27). Similarly, Ghedini et al. (undated) reported on a project to illustrate how centre-based childcare services can support and encourage increased participation by fathers in the care and upbringing of children. The employment of men workers, along with other strategies, was seen to encourage fathers' involvement in services their children attended. In addition, by mothers and fathers examining parental roles and expectations, it was demonstrated how services can play a role in enabling a more equal sharing of family responsibilities.

However, the community does not only encourage men workers. It can also be suspicious of them. Christianson (1994) reported that a US Headstart programme tried to employ men early childhood teachers, but found that the community did not support the concept of men working with young children, principally because there was a widespread fear that cases of child abuse would emerge through their employment. Murray (1996) reported that some US childcare centres feared parents' possible perceptions of employing men, so they adopted working practices and unwritten policies designed to protect men from the likelihood of parental accusations. For example, men were excluded from some activities. Specifically, men were 'more restricted in their freedom to touch, cuddle, nap, and change diapers for children' (Murray, 1996: 378). Some parents were reported as not enrolling children in centres they had visited because they saw that men were employed.

Suspicion of men workers has also been recorded in British studies. For example, in Ruxton's (1992) study, men workers were perceived to be virtually synonymous with men abusers. This was partly because many of those attending family centres had in the past been, or were currently, subjected to male violence, and partly because there was a widespread concern about the issue of physical contact with children stemming from a climate of fear about child abuse (Ruxton, 1992: 29). Smedley (1997) and Skelton (1991) also noted a suspicion of men nursery and primary school student teachers that translated into exercising caution in their physical contact with children.

Lastly, the issue of self-monitoring practice is also noted by King (1994) in relation to sexuality. He argued that 'a public perception is that men who teach primary grades are often either homosexuals, paedophiles, or principals (in training)' (1994: 4). In this study gay teachers monitored their own practice, particularly their physical contact with children, in order to avoid allegations about their sexuality. The relationship between childcare centres and their communities over the issue of men workers is thus riven with tensions, particularly in Britain and in the USA. The contradictions are plain: on the one hand, valuing and encouraging men workers so as to improve gender equality, and on the other suspecting their involvement in something damaging to children. The literature, it would appear, has not yet resolved the question we posed for men childcare workers: how to be?

These studies do, however, provide useful descriptive accounts of the different ways men (and, to some extent, women) interpret their employment in childcare, and the ways men's employment in childcare in particular is interpreted by others in the community in various national contexts. Our analysis evolved from these studies. In particular, we noted the different meanings men appeared to make of the notion of 'career' and the tensions that arise for men, women and the community when men disrupt the established order by both 'being there' and by attempting to import their masculinity or their identity as men into their work. This twin focus on childcare as a job in a segregated labour market and the meanings attached to the work, and how this then related to the implications for the work of the institution came to characterise our analysis. In what follows, we outline the perspectives we have adopted on gender, work and identity, and on childcare work in particular, to begin an explanation of gender within childcare work.

Gender Segregation and the Labour Market

In Britain, as with other Western societies, there has been a longstanding division of jobs into 'women's work' and 'men's work'; reflecting pay, status and conditions of employment. In parallel, there has existed an ideology of 'separate spheres', so women were not just poorly rewarded in the labour market, but ascribed a particular role in domestic work, in the main, child rearing (Crompton, 1997). Today, only a small proportion of jobs reported in the Labour Force Survey (LFS) are mixed gender (only 12 per cent have a balance of between 40 and 60 per cent men and women), so gender segregation is still a significant feature of the labour market (Cameron and Moss, 1998). Gender segregation operates both horizontally and vertically: not only are women and men largely to be found in different jobs, but their relative occupation of positions of seniority within an occupation is distributed on gendered lines, so that men are more likely to be in positions of power and authority. Although the fact of occupational gender segregation appears to be enduring, even where social policies emphasise matters of equality between the sexes (e.g., Sweden), individual occupations can change their gender identity over time. For example, in North America, teaching as an occupation has shifted gender from largely male to mainly female over the course of the 20th century (Williams, 1995).

Three other gendered features of employment stand out. First, more women than men work part time, with often adverse consequences for their rates of pay and conditions of employment. Second, women have developed a pattern of employment around childrearing responsibilities, so that they spend periods of time out of the labour market altogether, with adverse consequences for earning power and access to positions of seniority, whereas men's employment is traditionally seen as continuing over a lifetime. Third, married women with young children have been entering the labour market at a faster rate than any other group over the last decade, with implications for the demand for childcare facilities. In sum, men's employment is often seen as 'standard work' characterised as full time, providing a 'family wage', as lifetime in duration, with progressively higher wages and greater responsibility. Women's employment, on the other hand tends to be 'non-standard' with peaks of participation before and after child rearing (Crompton, 1997).

The question at the heart of explanations for the continuing gender division of market (and domestic) labour is, are women constrained to these occupations and this position in the labour market, more than they choose to occupy these positions? Or, in other words, what is the relative contribution of structure and agency to explaining women's position? Those who argue that structure is largely responsible point to the processes of capitalism and patriarchy which have operated to create value for waged work and then ascribed different values to men's work and women's work. For example, Hartmann (1982) argued that the traditional domestic divisions of labour were transferred to the waged economy to ensure that men did men's jobs and women did women's jobs such as light industrial work, caring work and low level office work – roughly following the gendered divisions of labour in the home, and in the process women's economic independence was curtailed. On the other hand, there are those who argue that individual preferences explain gender segregation (e.g., Hakim, 1996). Different levels of work commitment and different types of women are thought to explain women's differential participation in the labour market, and factors which structure women's access to employment and earning power are less important than their individual choices. Women are thus portrayed as a heterogenous category. Crompton (1997) emphasised that a 'multi-stranded' approach to an explanation of gender segregation is appropriate and the interdependence of household/domestic work and paid employment is central to an explanation.

So far the discussion of gender segregation in employment has centred on women. Nearly all discussion of men's paths through employment assume their advantaged position as 'breadwinner' and that their access to different forms of employment is unproblematic. Our study recasts men as the apparently disadvantaged party in one form of employment, childcare, although, as Williams (1995) shows, men tend to emerge with advantages in 'women's work' too. Wharton and Baron (1987), summarising literature on men in 'women's work', argued that men should 'express relatively high levels of psychological wellbeing' compared to women, 'because 1) male tokens are likely to receive superior treatment in the workplace and thus perceive themselves as better off than their female counterparts and 2) these men enjoy privileges within the larger society associated with the master status of being male' (Wharton and Baron, 1987: 576).

Gender and Organisations

How is gender produced within organisations or work institutions such as childcare centres? Hearn and Parkin (1992) argued that gender has traditionally been neglected in studies of organisations. The 'male' character of organisations has been assumed. Most sociological analysis of gender in organisations is about the structuring of the experience of work along gendered lines (Hearn and Parkin, 1992). For example, Kanter (1977) studied men and women in corporations and showed how the structure of large organisations shapes gendered experiences of work, so that women are 'crowded in dead end jobs at the bottom and exposed as tokens at the top' (Acker, 1991: 164).

Acker (1991) has argued that 'gendering' occurs in at least five interacting processes within work organisations. These are: divisions of labour, physical space and power along gendered lines; the construction of symbols and images that maintain and express these divisions; interactions between the genders that 'enact dominance and submission'; procedures which help to 'produce gendered components of individual identity'; and 'the fundamental ongoing processes of creating and conceptualizing social structures' (Acker, 1991: 167–8). Our data will shed light on these kinds of interactive and hierarchical processes in childcare institutions. However, whereas Acker's analysis assumed that men and masculinity would be dominant, this is not the starting premise for our study. We are looking instead for a multiplicity of gendered identities, within which the dominance of one gender may or may not be in evidence.

Identities and Gender

The above discussion has argued that it is necessary to combine the individual and the institutional in any sustainable account of gender in a work context. Gender is, then, a lived experience, constantly subject to construction and reconstruction, it is embedded within workplace institutions and provides a framework for how to be. Although gender in a work setting has usually been analysed to deconstruct women's experiences and to raise important issues of equality and gender differences, the ideas generated about how gender is situated or produced are relevant for our enquiry into men's and women's experiences in the nearly all-women domain of childcare.

Specifically, the idea of a gendered institution as one where not just members, or, in our case, workers and children, are inhabitants of one gender or another, but also where the formal and informal rules of operation are embedded with gendered understandings of practice seems highly relevant to childcare institutions. But although we have a convincing account of how gender permeates work and institutions, what is less convincing is the relative importance of gender to identity in the work context. This is important for our study because we use workers' experiences and their reflections on what happens as the main tool for uncovering gendered practices. The workers' agency, their ability to act and influence what happens, is seen as key. They are not seen as 'empty' holders of 'positions' (Acker, 1991), but their identity as workers, the meaning they bring to the work and their interpretation of the work in the context of their selves is seen as a key constituent of both the work itself and the research process.

Our understanding of gender, as we have already noted, is subject to changing component parts. We may feel differently about our gender at work, at home, when walking the streets late at night, when changing a tyre by the roadside, when putting curlers in an elderly lady's hair, or when cuddling a baby. Gender, once seemingly fixed and immutable, here becomes somewhat slippery. Critically, it is a relational attribute (Connell, 1987), and identity, argued Hall (1996), is subject to similar malleability. The concept of identity 'does not signal that stable core of the self, unfolding from beginning to end through all the vicissitudes of history without change' (Hall, 1996: 3). Rather, identities 'are about using the resources of history, language and culture in the process of becoming rather than being' (*ibid*, 1996: 4). Critically, identities are constructed within discourses, enunciative strategies, and produced in specific historical and institutional sites through specific discursive formations. Identities are constructed through difference. They require the marking of Others, and practices of exclusion.

The idea of the Other has been considered across feminist theory (e.g., de Beauvoir, 1983) and history-philosophy (e.g., Young, 1990). The central idea is that groups or categories of people demonstrate their master status (such as being male, or being white, or being an imperial power) through marking out other groups as Other (women, black people, poor countries) in relation to the master status. These Other groups can then be appropriated or assimilated by the dominant party. The marking of Other is not just a method of providing a distinction between two groups, but a way of institutionalising hierarchical difference and power: an Other can be reduced to a 'nobody'. Theorists have pointed out that the problem is how to both know and respect the difference that the Other represents, without assimilation or appropriation (Young, 1990).

We have found these ideas about gender and how it 'works' in both institutions and lived experience helpful in framing our analysis of gender in childcare work. To complete this introduction, we will briefly discuss two specific themes about children, childcare work and ideologies of gendered caring that we return to throughout the book.

Mothering, Fathering, the Self and Work

We referred briefly above to the connections between childcare work and the gender of the workforce. Childcare work with preschool aged children has long been regarded as 'women's work', not only because women do the work, but also because it is conceptualised as appropriate for women to be childcare workers, due to women's status as mothers. We pointed out that such a conceptualisation of childcare as like mother-care created a difficulty for men entering the profession as there is no equivalent model for men. The relationship between work status, dominant ideas about motherhood and fatherhood, and the work within a childcare institution forms the core of the first central theme.

Predominant ideologies of motherhood position the mother as the ideal carer of young children. There has been a historic investment in the role of the mother as the rearer of physically healthy infants (Davin, 1978), and in postwar theories of attachment, the infant's psychological bond with the mother was required to be nurtured in order to raise well-balanced children (e.g., Bowlby, 1951). Ideologies of motherhood have been a pervasive influence on British policy on childcare services. For example, the provision of childcare services for young children was seen to be only necessary when mother's labour was required for a war effort, and otherwise to be a private parental responsibility, thus reinforcing the message that mother's work was nurturing infants within the domestic setting. Ideologies of motherhood have had to accommodate the reality of mother's employment outside the home: now most children receive some kind of preschool service away from home (Holtermann *et al.*, 1998; Meltzer, 1994). By contrast, the state of 'fatherhood' has had far less policy attention, but has recently been subject to question and confusion (Collier, 1995; Williams, 1998). In particular, problems of father absence from children and problems of father distance in their relations with children have been noted. More generally, the relationship between 'men' and children is seen as potentially problematic (Burgess and Ruxton, 1996).

These predominant ideas of motherhood and fatherhood form the cultural backdrop to our view of an interweaving of conceptions of self, of constructions of the role and purpose of childcare institutions, and of ideas about domestic caring relations, that operates in the reflections of workers and parents about the activity we call childcare. This 'interweaving' works by drawing on dominant discourses that offer an interpretation of the way the gendered self relates to those dominant discourses about acceptable childcare practice. In this way, an individual worker can look to the world 'out there' to provide an explanation, albeit a contradictory one, of, for example, his own occupation of a role theoretically reserved for women.

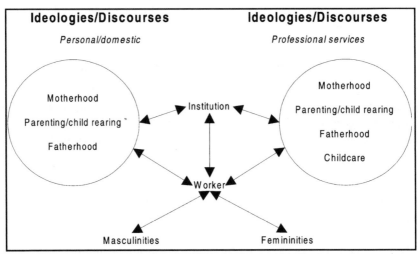

Figure 1.1 An interweaving model of self, institution and ideologies

Figure 1.1 demonstrates the complex web of interconnections between self, or gendered identity, and work or the institution. This emphasis on the sense of self connecting with the work self has parallels with the literature on informal caring. Informal caring is a term used to describe chronic unpaid caring, often for kin, such as elderly relatives. It is an activity largely performed by women, although not entirely (Baldwin and Twigg, 1991). One explanation for the heavily gendered division of this labour, argued by Graham (1983), is that women's self identity is constructed largely around the giving of care, whereas men's self worth is achieved through the attainment of personal non care-oriented goals. While we would not want to claim any essentialist differences between men and women, the premise of this argument, that personal psychology plays a part in the choice of, and satisfaction from, work environments has resonances with the position we adopt here.

The Purpose and Ethos of Childcare Institutions: Management Style and Reflexive Practice

The second theme that we return to repeatedly is that of the purpose and ethos of childcare institutions. What are they for? On what principles, theories and relationships do they operate? A social constructionist perspective views childcare institutions as

> a community of human agents, originating through our active interaction with other people and with society . . . [Childcare] institutions and pedagogical practices for children are constituted by dominant discourses in our society and embody thoughts, conceptions and ethics which prevail at a given moment in a given society.
>
> (Dahlberg, 1997, quoted in Dahlberg *et al.*, 1999: 62)

There is therefore a contingent character to childcare institutions: nothing about them is essential or self-evident – neither the purposes of the institutions, nor who the children are who attend, nor indeed who the workers are. Instead, there will be different understandings or constructions held by different people, understandings that are always contestable and value-laden, and which need to be made visible so that they can be the subject of dialogue, argument and reflection.

Dahlberg, Moss and Pence (1999) argued that understandings of the childcare institution interact with understandings of the young child itself. In their work, they explored three constructions of the young child, the first two of which have been, and are, influential and related constructions of the child, especially in the Anglo-American world. The first understands the child as a knowledge, identity and culture reproducer, starting life with and from nothing – as an empty vessel or tabula rasa.

> One can say that this is *Locke's child*. The challenge is to have her 'ready to learn' and 'ready for school' by the age of compulsory schooling. During early childhood, therefore, the young child needs to be filled with knowledge, skills and dominant cultural values which are already determined, socially sanctioned and ready to administer – a process of reproduction or transmission – and to be trained to conform to the fixed demands of compulsory schooling.
>
> (*ibid.*, 1999: 44)

The second image, powerfully influenced by the discipline of developmental psychology, understands the young child as an essential being with universal properties and inherent capabilities, whose development is viewed as an innate process – biologically determined, following general laws – unless, of course, the child has some abnormality. That, we say, is the way children of that age are, that is their nature, that is what they can and cannot do if they are 'normal'. This is *Piaget's child,* since Piaget's theory of stages has surely been very influential for this construction, even though Piaget himself never put much stress on stages.

(*ibid.,* 1999: 46)

But in the third construction, the young child emerges as *co-constructor,* from the very start of life, of knowledge, of culture, and of his or her own identity.

Rather than an object that can be reduced to separate and measurable categories (e.g. social development, cognitive development, motor development and so on), through isolating from one another processes which are very complex and interrelated, the young child is understood as a unique, complex and individual subject. This construction produces a child who, in Malaguzzi's words is 'rich in potential, strong, powerful, competent'.

(*ibid.,* 1999: 50)

This last quotation, from the first head of the famous early childhood services in the Italian city of Reggio Emilia, illustrates an important implication of adopting a social constructionist perspective. It implies that we make choices about how we see and understand children, implying an ethical dimension, and that these choices are immensely significant because of their links to policy and practice. The pedagogical work in Reggio has been based on a very deliberate choice to see the 'rich child', who is a co-constructive learner from birth. Learning is understood as a cooperative and communicative activity, in which children co-construct knowledge, and make meaning of the world, together with adults and, equally important, other children – what Malaguzzi summed up as a 'pedagogy of relationships'.

Dahlberg *et al.* (1999) go on to contrast two possible understandings of the childcare institution. The first they consider to be a dominant view of the institution as

a producer of care and of standardised and predetermined child outcomes. Linked to the modernist constructions of the young child, in particular as reproducer of knowledge, identity and culture, the broad and increasingly important task of these institutions as producers is to fill the empty vessel that the young child has often been understood to be.

(*ibid.,* 1999: 63)

The second understanding sees childcare institutions as having the potential to be 'forums in civil society, where children and adults can engage together in projects of social, cultural, economic and political significance', one of the many possible projects being learning understood as co-construction of knowledge, culture and identity in relationship with children and adults.

This discussion has profound implications for childcare workers, as well as the ethos of childcare institutions. Not only are there different understandings or constructions of who the childcare worker is, might, or should be, which are enormously productive in terms of training and practice, but these constructions of the worker are related to constructions of the young child and the childcare institution. If young children are understood as reproducers of knowledge and subject to biologically-determined processes of development, and if institutions are understood to be producers of predetermined outcomes, then the childcare worker is likely to be seen as a *technician*, whose task it is to ensure the efficient production of the institution's outcomes, however framed. For example, the worker's job could be transmitting a predetermined body of knowledge to the child or supporting the child's development to ensure that each milestone is reached at the correct age. The technology she administers incorporates a range of norms or standards: where the child should be at his or her current stage of development and where s/he must get to; what activities are appropriate to the child's stage of development; what the answers are to the questions she puts to the child; and so on. The outcomes are known and prescribed, even though the child may be allowed some choice and freedom in how she gets to them. As a technician, the childcare worker's task is to apply a technology and ensure the product conforms to set standards – to be an efficient reproducer.

Similarly, if the childcare institution is also seen as a substitute home, and the childcare worker as a substitute parent, or more precisely as a substitute mother since mothers are understood to be the main carers of young children, then this may contribute to the production of a gendered workforce.

But if the child is understood as an active learner, co-constructing knowledge in relationship with other children and adults, and if the institution is understood as a complex forum in civil society where many and varied projects take place, a public space quite different to the home, then the childcare worker can be understood as a co-constructor of knowledge and culture, both the children's and her own, in a pedagogy that 'denies the teacher as neutral transmitter, the student as passive and knowledge as immutable material to impart' (Lather, 1991: 15). The childcare worker mobilises children's meaning-making competencies, offering herself as a resource to whom children can and want to turn, organising space, materials and situations to provide new opportunities and choices for learning, assisting children to explore the many different languages available to them, listening and watching children, taking their ideas and theories seriously but being also prepared to challenge, both in the form of new questions, information and discussions, and in the form of new materials and techniques.

This role, and more generally a perspective that recognises the complex, contestable and interpretive nature of childhood and pedagogical work also requires that the pedagogue is seen as a researcher and thinker, a reflective practitioner who seeks to deepen her understanding of what is going on and how children learn, through documentation, dialogue, critical reflection and deconstruction (Malaguzzi, 1993; Rinaldi, 1993). The question of gender can be seen in this context as a complex issue of identities and relationships, rather than as an essential identity to be reproduced, and as a constantly contestable issue, which requires to be made visible, and made the subject of dialogue and reflection. Indeed, this is one of the main and pervading themes of our analysis:

that gender in childcare institutions, in its many settings and manifestations, needs to be made visible and treated reflexively, to open up the practice of the institution and its workers for critical enquiry and discussion, as the best means to develop a self-conscious and responsible practice, aware of gender but not gendered. The question here is, do childcare institutions have the space, the resources, the commitment, the ethos to enable reflective and critical practice and to 'work the tensions' between theory and practice?

Notes

1. We understand 'discourse' to refer to conventions of language used to name and talk about objects. Because conventions convey an element of predictability (what 'should' happen), they are powerful tools in constructing our understandings of 'how things are done'. Discourses organise our experience of the everyday world and help constitute the 'truth' at any given time. They also exclude alternative ways of understanding the world (*cf.* Dahlberg *et al.*, 1999).
2. Dominant ideologies refer to the overarching system(s) of values and beliefs in a culture that we use to define what is 'right' or 'the truth', so that it appears to be beyond challenge. For example, a dominant ideology about early childhood is that 'parents know their children best'.

2

Mapping and Sourcing

Working with children tends to be seen as a predominantly female occupation. Yet male carers have much to offer. . . .

(DfEE, 1998)

In this chapter we do some scene setting for the rest of the book. First, we will do some mapping, both of the broader field of early childhood services in Britain, in which childcare services play a major part, and of the structure of the workforce for those services. We will compare the British scene with that in some other European countries, and by so doing show how the British scene is in many important respects rather particular – both in the way of services and with respect to the workforce. In the second part of the chapter, we set out the research context and process in our work on gender in childcare centres.

Early Childhood Services in Britain

The landscape of early childhood services in Britain has been shaped by three main forces, which cumulatively have produced a set of services with rather unusual characteristics, at least viewed from a broader European perspective. First, the period of 'early childhood' is short, as a result of a decision made over 100 years ago to set 5 as compulsory school age: in most other European countries the age is 6 (for a fuller description of how this decision came about, see Moss and Penn, 1996). Indeed, early childhood is truncated even further because many 4 year-olds are admitted into primary school reception classes, on a voluntary basis.

Second, early childhood services have had a low priority in public policy for many years, leaving something of a policy vacuum (discounting a temporary flurry of interest during the Second World War, when public nurseries were provided to enable women's employment). As a result, a complex mix of services has emerged, each one the product of a very particular historical context and process. Since 1997, as we discuss later, Britain has entered into a new phase of more active public policy for early childhood services.

Let us take some examples. In response to low levels of nursery education, the playgroup movement (which had originally started in New Zealand) took root in Britain in the 1960s and grew rapidly, offering part-time provision mostly to 3 and 4 year-olds. In 1965 there were 500 groups in England, by 1972 over 15,000. Then from the mid-1980s onwards, in response to a surge in employment amongst women with young children (Holtermann *et al.*, 1998) which coincided with a period of neo-liberal, market-oriented government, private (mainly for profit) nurseries rapidly increased in number, there being a five-fold increase between 1987 and 1997 (from 1,143 to 5,500). At the same time, childminders, always the most common form of 'formal' childcare for working parents, also increased substantially in number. Within a matter of a decade, therefore, a private market of independent childcare providers became firmly established as the means of providing for the childcare needs of working parents. Filling the vacuum was not, however, left only to independent providers. In the face of limited nursery education provision, and anxious to fill spaces, primary schools have steadily increased their intake of 4 year-olds into reception classes, the numbers increasing from 116,000 in 1947 to 344,000 some 50 years later.

It would be wrong to suggest that there has been a complete policy vacuum since the War. There has been a steady increase in nursery education places, mainly due to an expansion of nursery classes attached to primary schools; nursery schools, by contrast, have declined in importance as official policy has moved to favour nursery classes. Although nursery provision was initially discouraged after 1945, so resources could be concentrated on the education of older children, policy did shift in the 1960s. Following the recommendations of the 1967 Plowden Report, an Education White Paper in 1972 set as a ten year target (unfulfilled in the event) a place in nursery education for all 3 and 4 year-olds whose parents wanted one. However, this form of provision and its expansion has taken a distinctive form: most children attend nursery education part-time, places being used on a shift basis as a matter of deliberate policy rather than expediency 'since the majority of educationalists regard part-time attendance at school as sufficient, indeed preferable, for most children until they reach compulsory school' (Department for Education and Science, 1972: 6). The official belief that part-time is best has become (like school starting age of 5) one of the prominent and taken for granted features of the early childhood scene (for critiques of this form of time governance of children's lives, see Moss and Penn, 1996; Dahlberg *et al.*, 1999).

The third force shaping today's early childhood services in Britain has been a long history of these services being split between two systems. Nursery schooling and reception class provision for 4 year-olds have been part of the education system, school-based and the responsibility of education authorities and government education departments. Other services – playgroups, nurseries, childminders and so on, referred to as 'day care services' in the Children Act 1989 or more generally as 'childcare services' – have been part of the social welfare system, and responsibility for their regulation, coordination and provision has usually been held by local social services departments and government departments concerned with health and personal social services.

In fact, this group of 'day care services' is itself further split. Some services, notably playgroups, have emphasised their function as primarily educational; others, notably private day nurseries and childminders, have been primarily concerned to provide 'childcare for working parents'; while yet another group of services, notably council day nurseries and a range of family centres, have been primarily concerned with providing for children defined by welfare authorities as 'in need' and support for their families. In practice, of course, things are not so clear-cut: some 'children in need' are placed by local authorities with childminders, playgroups or private nurseries; an increasing number of playgroups offer longer hours geared to the needs of working parents; private nurseries and childminders increasingly recognise an educational role. Nevertheless, the system of childcare services that has emerged has tended to be specialised in purpose and selective in access.

Overall, in 1996 there were nearly one and a half million places (1,472,700) in early childhood services in England (Department for Education and Employment, 1997; Department of Health, 1997). Just over half a million of these places (530,000) were in the education system, in nursery school (30,411), nursery classes (170,249) and reception classes (329,428)[1]. Nearly a million places were in the welfare system (942,700), with similar numbers at childminders (365,200) and in playgroups (383,700) and the remainder in day nurseries (193,800), most of which (90 per cent) were in private rather than local authority day nurseries (this figure does not include places in family centres, for which no statistics exist; nor are there any figures for the small number of 'combined centres' that attempt to straddle the divide by bringing together education and childcare).

There is no means of knowing how many children use these places. We do know, however, that many children attend services on a part-time basis, so that many places are used by more than one child. For example, 90 per cent of children at nursery school or nursery class attend part-time. Similarly many playgroup places are shared; the Pre-school Learning Alliance (PLA) estimated that in 1993 there were 1.8 children using every one place, while a survey of private nurseries reported that four-fifths of places were used part-time, the number of children attending per nursery averaging 56 compared to an average number of 36 places (i.e. 1.6 children per place) (LGMB, 1999). The number of children attending some form of early childhood service is therefore likely to exceed the number of places quite substantially.

The Early Childhood Workforce in Britain

How many staff?

Just as we cannot be certain about the number of places in early childhood services, nor the numbers of children attending, so too we cannot quantify the workforce precisely. We have to make some rough estimates. In the education system in England in 1996, there were 18,104 staff working in nursery schools and classes, of whom just under half were teachers, the rest mainly classroom assistants (Department for Education and Employment, 1997). There are no figures, however, for staff working with 4 year-olds in reception classes. But given the higher number of places in reception classes than nursery classes, it would be surprising if the number of reception class staff was not at least equal to staff in nursery classes even allowing for the possibility that levels of staffing in reception classes are on average lower than in nursery classes.

In welfare system services, we only know for certain that in 1997 in England there were 3,200 staff working directly with children in council day nurseries, and we have not even an estimate of the numbers of staff working in family centres (Department of Health, 1997). The LGMB (1999) survey estimated that, in January 1998, private day nurseries employed some 43,290 staff working directly with children (85 per cent of the total workforce, the rest consisting of kitchen, domestic and administrative staff); 29 per cent of these staff working with children had part-time jobs. A parallel survey by LGMB of playgroups reported 24,700 paid workers from a 29 per cent response rate, suggesting a total paid workforce in playgroups of around 85,000: nearly all, however, work part time. Finally, in 1996 there were some 98,500 registered childminders in England (Department of Health, 1997), although another LGMB survey reported that 9 per cent of registered childminders had no children attending at the time of the survey. These figures, rough as they are, suggest a workforce in early childhood services (excluding staff in reception classes and family centres) of around a quarter of a million.

Training and Qualifications

The education/welfare split pervades and affects many aspects of early childhood services, but nowhere more obviously than with respect to staffing. School-based early childhood services in the education system are staffed by a cadre of teachers, most of whom have completed a four year degree level training, usually to work with children of nursery class and primary school age, and with pay and conditions similar to other teachers in primary school. By contrast, early childhood services in the welfare system are based on staff with much lower levels of training. The most common form of training found in nurseries is a two-year post-16 level qualification: the 1999 LGMB survey of staff in private nurseries found that 39 per cent had the CACHE/NNEB diploma in nursery nursing, 11 per cent had childcare and education S/NVQs at levels 2 or 3, and 10 per cent had the BTEC/EdEXCEL Diploma or Certificate in nursery nursing, all at this level; a quarter of the staff surveyed had no relevant training. The LGMB's parallel survey of playgroup staff found that a quarter had no relevant qualification, and that the most common qualification was from one or other of the PLA's own courses, which are at a lower level than the CACHE or BTEC diplomas. Most childminders (68 per cent) had no relevant qualification, the most common qualification was the CACHE/NNEB nursery nurse diploma (8 per cent) and the PLA Foundation Course (6 per cent).

Of course, on the ground matters are not so clear cut. Teachers working with under 5s in school settings are usually assisted by staff with one of the main two year, post-16 'nursery nurse' qualifications. Some staff in private day nurseries (4 per cent according to the LGMB survey) and playgroups (6 per cent) and some childminders (3 per cent) have a teaching qualification, while some staff in public day nurseries or family centres may have various higher level qualifications from social work or other welfare fields. But despite these reservations, it is still basically the case that the split system of early childhood services in Britain has produced a split and two tier system of staffing: a teacher based staffing for schools, and what might be called a 'childcare' based staffing, based on nursery nursing and playgroup qualifications, for welfare system services.

Pay and Conditions

Another feature of this two tier system, which parallels training, is large differences in pay and conditions. Teachers in the school system have the same salary and working conditions as their colleagues in primary school, and classroom assistants, although paid less, are covered by nationally negotiated conditions and work school hours. Within the welfare system, the data is weak, since there are no collective agreements or regular surveys of pay and conditions. What indicators we have, however, suggest that levels of pay are often low, although there may be some variation between individual nurseries. For example, in a study of ten private nurseries, Penn concluded that conditions of work were 'mostly poor with low pay, no pension rights, frequently no sick pay, no maternity leave, limited holiday pay and limited job security' (Penn, 1995: 33). In another study of 95 private nurseries, salaries varied according to levels of training, but were generally well below average earnings at the time for full-time non-manual employees (Vernon and Smith, 1994). More recently, the prospect of the introduction of the national minimum wage has drawn attention to the fact that some staff in private nurseries are currently paid below the proposed minimum wage limit: 'nursery managers are busy juggling with figures to count the cost of maintaining their staff ratios while paying the national minimum wage when it comes into force' (Evans, 1998: 24). Similar concerns have been expressed by the playgroup movement, for although 'most pre-school leaders are already paid above the monthly recommended minimum wage, as many as 50 per cent of pre-school assistants may need to receive pay increases to bring them up to the necessary level' (Preschool Learning Alliance, 1998: 14).

Britain in a European context

European comparisons have become quite voguish in the early childhood field in recent years, often involving league tables of provision showing Britain's lowly place in terms of publicly-funded provision. This may have contributed, in a small way, to the raised priority for early childhood services in public policy in the 1990s, although at best playing a small part in a complex process.

But there are other reasons for looking at Britain in relation to other countries, for example the way that working comparatively can help make visible, and therefore make subject to question, assumptions and practices deeply embedded and taken for granted. The issue here is using other perspectives to help critical thinking and the process of problematisation – what Michel Foucault described as 'trying to grasp how "that which is" might no longer be "that which is" . . . to show how "that which is" has not always been . . . [and] to show that things are not as self-evident as one believed, to see that what is accepted as self-evident will no longer be accepted as such' (Foucault, 1988: 36, 37, 155).

Britain is not unusual in having had a split system of early childhood services; many other countries have had a similar structure. What makes Britain unique is the combination of a split system with the other features outlined above: early admission to school and a complex mix of services that have emerged largely in response to a lack of active public policy. What has emerged over the last 50 years is an education based system essentially offering older pre-schoolers a short period of preparation for primary school, publicly funded and led by a teacher-trained workforce; and a much larger welfare based system, mainly dependent on parental fees and consequently constrained in what it can pay its 'childcare' led workforce and, as a consequence, the level of training it can support among that workforce.

The singularity of the British system of early childhood services becomes clearer when compared with other member states of the European Union. With a few exceptions (notably Ireland and the Netherlands), a general pattern can be discerned: school starting age of 6, preceded by universal provision of publicly-funded provision for at least three years in one or at most two types of centre-based early childhood provision, with places often available on a full-time basis. Before the age of 3, the situation is more disparate, varying from low levels of publicly-funded provision in countries such as Germany to high levels of provision, at least for children over 12 months, in Scandinavia (in both Finland and Sweden children under 3 are entitled to places in publicly-funded services). Some of the Scandinavian countries have well-established integrated early childhood systems, in which all services are the responsibility of either the social welfare or the education system; other countries, for example, Spain, are working towards the achievement of an integrated, education-based system. In these cases, the integrated system is reflected in an integrated early childhood profession, with a relatively high level of training (at least three years post-18 level), and pay and conditions equal to or close to those of school teachers. Many countries however operate a split system like Britain, in which case there is also a split workforce, divided between teachers and others.

To illustrate these patterns of provision in other European countries, and their staffing consequences, we look below at three 'cases': Denmark, with an integrated, welfare-based early childhood service; Spain, with an emerging integrated education-based early childhood service; and France with a split system, in which children under 3 are mainly within welfare-based services while children over 3 are in the education system, the great majority receiving three years full-time nursery schooling (quite separate from primary school).

Denmark

Government responsibility for early childhood services is held by the Ministry of Social Affairs[2]. This is a long-standing, well-established and almost universal system. Services are largely publicly funded (parents contribute about a fifth of total costs) and locally managed by local authorities and individual centres – each centre has its own management board including a parent majority. Even standards for centres are not nationally prescribed but determined by the local authority often in negotiation with the trades unions. While generous parental and maternity leave schemes mean many children under a year are cared for by parents, 55 per cent of children attend publicly-funded services: of these, just over half go to publicly-organised family day care, the remainder going either to nurseries for children aged 0 to 3 (*vuggestuer*) or to age-integrated institutions taking children from 0 to 6 or older. Children aged 3–6 are largely in centres – two-thirds going to kindergartens (*børnehaver* – centres exclusively for children from 3 to 6) and a quarter going to age-integrated institutions (centres taking children from 0 to 6 or older) – with just 7 per cent in organised family day care. All services are open all year and on a full-day basis, reflecting the high employment rate among mothers and fathers.

There are two types of worker employed in centre-based services: *pedagogues* and untrained staff. Nearly two-thirds of staff are *pedagogues*, and most untrained staff are gaining experience prior to training as *pedagogues*. *Pedagogues* are qualified to work across a range of services for children, both of school-age and younger, and indeed with adults. Although the *pedagogue* is seen as quite different to the school teacher, pay and conditions are slightly worse. *Pedagogue* training lasts three-and-a-half years and takes place in 32 specialised colleges funded by the Ministry of Education. Although the training covers a wide age range, there are possibilities to specialise once the course has begun.

Early childhood services have been undergoing expansion and there is a new enthusiasm for the *pedagogue* training. For example, in 1997 there were 21,000 applications for 5,000 places. Moreover, the workforce being trained is relatively mature: while the minimum age for training is 18, the average age of students is 27. Denmark has pursued an active campaign to recruit men into *pedagogue* training: in 1995 22 per cent of the intake were men (see Table 2:1 page 38).

France

Early childhood services in France are well-established and long-standing but differ from those in Denmark in that overall responsibility is split between government departments. The Ministry of Employment and Solidarity, and welfare departments in local authorities, are responsible for services for children from

0 to 3 years, including nurseries and organised family day care. The education system is responsible for an extensive network of nursery schooling (*écoles maternelles*) for children aged 2 to 6 years. This service is the responsibility of the national Ministry of Education, although local authorities are responsible for providing various inputs. There is therefore some overlapping responsibility, in particular 2 year-olds who may be in welfare or education system services.

Much provision is heavily and directly publicly funded. Nursery education is free at the point of access to parents. Parents contribute to the cost of welfare system services for children under 3, the amount varying according to the type of service and levels of family income; the average in 1996 for *crèches collectives* (nurseries for children under 3) was 23 per cent. In addition, there is an extensive system of demand subsidy for parents, such as grants and tax relief to assist with costs of using particular services.

Just under a third of children under 3 attend publicly-funded services, but a substantial number in addition attend private services, mainly family day care. Virtually all children aged 3 to 6 attend publicly-funded *écoles maternelles*, as do many 2 year-olds. Indeed, more than half of children under 3 in publicly-funded services are 2 year-olds attending *écoles maternelles*, the rest attending either various kinds of nurseries or publicly organised family day care. Welfare system services are open all year and on a full-day basis. *Écoles maternelles* are open during term-times only.

There are two systems of staffing. Within the welfare system, in nurseries and other centres, there are three types of worker: the director, who traditionally has a nursing qualification; assistants; and more recent additions are staff with an education training. By contrast, staffing in *écoles maternelles* primarily consists of teachers, with some help from assistants. The split staffing regime is reflected in staff training. Within the welfare system, the director will have trained as a medical nurse specialising in paediatric work; this is a four-year, post-18 training. In contrast, the assistants will have a one year, post-16 training at a specialist school and the education worker will have a post-18 training lasting two years and four months at a non-university training centre specialising in this particular training. Teacher training was reformed and upgraded in 1991: the qualification is to teach children from 2 to 11 years. It takes five years – a three year university degree course leading to a *licence* followed by two years professional training at an *institut universitaire de formation des maitres (IUFM)*.

Spain

In Spain a law reforming the entire educational system was passed in 1990 (LOGSE). Under LOGSE, the period from 0–6 years is recognised as the first stage of the education system (*educación infantil*), which in turn is divided into two cycles – 0 to 3 years and 3 to 6 years. Spain, therefore, was the first European country to officially designate centres for children under 3 as part of the public education system. This has involved a major change in how services for children under 3 are conceptualised: they are recognised as both an educational and public issue, and not just a welfare issue concerned only with parents working or disadvantaged children. More generally, Spain is the first European country to opt for an education-based integrated early childhood service covering the age range 0 to 6 (the second country is Sweden, which has recently transferred responsibility for early childhood services from social welfare to education).

The National Ministry of Education and the Departments of Education in the regions have responsibility for education. LOGSE has led to a new national curriculum for the 0 to 6 age group (*Diseño Curricular Base: Educación Infantil*); a reform of staff training; a generic title for all services for children under 6 (*escuela infantil*); and, for the first time, a national system of regulation for all services for this age group, with minimum standards. For children under 3 years, a third of staff must be trained teachers, while for children from 3 to 6 years there must be four teachers for every three groups or classes of children. Some autonomous regions and local authorities however operate higher standards.

LOGSE states that 0 to 6 is not a compulsory stage of education. In practice, however, the government's priority has been to provide universal provision for children aged 3 to 6, and services for children under 3 have received less attention; places for this age group are not yet available on request. Although some centres are age-integrated, for children from 0 to 6, most are either for children under 3 or over 3. There are no official statistics on attendance rates for children under 3 years. Estimates by trades unions, however, suggest that 20–30 per cent of this age group attend some form of centre, but that only about 5 per cent attend centres that are publicly funded. Parents earning below a certain income receive some subsidy for their payments through tax relief. Most children (84 per cent in 1993/94) aged 3 to 6 attend services, nearly all 4 and 5 year-olds and just over half of 3 year-olds. Most of these places are in publicly-funded schools.

Non-school services are open all year and on a full-day basis. School-based services are open during term-times only, with a three hour midday break, although an increasing number of schools offer supervised meals during this period. Spain has one of the lowest levels of maternal employment in Europe.

Under LOGSE, the staffing of Spanish services has moved from a system of teachers specialising in work with 3 to 6 year-olds, and less highly qualified workers for children under 3, to a system based on an early childhood teacher specialising in work with children from 0 to 6. In addition to teachers, there are 'senior workers in early childhood education'. Only teachers can work with children aged 3 to 6 years, but both types of worker are found in services for children under 3 years; in the latter case, teachers are normally in the minority except where the management has decided to have a high level of teacher-trained staff. The *técnico superior* may be responsible for a group of 0 to 3 year-olds.

Post-LOGSE, the early childhood teacher has a three year post-18 training to degree level in a university-based teacher training institute; the training, pay and status is at the same level as for primary school teachers. Early childhood is one of six possible areas of specialisation in teacher training. The other workers – *técnico superior en educación infantil* – have a post-18 training lasting 2,000 hours, of which 1,600 hours are allocated to theoretical subjects (e.g. psychology, pedagogy, sociology, etc.) and the remaining 400 hours to practical work in centres. Following LOGSE, special training programmes have enabled existing staff to 'top up' their basic qualifications through in-service training, for example to become early childhood teachers. In Barcelona, which has been very committed to the principles of LOGSE, this meant that over a five-year period the number of teachers in centres for children under 3 rose from 20 per cent to 80 per cent.

New Labour, New Early Childhood Services?

It could be argued that the picture of early childhood services in Britain painted at the beginning of this chapter has been superseded by recent developments. Certainly the first two years of the present Labour Government have seen unparalleled attention, resources and initiatives devoted to early childhood services. Educational provision has been made for all 4 year-olds, and is to be extended to at least two-thirds of 3 year-olds by 2002; a National Childcare Strategy has been proposed, to be implemented by early years development and childcare partnerships, informed and guided by childcare audits and local early years development and childcare plans; the Sure Start initiative will target children under 3 and their families in the most disadvantaged areas; a pro-gramme of Centres of Early Excellence, intended to highlight 'best practice', has been launched; new sources of funding have been provided, including a childcare tax credit to be introduced in October 1999; both the regulation of early years education and childcare and the desirable learning outcomes are under review, the latter by the Qualifications and Curriculum Authority (QCA); and the QCA, together with the National Training Organisation (NTO), is taking forward work to develop and implement a framework for qualifications and training in the early years education, childcare and play-work sector.

Yet, it has been argued, that the changes, important and historic as they are, add up to a process of reformation rather than transformation (Moss, 1999). To take three examples. The truncated period of early childhood – in practice running from birth to school entry at 4 – has not been reviewed, but continues to be taken for granted. At national level, the important step has been taken by the Labour Government of transferring responsibility for 'day care' services from the Department of Health to the Department for Education and Employ-ment: but responsibility continues to be divided between two parts of that Department – the 'early years division' and the 'childcare unit'. So, while government policy certainly emphasises the close relationship between care and education, administrative practice and underlying thinking appears to remain compartmentalised to a significant degree, reflected in the continuing use of the language of 'childcare' and the emphasis attached to a 'National *Childcare* Strategy'.

This continuing split in the administration and conceptualisation of early childhood services has implications for the third example, and the one most relevant to this book: the staffing of early childhood services. The work being undertaken by the QCA and NTO to develop a framework for early years qualifications and training is again essentially reformatory. It starts with existing occupational groups and 'job roles' in early years work (with the major exception of teachers, who are excluded presumably because the brief for this exercise arises from the National Childcare Strategy), then moves on to discuss standards, qualifications and training. What is missing is any prior analysis and discussion of the nature of the work in an integrated and coherent early childhood service concerned with education, care and a wide range of other functions – and what type or types of worker might be needed to undertake this work.

The present system of staffing which we have described above, and which is replicated in government documents, involves a disparate mix: an élite corps of teachers in nursery and reception classes; and a much larger army of various types of 'childcare workers' (again the explicit language of recent government documents), with a training at a lower level than teachers but covering the full early childhood age range. But as Denmark and Spain illustrate above, there are other basic options for early childhood work, for example the *pedagogue* trained to work with children from 0 to 6 (and sometimes also with older children in non-school settings), envisaged as equal to but different from the school teacher; or the *early childhood teacher*, trained to work specifically with children from 0 to 6 within the education system. In terms of basic training, both options assume at least three years at a post-18 level, with a focus on the whole early childhood age range, as the benchmark for early childhood work. As we show in later chapters, making the issue of gender in childcare practice visible begins to raise more general questions about who the early childhood worker is and how they work, which in turn could beg wider questions about how she or he should be trained.

Gender and the Early Childhood Workforce

Despite the complexity of the early childhood scene in Britain, and the differences between Britain and some other European countries, one common thread runs throughout. Early childhood services, of all sorts and in all places, are overwhelmingly staffed by women. As we show in Table 2.1 (page 38), which compares the gender composition of the childcare workforce in Britain with other caring occupations and in other countries, British surveys point to around 2 per cent male workers (Cameron and Moss, 1998; LGMB, 1999), and a similar proportion of childcare students and college lecturers (Cameron, 1997b). Elsewhere, there are either no statistics or else the figures point to 90 per cent plus women workers. In Scandinavian countries, the proportion of men seems to be somewhat higher, but it is still low: 3 per cent in Sweden

(1994); 4 per cent in Finland; 5 per cent in nurseries for under 3s and 9 per cent in kindergartens and age-integrated institutions in Denmark; 5 per cent in Norway. Given the higher levels of training and better pay and conditions in these countries, compared say to Britain, these figures certainly question simplistic explanations concerning the gendered nature of the childcare workforce based on poor pay and status.

However, at the same time, it is clear that the gendered nature of the workforce is recognised as an issue in Scandinavian countries. There is widespread agreement that more male workers are needed in order to improve equal opportunities for men and women and improve gender equality for children; the problem is *how* to achieve this. The Norwegian government has actually set a target of 20 per cent male workers by 2001, and has developed a programme of action to attempt to achieve this (Haugland, 1999). As already noted, Danish colleges training pedagogues are also working to increase male students, with some success (Ærø, 1998).

Table 2:1 *Percentages of men workers in childcare and other caring work*

Country	Occupation	% Men	Source/Date
England/GB	Childcare and related	2	Owen *et al.*, 1998
	– Nursery nurses	1	
	– Playgroup leaders	3	
	– Educational assistants	4	
	– Other childcare	1	
	Independent day nurseries		LGMB, 1999
	– Managers	3	
	– Childcare and education staff	2	
	– Placement students	4	
	Childcare college		Cameron, 1997b
	– Students	2	
	– Lecturers	2	
	Primary and nursery teachers	15	EOC, 1998
	Nurses	10	EOC, 1998
	Care assistants and attendants	8	EOC, 1998
Norway	Pedagogues (leaders/directors)	5	Hauglund, 1998
	Assistants	5	
	Students	12	
Denmark	Centres for children 0–6	8	Jensen, 1996
	Students	20–30	Ærø, 1998
Sweden	Centres for children 0–6	3	Jensen, 1996
Spain	Centres for children		Jensen, 1996
	– Madrid 0–6	8	
	– Barcelona 0–3	4	
Belgium	Centres for children 0–3	1	Jensen, 1996
	Family day care	4	
USA	Centres and family day care	3	Whitebook *et al.*, 1993

The issue has also begun to receive some government recognition in Britain. The Government's recent Childcare Strategy document, in a section headed 'boosting supply and recruitment of suitable staff' acknowledged that 'working with children tends to be seen as a predominantly female occupation. Yet male carers have much to offer, including acting as positive role models for boys' (DfEE, 1998: 2.25). The question now is what measures could, or will, be taken by Government to support the development of a more mixed gender workforce – recognising that the issue of men working with children arouses far more ambivalent feelings and views in Britain than in the Scandinavian countries. For in Britain we are still asking *whether* rather than *how*.

The Research Context

This study of gender in childcare services asks how and in what ways mixed gender childcare workforces 'work', together as staff teams, with children and with parents. It examines what happens within the childcare centres as well as how the work is represented to the wider world. It is concerned with the self, ideas of identity and how this might relate to employment in childcare. The research context was, as we briefly referred to earlier, part of a larger programme of work on staffing and gender issues in early childhood services. Elements of this larger study informed and preceded the interview study of workers and parents and consisted of three smaller studies, two surveys and secondary data analysis.

The first survey examined the views of 269 childcare college lecturers who taught in English colleges of further education (and similar insitutions) such courses as CACHE and BTEC Diplomas in nursery nursing and early childhood studies (hereafter referred to as 'the college lecturers' survey') (this represented 44 per cent of the English colleges). The second survey was of 96 English local authorities' child protection policies (this represented 90 per cent of English local authorities). In particular we asked what was included under child protection policies, and whether, for example, a concept of protection for workers was incorporated (hereafter referred to as 'the local authority survey'). The secondary analysis was of the Labour Force Survey (LFS) and characteristics of childcare occupations included within this data set.

We also reviewed the international literature on both the staffing of childcare services (Cameron, 1997) and men as childcare workers, and the material reviewed is incorporated where relevant. Two further sources of inspiration for the present study were contact with colleagues in Scandinavia (e.g., Jensen, 1996; and a study visit to Norway and Denmark in early 1997) and Britain (e.g., Penn and McQuail, 1996) and the effect of organising an international seminar on the issue of men as workers in childcare services, the proceedings of which were subsequently published and are referred to in this book either by individual contributing authors or as Owen *et al.* (1998). Together with the interview study of workers and parents described next, these studies, contacts and discussions form the data sources used in this book.

Designs and Design: The Centres and the Respondents

The interview study with workers and parents was designed to uncover the nature and dynamics of gendered practice. We initially tried a case study approach to the examination of gender in childcare centres to demonstrate the art of the possible. We thought we would be able to identify centres with a staff group composed of equal numbers of men and women and spend a period of time in each trying to understand how gender was 'lived out' in everyday childcare work. We could, however, only find one centre with such a staff composition (Sheffield Children's Centre). Even at the end of the period of study we only know of one other childcare centre in Europe with a gender balanced workforce, the Equal Rights Childcare Centre in Gothenburg, Sweden (Sundqvist, 1998). We next tried a second approach using a case study method, which was to compare four childcare centres with differing levels of 'gender awareness', seen in their history of recruiting men, their policies on gender and so forth. For varying reasons, the centres identified felt they could not commit themselves to such a study: for one it was a question of the methods proposed; for others it was a matter of being unable to incorporate a research project into the centre when already working under intense pressure.

As a result of these early difficulties with the design of the study, and an awareness of a gap in the British literature on men and caring work, we decided to make *workers* instead of *centres* the focus of the study. We set about finding a group of men and women workers employed in childcare settings for pre-school age children to interview about their personal backgrounds, their employment experiences and their views about gender differences. Because the issue of child sexual abuse often seems to arise when one discusses men and childcare work in Britain (and the USA, but not in Scandinavia), it seemed important to discuss this with workers and to elicit any differences in views or experiences between men and women workers.

Contacting Workers

The change from a centres-led case study design to an interview based design limited the centres' involvement with the study and, once we found men workers, there were few problems with either men or women workers' participation (only one centre we approached declined to take part). We contacted workers through their managers, and we found managers through professional contacts in the early years field, and through contacting London local authorities and the large voluntary sector childcare providers. Through the managers, we also gained permission to contact parents. We knew that in other countries, such as Denmark, men working in childcare enjoyed popular parental support:

we wanted to know whether parents in England were similarly supportive. Resources would only permit a small sample of parents, and, as we were interested in views and experiences (rather than solely opinions), we decided to contact parents whose children attended the centres where we interviewed men and women staff, as this would both ease our contact with parents and maximise the potential for a range of views on the subject of men workers and gender more generally.

Within the constraints of a professional contact method of finding men workers and a matched group of women workers, we also wanted to encompass a range of varying indicators about childcare work. These indicators included geographical location; degree of experience in the field; whether the work was primarily constructed as 'education', 'childcare' or 'family work'; and the centre 'auspices', or whether the institution was located in the private, voluntary or public sectors. In the event the group of 21 respondents came from ten institutions all including children aged 3 and under. These institutions included three from the private sector: two day nurseries and a Montessori school; three from the voluntary sector: two family centres (run by a national organisation) and one children's centre (a worker's co-operative); and four from the public sector: three day nurseries/combined centres and one family centre.

Although we had intended to recruit a group of workers with less than two years of childcare employment experience on the one hand, and over five years experience on the other, it did not quite work out this neatly, because we were led by the characteristics of the men workers we could find, and there was very limited choice. By focusing on length of experience and asking managers to supply respondents who were either 'new recruits' or 'old hands' we did achieve a group representing some senior and some junior positions, but not two neat groups. In one institution, there were two men employed for an equal length of time and equally senior and it proved impossible to choose between them, so we interviewed both, thus ending up with a group of ten women and eleven men childcare workers (details of the worker respondents are in Appendix 1).

The Centres

We did achieve some geographical spread. Six of the childcare institutions were in London, and three in the surrounding counties. One was in a northern city (see Appendix 2). All the institutions cared for children under 3 years of age, although as might be expected from the centre types listed above, there were variations in the primary purpose of the institutions. The private day nurseries were commercial enterprises designed to provide a care plus education service to children aged 0–4 years of working parents. They were open for long hours (8am to 6pm and 7am to 7pm) to accommodate parents' working hours. They were costly (£930 and £860 per month for a full-time place for a child under 2 years of age), although one had a scheme for subsidised fees for parents working at the adjacent superstore. The private Montessori nursery school, also fee paying, offered education plus care for children over 2 years of age, term time only, either all day or in two sessions according to parental preference. It did not offer childcare as such, and the children either had a mother at home, or those with working parents were collected by nannies.

Both the voluntary and the public sector family centres were for families with children in need: in some cases the level of need was severe. All three of the family centres in this study were of the therapeutic type (DoH, 1991) although various models exist (Smith, 1996). All the family centres had as a principal aim engaging parents both as individuals and in groups in order to improve their parenting skills. The families were mostly referred to the centres by health and welfare agencies, but in one centre there were groups where mothers and fathers could attend on a self-referral basis. Children attended crèche facilities when their mothers (or, rarely, fathers) were in group sessions. As part of welfare services, parents were not charged fees for the childcare sessions.

The public day nurseries varied in their emphasis on care and/or education. Two centres, one an under-3s centre, and one a combined centre, were run by education departments and were wholly or partly inherited from social services departments. Both of these employed teachers and emphasised the curriculum and its planning. The under-3s centre took children from the immediate neighbourhood, and a proportion of places was reserved for children in need. Some places were also available to working parents on a fee paying basis. The combined centre took the full range of pre-school age children. Alongside sessional and all-day nursery education, it also offered all day care for children under 2 years, and wrap-around care for older pre-schoolers whose parents worked. Parental fees were charged for the care element of the service. The third public day nursery was run by the social services department, and had a more traditional outlook, offering care and a broad curriculum where access was based on admission criteria such as social need.

The remaining centre was the most unusual of the institutions. This was Sheffield Children's Centre, a worker's co-operative that offered all day care for pre-school aged children, specialist therapy services for children in need, an after school club, and training for workers, as well as a peripatetic crèche service. While the other nine centres had one or two men on the staff, this centre employed a total of 77 staff, half of whom were men and half women. This was the result of a deliberate recruitment policy over some years. Other features of the centre were the democratic structures in place to debate policy and practice, a very low staff turnover, a high degree of parental involvement in the centre, and low staff salaries. Because this centre was so unusual, we carried out an additional interview with the coordinator of the service, referred to as 'additional interview material'. We have made extensive reference to the methods of Sheffield as it offers an excellent point of contrast to childcare work in general. With their permission, the usual practice of concealing the centre's identity has been abandoned. By way of comparison we have also made extensive reference to another unusual centre, which, while not employing so many men as Sheffield, has developed a consciousness of gender in its work. This centre is Pen Green Centre for Under Fives and Families and their work is referenced through published sources.

The Parents

For the group of parents, we intended to recruit the mothers and fathers of five children in each of the ten settings, thus making a potential total of 100 parent interviews from 50 households. In the event, from 50 households we had 77 interviews, 52 from mothers/co-mothers, and 25 from fathers. The shortfall of fathers stemmed from difficulties recruiting them in 16 families where the mother was the main or sole carer, and nine families where the fathers worked long hours or overseas. In these circumstances contacting them was either insensitive or impractical. We took the opportunity of visiting the centres to approach parents on the premises to introduce ourselves and obtain permission for a subsequent interview. The institutions varied in the extent of their involvement in this part of the process. All were sent introductory material about the study: some chose to display this on noticeboards, others did not. Some recruited parents for us, others did not. In some institutions it was more difficult than others to get parents to agree to be interviewed, which meant that there was over-representation by some institutions and under-representation in others (details of the parent sample are in Appendix 3).

On Representativeness

The objective of the methodology was to find centres employing men childcare workers, and through this to find women workers and parents of children who attended. Interviews were designed to produce accounts of practice and reflections on practice as well as views about men workers more generally. The kind of information wanted and the scarcity of sources mean that we did not seek a representative sample of the childcare workforce, or to achieve a representative sample of the distribution of the different types of childcare services in England. Instead we tried to maximise the variation in types of setting, in auspices and in some characteristics of the workers, in order to maximise the range of institutions included. As reported below, the significance of the centre became more evident through the research process.

The Research Process

Through the managers of the ten institutions we found with men employees, we obtained permission to visit the centres and interview the man (or, exceptionally, one of the men) and a woman colleague, and to approach parents who were collecting children to seek their permission to be contacted by telephone at a convenient time. The worker interviews were tape recorded for later transcription according to a prepared schedule. The respondents were encouraged to elaborate on their answers where they had relevant experiences to relate.

The interview schedule covered the respondents' work and educational histories; their experience of staff dynamics and support; their views about gender differences in working with children; and working, or contact, with parents. We asked them about workers as role models, and we asked them about allegations of child abuse and strategies for the protection of children and workers. We asked the workers about their satisfaction with their work, and for their views about moving towards a more mixed-gender workforce as well as some biographical details. The parent interviews were shorter and simpler, focusing on their views about employing men as childcare workers as well as collecting some biographical data. Responses to the questions were written onto the interview schedule for subsequent coding and analysis.

Interview Themes

The interview questions were structured to explore three main concerns. First, we wanted to move away from a focus merely on men, which would encourage a study of the unusual (or the 'freak' as one respondent put it), towards a focus on the pervasiveness of gender within childcare work. Second, we wanted to explore issues emanating from a reading of the literature on men in childcaring work and the broader field of men in non-traditional occupations. For example, we wanted to know whether, and in which ways, men and women childcare workers employed in England considered themselves role models, and whether the idea of men workers providing an integral welcome to fathers, as frequently asserted in the literature, was the case in English centres.

The third concern was to pick up on ideas being developed about gender differences in Scandinavia. For example, in Denmark the idea of gender pedagogy has been developed in childcare work (Jensen, 1996). This refers to a consciousness of gender in the structuring of children's daily lives, 'which respects and values every individual girl and boy, and which creates physical environments and activities all of which oppose limited gender roles' (Jensen, 1996: 15). Gender pedagogy evolved from the realisation that the prevalent gender neutral approach did not effectively promote equality of opportunity or break down traditional gender roles. The new approach drew on the Danish philosophy of children's autonomy and self-determination in their learning and development (ibid.). In Norway, there is a debate about evolving a definition of 'masculine caring' (Cameron, 1997c). We wanted to explore the relevance of these ideas to a British childcare workforce.

Analysis

After the worker interviews were transcribed, and the parent interviews coded and entered into SPSS, the material was initially subjected to the 'Framework' method of analysis (Ritchie and Spencer, 1995). This meant a sample of the worker interviews were read, and an index of codes drawn up to reflect the main topic guide headings plus additional headings emerging within the interview data. These index codes were then written onto the margin of each transcript and transferred to a series of charts, so that all the data relating to a particular heading or group of headings could be readily handled on a series of A3 sheets. The comments from the parents' interviews were collated onto grouped A4 sheets of paper so responses to each question could be easily compared. Then the process of synthesis, of making connections, identifying themes and relating the worker data to the parent data, began. Chapters 3, 4 and 5 draw mainly on the worker data, Chapter 6 mainly uses the parents' data and Chapter 7 combines both interview data sources, and draws on the college lecturers' survey and the local authority survey. Throughout the book we have interwoven respondents' thoughts and reflections with other literature in order to compare our data with that from other relevant sources so far as we are able.

From Data to Theory to Data

As we began the analysis and drew on the wider literature it became apparent that the study was shifting from being a descriptive study of gender in childcare institutions to one which would critically and thematically examine the production of a gender discourse within the institutions, and between the institutions and the outside world, through the views of parents and staff. By the 'production of a gender discourse' we are referring to the ways in which matters such as gender differences, gender identities and gender relations are discussed (or not), thought about (or not), considered relevant or irrelevant, and how this positioning is then translated into childcare work. A key question emerged early in the analysis about how gender underpins and is woven into the fabric of work in childcare services, and how this relates to the inter-relationship between workers' sense of self-identity and that of the institutionally prescribed or evolved work role. This interweaving of self, work/profession and institution was a constant theme in the research process.

The theme of workers' sense of self as workers drew the analysis away from a sole focus on men and the production of gendered identities such as masculinities, towards a focus on the production of a gendered discourse within childcare work. A focus on men would have emphasised their novelty while at the same time obscuring the differences between men that we found to be so evident. 'Men', as we found again and again, are not a unitary category. The idea of 'men' in childcare work may indicate an unusual and perhaps readily compartmentalised unit of study, but, in fact, we found that the relations between men and women workers, between men and their employing childcare centres, both in terms of the position occupied and the philosophy or policies of the centre, and between men and parents, to be mediating the experience of being a 'man' or being masculine within childcare work.

In the course of making gender visible we found women workers' views and experiences, and the ethos and philosophy of the centres as a whole, to be equally productive of a gendered discourse as the employment of men. We argue therefore that enduring ideologies of motherhood are an important factor in structuring the production of gender in childcare work. Our analysis of men and women workers and of parents led us from the particular to the general in two ways. First, there appeared to be consequences for childcare work and childcare institutions as a whole of consideration of issues of gender so that, regardless of the gender balance of the workforce, gender is a salient issue in defining the character of work with young children and their parents. Second, analysis of the production of gender appeared to lead to an analysis of organisational practices and management styles and in particular the issue of reflexivity in childcare practice as discussed in Chapter 1. We draw upon the work of Dahlberg *et al.* (1999) in this area of analysis.

Notes

1. Statistics for service in the education system are expressed in terms of pupils attending, while statistics for service in the welfare system show numbers of registered places. The figure for education system places is an estimate based on the assumption that two pupils attending part-time occupy one full-time place. The figure given for places is probably a small under-estimate as it makes no allowance for places that are not being used.
2. The location of early childhood services within the welfare system in Denmark should be seen in the context of what Esping-Anderson (1990) has defined as the Scandinavian model of the welfare state, with a commitment to redistribution, universality and high levels of benefits and services. Location within the welfare system therefore does not mean selective services targeted on particular groups of children, e.g., with working parents, from disadvantaged backgrounds or defined as 'at risk'.

3

How do Men and Women come to be Childcare Workers?

They had a childcare course at school, like the GCSE childcare and that sort of thing, but it was open to . . . like the girls basically, so I mean it was offered to them first. So I'd wanted to do it from then and I actually spoke to the school.
(Male worker)

What makes a man and woman a childcare worker? What are their career paths and qualifications for the job? Does gender make a difference to career choices in the childcare field? In this chapter, we will examine the signposts along the paths of childcare careers for men and for women. We will document and compare workers' motives for entering childcare work; their qualifications; their employment routes and their ambitions for their careers. We will identify gendered differences, and similarities, and offer some explanations for these.

Entering Childcare Work

How did the men and women we interviewed arrive at their childcare jobs? Among the women, the largest group were those who decided to enter childcare work while still at school. Five of the sample of ten women grew up with the idea that they would work with children. A sixth woman made the decision while at university. Typical comments from this group were: 'I always knew I wanted to work with children' and 'I never wanted to work in an office, I always wanted to do something else, so I think it was children or animals, which is quite normal, but yeah, it worked out to children'.

Two more women had worked in related fields – residential work and as a school helper and at playgroups – before obtaining childcare work. The remaining two women changed careers after some years in fashion and design work, and had decided to retrain for work in childcare during a period of unemployment.

None of the men grew up with a similar sense of certainty about wanting to work with children. Two knew they were interested in childcare work, but never had an opportunity to do childcare courses while at school. The only comparable phase for decision-making among the group of men were spells of unemployment. Six men, including the above two, decided to try childcare work while they were unemployed. Three of them went onto training courses and from there into employment. A fourth relied on his childcare related voluntary work to obtain employment, and a fifth relied on his full-time fathering as well as part-time youth work to gain employment. The sixth entered childcare work through his experience as a family liaison officer with the military, and through his experience as a father.

The remaining five men represented a similar range of backgrounds to those held by the women. Three men had worked in childcare related employment – in residential social work, as a teacher in a refugee camp, and as a primary age teacher – before obtaining their present jobs, and one had worked as an actor, not with children at all. Only one, Nick, consciously chose the preschool age group while undertaking a professional qualification, a PGCE in primary education.

Why Did they Choose Childcare?

For six women workers, the choice of childcare work was an extension of skills learned earlier in life. Women workers described having an 'activities drawer' as a child to entertain cousins and neighbours, forcing sisters into playing 'school', and, more than anything, being around children in large families where they felt their role was comfortable and 'natural'. With this background, choosing to work with children was not difficult; it was part of a lifelong commitment to them.

For a further six workers, four men and two women, the choice of childcare was made during an employment hiatus in their lives. They were typically unemployed, and casting around for a career or a second career. Hitting on the choice of childcare work seemed to draw on earlier inclinations and experiences of being around children. The two women in this group, for example, had trained in the design world, and found employment therein unsatisfying and unpredictable. For one, the option of childcare work had been explored while at school, as she said she had 'always loved being around children', but had been discouraged by advisers in favour of pursuing her skills in art and design. The second woman began helping her sister at a playgroup when she became unemployed, and her sister encouraged her to retrain in childcare. She found that this voluntary experience reawakened previously developed skills and enjoyment in being with young children.

This theme of taking up childcare later on in one's career and it tapping into earlier, familial experiences of children ran through some of the men's stories, too. Two men, while unemployed, were able to take up places on childcare training schemes. They did so both because they were offered the opportunity, and because they realised they had enjoyed being with children during their childhoods. One of them said he had considered childcare work when at sixth form, but had been discouraged in favour of clerical work.

A third man, also when unemployed, had became convinced during a spell as a volunteer in Romanian orphanages that working with children was 'the natural thing to do' on his return. The fourth man, while unemployed after being made redundant by a training company, chanced upon an advert for a job he thought he could do on the basis of his experience as a father, and previously as a family liaison officer in the military, and applied.

The third group of workers moved into childcare as a deliberate change of career. The motivations for changing career were a mixture of the philosophical, the intellectual, the personal-political and the practical. This group comprised seven men and two women. For example, two men trained as primary school teachers and moved into work with younger children. Trevor initially worked both overseas and in multicultural support teams serving a number of primary schools. He gradually realised that he found the age group and subject based teaching less fulfilling than the stimulation of the process of children's learning. He said, 'I think I became interested in youger children because I mean I think I find children interesting and how children learn interesting and I'm less interested in teaching a subject.' The second teacher, Nick, was motivated by his commitment to philosophies of progressive education which he thought incompatible with classroom teaching, but more possible in childcare centres with young children. He said:

> It was becoming clear to me that principles I thought were important were possible to put into practice in nursery settings . . . in terms of offering children lots of choice and access to equipment and flexibility indoors and outdoors and looking at the whole child rather than just having one person with 30 children. I thought it was important to have an all round perspective and to offer children that sense of choice, autonomy, responsibility, that's what really attracted me to working with under 5s.

After qualifying as a teacher, Nick began work in a childcare centre.

Fred, who trained in drama, found acting ultimately unfulfilling, and wanted a method of teaching that was congruent with his own philosophy, and so retrained in Montessori education. He said:

> I was doing drama, acting and drama education. I began to realise that the education side of it was more interesting to me than the acting side. I began to explore this and look around for educational philosophies that I liked. I came across Montessori and it seemed to fit what I believed anyway. I had some reservations about the age group. I thought 'do I really want to be surrounded by a bunch of screaming 3 year-olds?' I went to visit some nurseries and found that I could relate to the children and they seemed to respond to me. I liked it. So I did the Montessori training.

Oliver held a personal commitment to a particular childcare organisation through his church, a commitment sustained through voluntary activities such as youth work. When he had the opportunity following redundancy from a career in financial services, he applied for and got a job at the centre, thus pursuing an alternative career in childcare begun in a voluntary capacity. A fifth man, Lloyd, who had many years of experience in residential social work, gradually found himself attracted to work with younger children so as to 'hit the problems before they developed'. Last, Yusuf, who originally trained in Pakistan as a teacher, was working in a refugee camp as a volunteer at weekends and was inspired by a meeting with the head of the workers' co-operative children's centre and managed to arrange to move to England to work there. He said that working with children was from 'something in my heart'.

Three workers moved into childcare work for practical reasons. Two (one woman, one man) had been full-time parents and doing part-time childcare related work such as youth work, playgroup work and as a school helper. They found childcare work to be a more stable form of employment. The third, a woman, an ex-residential social worker, found the daytime hours of childcare work domestically more convenient.

To summarise, the women were more likely than the men to choose to work in childcare because they held a lifelong commitment to work in this field. The men, on the other hand, were more likely than the women to pursue a childcare career for individual or philosophical reasons. Quite a high proportion of this group of workers moved into childcare work through the experience of unemployment and/or redundancy. This idea of childcare as a 'second chance career' has been noted (Williams, 1995; Penn and McQuail, 1996) as a significant route into the work for men, but this data shows that women also move into childcare as a change of career. However, as we shall see, the 'choice' of working with children is made in the context of educational background and qualifications, of the support or lack of it from family and friends, and in the context of ambition and contentment at work.

Educational Background and Qualification

British childcare workers hold a great range of qualifications, reflecting a lack of consensus on the relative balance of experience and qualification thought necessary on the one hand, and the appropriate blend of caring and teaching skills required for young children on the other (Moss and Penn, 1996; Suffolk County Council et al., 1998). Research shows that the level of qualifications held by childcare workers in Britain is not high (Moss et al., 1995). The workers we interviewed were more highly qualified than childcare workers are on average: indeed all held a relevant qualification or training background. However, in keeping with the national picture, and the institutions represented, the range of qualifications was broad.

There was no difference between the men and the women in their school leaving achievements. Within each gender group, three held 'A' levels on leaving school and six held 'O' levels/GCSEs. One man had left school with no qualifications[1]. Workers' attainments within the further and vocational education sector are less easy to describe. Some workers held more than one vocational qualification; others did not hold any. As a general picture, the women were twice as likely as the men to hold a specific childcare qualification such as an NNEB, or BTEC, in Nursery Nursing or equivalent. Six women but only three men were so qualified. Other relevant qualifications held were the City and Guilds in Childcare, the NVQ in Childcare Levels 1 and 2, and the NVQ in Playwork Level 3. Also represented were qualifications and short courses in residential care, in youth work, in social work and counselling. Two workers, one man and one woman, held Montessori teaching qualifications; the woman also held a drama qualification.

Four men and two women had higher degrees (a third woman was studying for a Diploma in Social Work). The degrees held were in teaching (two men), in education, training and development (one man), in psychology (one woman), in drama (one man), and in fashion design (one woman). As will be apparent from the degree subjects, the extent to which the workers relied on their formal training in their childcare work varied. To some extent, the breadth of qualification backgrounds related to the range of institutions represented. For example, the workers employed in family centres in particular held qualifications for childcare work drawn broadly from 'care' and 'people' type qualifications and short courses, and relied on parental experience rather than relevant formal qualifications.

Job Histories and Recruitment

It will be apparent by now that a linear progression into childcare work via predictable stages of vocational or higher education is reserved for a relatively small group; about half the women interviewed[2]. The connection between childcare as work and domestic or familial roles with young children is made by some women relatively early in their thinking about careers. Even the women who make these connections and foresee a fulfilling role for themselves in working with young children are often dissuaded from it and encouraged to take other kinds of employment. A few men, those with teaching qualifications, held fairly linear careers, but even these changed age groups from primary to nursery at some point in their careers. Most of our childcare workers, men and women, had a chequered employment history. Table 3.1 summarises the employment and voluntary work experiences held by workers.

Table 3.1 *Men and women childcare workers' work experiences*

Childcare related employment	Childcare related voluntary work	Unrelated employment
Nanny	School for children with	Shop work
School assistant	behavioural and	Warehouse work
Private and public nursery	emotional difficulties	Administration
officers/assistants	Drama group helper	Medical rescue work
Playgroup worker	School helper	Fashion design
Teacher	VSO teacher trainer	Graphic design
Residential care/children	Orphanage work overseas	Acting
Residential care/adults	Crèche worker/supervisor	Financial services
Bi-lingual classroom	Youth club helper/leader	Navy
assistant		Gardening
		Roofing
		Bus driving
		Post office manager

One example of a chequered job progression for a man went as follows. With few school leaving qualifications, William could not pursue his ambitions at the sixth form stage of doing a childcare course as his parents had recently been made redundant and he had to earn some money for the household. He became a solicitor's filing clerk and then a clerk for a tax firm for over three years. He was then made redundant. The employment agency advised him about the local TEC and the availability of childcare courses. He completed a six-month City and Guilds in Childcare course which included placements in nurseries. William then signed on with a childcare agency and worked in several nurseries covering for maternity leave and staff shortages. When he was offered a lucrative short-term contract in administration work he temporarily left childcare work, returning onto the agency books and temporary work before being advised of a vacancy in the chain of nurseries for which he now works. After ten years in the labour market, William entered his first permanent childcare job only a few months before interview.

The US childcare training organisation, NAEYC, has used the term 'lattice' to describe the levels of professional preparation and the sequence of sideways movements that typically characterise childcare workers' career moves. One of the women we interviewed illustrated this concept well. Straight after 'A' levels, Brenda got married and had three children. The first two were born close together and she was very busy. Once they were at school she worked in a shop, and then managed her father's post office business. The third child was born after some years and 'I just felt that I had the time and I sort of did things with him', including becoming involved in setting up the local playgroup. She then worked as a classroom assistant, both in a special school and as a bi-lingual assistant in a primary school. At the same time she completed two part-time BTECs (in Nursery Nursing and in Social Care), and, after one year of studying, she obtained her present part-time job in a family centre. Brenda's ultimate ambition is to become a social worker, and she began a full-time Diploma in Social Work soon after starting work at the family centre. She fits her employment hours around college requirements. Eighteen years after leaving school, Brenda is close to realising her ambitions for her career, having combined employment, further education and mothering responsibilities for a number of years.

The chequered career, or lattice, is the dominant picture in these workers' employment histories. The differences between men and women relate to two factors: first, the degree to which other (e.g. family) responsibilities impinge on the ability to seek a childcare career at the school or college leaving stage; and second, the degree to which the career expectations of family, school and self mesh to provide an avenue of possibility for childcare. One striking feature of these workers' job histories is the incidence of obstacles in deciding on, and moving into, childcare work. Some workers described specific experiences during their recruitment.

John reported that when applying for jobs he was subject to anti-male discrimination.

The minute they know you're a man it's 'Oh no, the job's gone', I mean I've had that so many times when I've phoned like for a job . . . I know I've been suspicious because they seem quite talkative about it until like a little while on . . . so I've asked somebody else to phone up and the job hadn't gone, so this happened quite a few times . . . not so much in social services . . . it's more private day nurseries, the smaller ones.

John was the only man to report such explicit bias against him as a man, but others reported difficulty getting work with young children. William took a sick leave cover job at his student placement childcare centre because 'I thought it would be a bit difficult, me being newly qualified, it might have been a little bit difficult to get a job'. Hannah, with an NNEB qualification, spent six months going for childcare job interviews before getting her present job: 'there was a lot of competition out there', she said. Rachel was given considerable help and encouragement from her placement supervisor whose daughter worked in a nursery and who told her about vacancies. Yusuf worked as a volunteer at a centre with school age children and concurrently did a part-time qualification before he was taken onto the paid staff to work with the younger age group.

On the other hand, some workers did report finding work with ease. Duncan said that when he moved to London and applied for local authority nursery jobs 'they were fighting over me' precisely because he was a man. Michelle got her first job as a nursery nurse in a school before leaving college. Fred got his Montessori teaching job through being on a student placement at the school where he eventually became headmaster.

The concept of the career 'lattice' rather than ladder appears to be borne out among both men and women. Although factors other than the personal characteristics of workers, such as economic buoyancy, will affect the ease with which childcare workers can get employment, several points emerge from this data to illustrate how men and women become childcare workers. First, to an extent the main relevant qualifications available support women rather than men entering the work. The NNEB and the BTEC Nursery Nursing are available from age 16 for those with some GCSEs, references and successful personal interview, and whose family backgrounds have given them an experience of being around children and which values their 'being around' children (Cameron, 1997b). The men who did these courses, and lower level childcare courses, did them usually part-time, alongside employment and at a later stage.

The availability of part-time courses at varying levels and offered by various accreditation boards would appear to help men entering the field later on in their employment careers. They do, of course, also help women 'returners' and women who change career, but, significantly, no man we interviewed had begun an NNEB or equivalent on leaving school and then entered childcare employment in the way that women did. Moreover, our survey of childcare college lecturers confirmed that men are a fairly marginal concern on childcare training courses. Fewer than 20 per cent of responding lecturers thought that the colleges aimed their recruitment material specifically at attracting men students; and only just over 20 per cent of respondents thought the number of men students applying to childcare courses had increased over recent years.

About 2 per cent of students were men and the most men students recorded in any college on a part- or full-time CACHE or BTEC Diploma was five, compared with 320 women recorded in one college on a full-time CACHE Diploma. For some lecturers, placing men students in practice placements had been a problem: about a fifth of respondents thought there were more difficulties obtaining practice placements for male students than for female. By far the majority of the respondents, however, said they would prefer the gender balance on their courses, and in the childcare workforce, to be more even.

Second, the role of employment agencies, both government funded and commercial, is worth noting. In two cases, employment agencies directed workers towards childcare courses as a prelude to employment; in five cases, childcare agencies put forward men's names alongside women's for childcare work, temporary work which became more permanent employment. William provided an example of a positive use of employment agencies for promoting men into childcare work. He said:

> At the time I was unemployed for a number of months and the employment agency asked me 'what would I like to do? If there was anything that I would like to do, what would it be?' And so I said 'well, I've always wanted to get into childcare, I've just never had an opportunity to'. So they says (sic) 'oh, well, we've just started this course' and I thought 'oh, thank you!'.

Given the way men (and some women) seem to come into childcare work at a later stage in their careers, often during an employment hiatus when they may be casting around for an appropriate career choice, the agencies they use to provide support and assistance have the potential to open up childcare work as a possible career choice to those who may not have considered it before. They also, of course, hold the power to reinforce gendered career expectations and to dissuade men and women from entering the profession.

The third point, however, is that it seems likely that men who know they want to work with younger children seek to obtain a teaching qualification, rather than an NNEB. This is a means of entry to higher paid and higher status employment than the NNEB allows, but, unless nursery education is specified initially, requires a later transition to work with under 5s. So, although men may have similar experiences to women in terms of their early exposure to children and formulating an idea that they may like to work with children, they tend not to act upon it in the same way. They tend to either go into something else on leaving school, and wait for a further opportunity; or they interpret their inclinations as a move towards teaching and enter higher education.

Support

The support received by workers from family and friends for their work choices was clearly gendered. Women won straightforward and wholehearted approval for choosing childcare work. For men, familial and peer support was patchy. None of the men entered the field with the committed backing of parents, spouse and friends that women enjoyed.

Support from Families

The terms used by the women to describe the response from their families about their work choices included 'pleased', 'proud', 'happy', 'appropriate for a girl', 'supportive' and 'completely behind me'. There was a strong sense that caring work with children was an obvious and excellent choice for women, even if they first entered another occupation. For example, Brenda's family supported her decision: 'I think there's this notion that mothers go into a caring field'. Few reservations about childcare work were expressed by family members. The low wages to be expected from the work were mentioned by Hannah's parents. She said that 'they did say to me "you don't earn a lot of money when you're working with children", this was when I was about 13 or 14, and I didn't . . . I'd rather do a job that I enjoy and got satisfaction out of . . .' The other reservation was not about childcare work so much as about employment itself. Fozia grew up in Pakistan and her father wanted her to follow custom and stay at home. However, when her parents separated, Fozia's father was no longer able to stop her: she left home to study childcare and then moved to England to work with her mother's blessing.

For the men, the response of family members was more likely to be one of surprise. Kieran said 'my wife was quite surprised, because, quite frankly, in 26 years of being in the military, I was rarely home . . . I missed many special days (in my children's lives)'. Fred said 'my mother was surprised that I wanted to give up acting. She very much felt that's what she wanted me to do and couldn't really understand it.' Some parents went further and didn't approve of the choice. John said 'My mum was fine, she knows how good I am with children. My dad, I still don't really get on with him . . . he's the sort "go out and get a proper job" . . . he thinks we sit around all day . . . I get so frustrated.' The theme of a 'proper job' was also echoed by William, whose stepmother was 'quite distressed, she didn't think it was a proper job for me'. Nick, who began a teaching career in a childcare centre, said he was 'not taken seriously' by his family, as the work 'wasn't a proper teaching job'. Other parents were reported as not understanding the work: Stuart said: 'I don't think my parents understand what I do, it's quite hard trying to explain sometimes . . . they're not critical . . . they are from a generation where they didn't have family centres.'

Some families were supportive of the men's choices, usually in the context of other factors. Many members of Trevor's family were teachers, so embarking on a teaching career was unexceptional for him. Oliver's family were similarly involved in caring professions and found his choice of work fitted in with the family model. Another influence on men taking up childcare work was family involvement in the church. Duncan's family were described as 'very supportive'. The family were all involved in the same church and 'because I was also doing Sunday School, they'd seen me working with young children, they knew (visiting) Romania had had a deep effect on me and a big impact on my life and . . . they were really pleased.' Lloyd, also from a committed church family, said his wife and children were 'very good, didn't have any qualms at all' about his change of career into childcare. Lastly, Yusuf was an example of family support for a career choice independent of other factors, which he thought unusual for his native Pakistan. He said his parents 'never pushed me to do it, they never pushed their choice to me'.

Support from Friends

The pattern of support from friends was similar to that from families. Women workers unanimously reported encouragement from their friends about the choice of childcare work. The response among the men's friends ranged from support and surprise, to ridicule and confusion.

Stuart said he changed his friends when he moved towns and left roofing work. Most of his friends now 'are quite supportive and think it's good for men to be working with children'. Similarly, Nick reported that he had 'met some good people through the work . . . most of (them) could appreciate why I was doing the work'. However, Kieran said that friends who knew him in the army were surprised at the transfer. 'I guess their perception of me in uniform is somebody that probably wouldn't have done this and I think they're surprised . . . they just see you as, you know, maybe a gruff old sergeant'.

William found that his women friends were more likely to question why a man 'would want to work with children'; whereas his men friends saw it as a 'natural progression'. On the other hand, John's men friends gave him 'a bit of stick when I first started . . . a lot of my friends are like builders and plumbers . . . it's like "oh, it must be like a really easy job where I reckon you just sit around all day and get paid for it". It wasn't done in a horrible way. It's more joking around . . .'

Trevor reported that 'sometimes people think it's a strange thing for a man to do . . . the common one one gets, you say you work in a nursery and they assume it's something to do with plants'. Duncan had also encountered some confusion about his job and gender status. 'When I say I'm a Nursery Officer (some people say) "so you work with flowers?"'. Duncan also reported coming across people when he was starting out who assumed that because he wanted to work with children he would be training to become a teacher. But overall, Duncan felt 'there was quite a few reserved judgements and quite a few (who said) "Go for it"' among his friends.

Two men said they didn't talk about their work much with friends, partly because of the confusion arising between their gender and the assumption that such work is woman-dominated, but mostly because of a risk of breaching confidentiality in a small local community.

In summary, it is unlikely that men workers made their choices about childcare work solely on the basis of approval or otherwise of friends or family. Moreover, none of the workers reported wanting to leave childcare employment because of comments from those outside the profession. Those who had met with opposition or resistance to choices perceived as unusual for their gender were keen to downplay the significance of comments from others, by saying 'it doesn't bother me', or 'they accept it now', or 'it was just joking around'.

It is arguably the case that universal support helps women childcare workers to feel the choice is a 'natural' one. Without support workers could feel isolated, or commitment to their chosen work could wane. But the effects of any lack of familial and peer support seemed to disappear with time. This seemed to happen both by gaining confidence in work, and by a gradual shift in friendships, so that the values and philosophies of their work were better reflected in their evolving peer groups. So the responses of family and friends could be an effective inhibiting factor in men taking up childcare employment, but once they are employed, their ability to withstand the confusion or challenge to their gender identity from others grows with duration on the job.

Staying Put and Moving On

Respondents were asked what they thought they would be doing in five years time. Childcare work has a high turnover rate (Cameron, 1997a; Whitebook *et al.*, 1998), and men workers in non-traditional professions are seen as transient workers (Williams, 1995; Clyde, 1994) who may add to that turnover rate. We were interested in the extent to which our sample of men and women were content with their work and their workplaces, or whether they held career ambitions which entailed planning to move on.

The men and women we interviewed spanned childcare work experience: their duration of employment, as well as gendered expectations of career, structured responses to our questions about where they saw themselves in five years time. Indeed, one man was due for retirement during this period. The most common response (11) was to see themselves doing the same as at present or doing some work relevant courses to maintain their interest and expertise. There were more women than men who saw this outcome for themselves (seven *vs* four). The gender balance was reversed among those who had specific career ambitions. Six men and three women saw themselves moving into specialist posts as a sideways move, becoming managers or owners of childcare institutions, or qualifying in a higher status profession, such as social work or psychotherapy. As we saw in Chapter 1, men in non-traditional occupations tend to use their minority status to further their career ambitions: this pattern was confirmed among the workers we interviewed.

The dimension of seniority affected ambition so that those workers occupying more junior positions tended to have higher career expectations. Of the five who already held senior positions, three saw themselves 'staying put', one envisaged a possible sideways move and one owning her own business, not necessarily in childcare. These five, plus Lloyd, who foresaw retirement, recognised where they had got to in their work lives and saw that other commitments would be taking precedence for a while. For example, Anne, a centre owner on maternity leave, envisaged having another child in the near future and 'keeping a watching brief' on the centre while she focused her time on her own young children before resuming her career. Fred, who was shortly to become head of a centre, predicted a period of consolidation of his leadership skills. He too had a young child and wanted to combine employment with being an active father-carer. Caroline, who held a senior position but frequently felt disempowered in her job, was the only one in this group to express ambition motivated by frustration and a lack of job satisfaction. She thought she would rather work for herself.

Wanting to move on or stay put is not a decision made out of context. Although some workers, men in particular, held personal and specific work goals from the start, others felt their particular, exceptional workplaces were a very good reason to stay where they were and were utterly content. Duncan was an example of an ambitious man who had devoted some time to considering his career path. He said 'it's always been my ambition to go into management . . . realistically, in five years time, I would like to be a deputy . . . if I'm still a Nusery Officer in five years time I'll be disgusted'. Duncan had an instrumental view of work; for him, the setting where he currently worked was a passport to fulfilling personal career objectives elsewhere. But for Fozia, the institution itself is the critical feature of her work satisfaction and decision to stay put. Fozia said:

> I love working with children and . . . under no circumstances I don't think I'll ever leave this centre and, you know, sort of look elsewhere or anything, 'cos I know I'll never sort of be able to work in any other provision maybe because I came here first and that I'm used to it now . . . I think, I don't know, again, I think it's the friendliness of the staff and lovely children.

These workers would appear to endorse earlier findings about men's transient presence in so-called 'women's work' (Williams, 1995) and their internalisation of ambition in childcare related professions (Skelton, 1991). Furthermore, Williams (1995) makes the point that men workers import into 'women's work' ideas of career and ambition more usually found in 'men's work'. For example, among this group of workers the process of thinking ahead about one's career and being overtly ambitious would appear to be a mostly male characteristic: most women thought they would either stay where they were or had vague ideas about 'going higher'. Two women were exceptions to this: Brenda and Erica, who both worked in family centres, had an instrumental view of their current work setting and saw themselves becoming a social worker and a psychotherapist respectively within a few years.

Discussion

Men and women come to be childcare workers by different routes. Although absolute patterns are rare, there are significant differences that can be ascribed to gendered experiences and interpretations of work and self. In this discussion, we shall try to elucidate the process of becoming a childcare worker through gendered eyes, while still remembering the exceptions in the detail.

Seamless and Rethought Careers

One important distinction in the process of becoming a childcare worker is that of 'seamless' and 'rethought' careers. Seamless careers are those where a decision is taken while still in education about a career to pursue and the steps, or jobs, along the way. An ultimate goal may, or may not, be in sight. Rethought careers, on the other hand, are those working lives where at some point through unemployment or redundancy, disenchantment or release from domestic responsibilities, a worker reviews the direction of their employment and may undertake some (more) training or qualifications and re-enter work. Among this sample, men were more likely to have rethought their careers in order to enter childcare than the women (nine men and four women). Two men (the teachers Nick and Trevor) and six women had had seamless careers.

This chapter has illustrated the importance of an 'employment hiatus' in recruiting men into childcare work. This represents a critical moment in re-thinking employment options and sources of work satisfaction. It also involves reviewing earlier experiences, such as 'being around' children and recognising that skills and enjoyment with children can be translated into employment. While this process would appear to come effortlessly to women, it is much more difficult for men. The effortlessness, or naturalness, of women viewing themselves as childcare workers undoubtedly contributes to women pursing a seamless career in childcare. The opposite is true for men: few connections are made between being around children and employment options for the future while in early adulthood, so entry into childcare work is usually a rethought career. The two exceptions in this sample were teachers, and even they had re-oriented themselves from primary age teaching to work with preschool age children. One finding, then, is that men do not grow up knowing they will work with young children: women do.

Wheels within Wheels: Families, Gender and Training in Childcare

The temporal proximity of childcare training to childhood affects men's and women's entry into the childcare field. The main childcare qualifications, the CACHE Diploma in Nursery Nursing and its equivalents, are available immediately after leaving school, at age 16, for those with a minimum number of GCSE passes plus satisfactory references and interview. As noted above, women take with them from childhood experiences of being around children when considering their childcare careers, whereas if men do consider working with children, they tend to interpret this as a teaching career. Families are an important source of career advice to young people (Banks et al., 1992). The responses from this sample of workers suggest that the influence of families works in two ways. First, by offering opportunities to try out being with young children both as parents (fathers as well as mothers), and as siblings, cousins, aunts and uncles. Several workers referred to always having children around, to caring for their siblings, to babysitting and to taking an interest in neighbours' children. This was the case for both men and for women in the sample.

The second way families influence career choices is by offering approval or otherwise for decisions about careers. For example, John's mother 'knew how good I was with children'; and Vera's decision was supported because 'childcare was already in the family'. However, the comments referred to earlier about men requiring a 'proper job', a term that excluded childcare work, suggests that families, whilst recognising individual skills, also discipline their offspring to conform to predominant societal understandings of gendered work. Would, for example, John's mother have needed to 'know' how good he was with children if John was a woman entering the work? Would it have been enough to have been a woman? Georgia said her parents had thought her choice was 'appropriate for a girl', suggesting that her gender was sufficient qualification to enter childcare work with parental support.

With this combination of practised skills and familial approval, it is not surprising that women take up childcare training opportunities at a point when, on leaving school, they can immediately build on their success to date. Moreover, the model of training traditionally focuses on infant care and simulating mother-care, thus further reinforcing the idea of domestic, familial caring roles that women usually occupy (Penn, 1996). But how do men respond to their experiences of children in childhood? Three respondents who had been around children gave some insight into this process.

John tried to get onto the GCSE Childcare course while at school, but found that all the places were filled by girls. He didn't know whether it was 'just pure chance ... or like restricted to girls'. He was also bullied at school, and eventually absented himself completely. He found his way into childcare through a YTS programme. William spent some years of his childhood in local authority care and looked after his siblings and other children. 'Because I'd always been around children (in care, this) was a big part of my life.' William admired his social worker and wanted to emulate him but thought he was better suited to younger children than older ones. He thought about childcare options while at sixth form, but his family could not afford for him to be at college rather than earning a salary. He eventually trained in childcare through the support of the employment agency. Yusuf came from a large Pakistani family where there was relatively little pressure on his choice of career. He said 'I think that was my nature' to work with children. But he started off training in medicine, and then, due to family responsibilities, he returned to his home town and studied for a BEd in primary teaching and from there moved into refugee kindergartens and childcare work.

For all three, their skills and experience with children were discounted in favour of other avenues of (un)employment on account of their gender. Several different kinds of masculinity can be seen in their stories. The first image is of a school truant, subsequently unemployed and unskilled, inhabiting a particular (sub)cultural role. A period of unemployment both prompted and permitted the transformation of his role by moving into 'women's work', albeit in a man's world (Smedley, 1997). In the second, there are twin images of the 'vulnerable yet caring young man', and simultaneously of the family breadwinner, not free to choose his own way into work. The third man was relatively advantaged within his native Pakistan, being able to choose his training and occupation. The images here are of family breadwinner, and of altruistic-political commitment, before pursuing his 'nature' of liking children as a form of employment. Men, it would seem, do not respond to their childhood by entering childcare training, but are motivated by images of masculinity, such as earning money for the household, or training for higher status occupations, or being unemployed.

So the proximity of childcare training to the childhood years builds upon influences within women's childhoods, but fails to tap so readily into men's experiences and expectations of their behaviour. Men and women are differently propelled towards, or away from, childcare work through their childhood influences, and through the construction of training. This finding begs the question of the content of the childcare training, and why it is attractive or 'natural' for women, yet not for men. It also suggests that childcare courses designed for mature students, and available alongside part-time employment, may be particularly appropriate for men. The evidence from our survey of college lecturers, however, suggests that training course providers will also have to address the question of mixed gender recruitment strategies. In addition, the role of employment agencies in promoting men's introduction to childcare work is important.

Contentment and Ambition: the Construction of a Gendered Career

Contentment and ambition are central to the stability of the childcare workforce. If workers are content, they more readily stay in workplaces providing the stability and continuity of relationships that are thought critical to high quality childcare (*cf* Cameron, 1997a). Ambition, on the other hand, with a focus on the achievement of personal work goals and self-fulfilment through promotion and greater rewards, tends to lead workers out of childcare centres. These two ideas about workers' perspectives about their work, that they must stay or go, can neglect the role of the institution. For example, if ambition was harnessed by centres, it could contribute to the enhancement of the scope and quality of childcare work. By the same token contentment can easily become stale and repetitive work: merely staying put would have consequences for the degree to which the environment was stimulating to workers.

Contentment and ambition also have gendered aspects. Crudely speaking, the women we spoke to were 'content' and the men more readily spoke of their 'ambitions'. A similar pattern was noted by Acker in relation to teachers in primary schools (Acker, 1994). Drawing this distinction neglects the career aspirations held by some women, particularly seen in those who wanted to move out of childcare altogether and into related fields such as social work, but it does serve to remind us of the need to consider ambition in the context of workers' lives, rather than just their work.

One key aspect of workers' lives relates to their domestic and family commitments. Combining employment and other commitments has been a continuing issue for women, and it may be emerging as an issue for some men, as well (Deven *et al.*, 1998). Studies of childcare staff turnover reveal that family and personal reasons account for a high proportion of the reasons staff leave their posts (Whelan, 1993). Brannen and Moss (1991) reported that many women with young children may want to 'mark time' in their careers while their children are young. This was in fact reported by two of our workers, Anne and Fred, both parents of infant children who wanted to both be active parents and pursue their childcare careers. There may be a case for extending the concept of 'ambition' to include such commitments, and not restrict it to work goals.

A second aspect of workers' lives is their sense of work fulfilment. It is this that leads to stability in employing centres, or, alternatively, to seek employment elsewhere. A good example of retaining staff is offered by the Sheffield Children's Centre where staff turnover is very low, despite the presence of conventional predictors of turnover such as low wages. Importantly, perhaps, they have a highly participatory management structure, a commitment to individual training and mentoring, as well as a wide range of services under their umbrella, so there is considerable scope to extend skills and experience. One effect of focusing on how workers' goals for personal-work fulfilment can be met within the service, therefore, is to redirect ambition into the services of the centre instead of allowing it to be dispersed elsewhere.

A second example can be seen in the work of support and training officers in Emilia Romagna regions of Italy. These and other staff (known as *pedagogista*) are assigned to a small number of childcare centres with a specific remit to develop pedagogical practice. Time is set aside for this reflective development and training work. By introducing a depth of analysis to childcare practice, leading to a deeper understanding about the purpose and practice of pedagogical work, the workers' full intellectual and team working resources are drawn upon and even demanded. This process may help staff remain committed to each other and their centres (Dahlberg *et al.*, 1999).

A third point we would wish to make about gender and ambition is that men workers' use of childcare employment as a vehicle for personal career ambitions highlights the difficulties childcare faces in recruiting and sustaining not only male workers but its workforce as a whole. Childcare does not lend itself to the even moderately ambitious, as it is low paid and has few opportunities for promotion. Work on the US childcare workforce suggests that workers often leave their jobs because they are disenchanted with features of the work such as stress and low pay (e.g., Whitebook *et al.*, 1993). It would seem that while ambition may be a reason for men to leave childcare employment, other factors may lead women to leave.

Summary

This chapter has shown that while both men and women childcare workers can often reflect upon early familial experience with children, gendered career paths tend to emerge early on. Women tend to interpret their experience with children as a career choice while at school or college; men tend not to make their choices until later, often while unemployed and reviewing their employment options. Families have a clear role in this gendering of careers: they offer the experience of being with children, but the ambivalent support offered to men showed that they can also act as a constraint upon men's choices of working in childcare.

The gendering of careers seems to continue in adult life. The current model of childcare training capitalises on women's early childhood experiences by providing a straightforward entry point at the end of compulsory schooling. Men's post-school education choices, however, show them responding to ideas about masculinity/ies that may steer them away from undertaking childcare courses. It may be that courses for mature entrants would be particularly attractive to some men who were considering childcare work options. Once in work, the men were more likely to want to move into management or higher status professions than the women, whose ambitions were more likely to be vague or to be content with their working environment. Finally, we argue that the role of the institution in meeting the ambitions of workers is critical when examining how to retain workers. For example, a centre that incorporates a wide range of services across the preschool and school age groups is more likely to offer the scope to develop workers' skills in different areas of practice and so 'keep them on board'.

Notes

1. The remainder were missing data (2).
2. Although, in terms of female childcare workers overall, this could be assumed to be by far the most dominant pattern.

4

The Institution: Gendered Practice

It not only affects the direct work with a man and the children, but also affects the whole dynamics of the team, because I do think there has been a difference, but I can't put that into words, and I don't think it's a black and white difference or a clear distinction, but I felt like [him] being introduced to the team would sort of throw us up, you know, it would create changes and challenges . . . and it has.

(Female worker)

Men and women pursue different routes to childcare work, but what differences exist in their experience of the work itself? This chapter begins by setting out the conditions in which men and women work, and then explores workers' views about, and experiences of, staff dynamics in childcare settings. The final section examines workers' perspective on the children's day within the institution. A theme running through the chapter is the question of whether differences are related to gender or individual personality. A second recurring theme is the feeling of being different, or an Other. As we noted in Chapter 1, the concept of Other has been developed in relation to a range of issues such as women's subjective experiences, colonialism and ethics, but is translated here to the experience of being male in a largely female workplace. We argue that gender is embedded in the workplace, and only becomes 'visible' when it is consciously invoked. One, perhaps partial, method of invoking gender relations is the employment of men workers.

Staff Conditions

Workers in this study confirm the findings reported by Penn (1995) and Vernon and Smith (1994) about salaries for childcare workers. Pay is low. Staff we spoke to working in the private sector, those without managerial responsibilities, and those employed in the workers' co-operative, all had salaries below average for women workers in Great Britain, which was £297 per week, equivalent to £15,400 per year for full-time workers (EOC, 1998). Table 4.1 summarises the average salaries paid in the different childcare institutions. For nursery workers and their equivalents in family centres such as family aides and project workers, salaries ranged from £8,200 to £17,000. For those with managerial responsibilities such as owners, managers and teachers in a senior management team, salaries ranged from £19,300 to £29,000. The highest salaries were paid to staff holding senior positions in public sector services and the lowest salaries were paid to nursery officers and assistants in the private sector, and in the workers' co-operative. Salaries paid in the public sector nurseries and family centres, and in voluntary sector family centres represented in this study, were similar.

Table 4:1 *Average salaries (£, annual salary, 1997)*

	Public	Private	Voluntary/Co-op	Average salaries
Day nurseries (junior/ middle level)	14,600	9,800	8,600	11,100
Family centres (junior/ middle level)	13,000	–	• 12,600	12,800
Senior positions	23,400	20,000	–	22,100

Workers were aware of their low wages relative to the degree of responsibility they held. Rachel compared herself to her sister who was a florist and had a better salary. She said: 'it's a big responsibility, I mean we're caring for children, it's not like caring for flowers, like my sister does . . . I think it's really awful the money we get paid actually.' Trevor thought he was paid less than his contemporaries in teaching because he worked in an under-5s setting where the career structure, and so his pay prospects, were limited as 'they are by nature small places . . . they're limited to how many senior staff or how many posts of responsibility you can actually have.' Lloyd, with a lifetime's experience in caring work, said he 'couldn't exist' on the salary he was paid: 'if I didn't have a pension I couldn't do the job, I don't get paid enough'. Fozia, however, who was the lowest paid worker we spoke to, said that the quality of her working environment offset the poor wages: 'we are all on (the same) low wage . . . we don't mind because we love our job and you know, I mean, our wages depend on the children's fees . . . but if we have any problems where finance is concerned, some of us do get help from the centre'.

Four of the staff we interviewed worked part time, all in family centres. Two of these were actively looking to increase their hours, preferably to full time. The other two could negotiate longer or shorter hours as necessary to fit in with college requirements. Brenda was completing a Diploma in Social Work alongside her employment so appreciated her hours; Stuart was looking to begin a similar Diploma course and wanted to cut his hours to suit the demands of this. Other than this, the workers worked full time, generally a 40-hour week. Some staff worked a full week over four days and were able to do overtime on the fifth day to boost their income. Some staff worked shift patterns to fit in with nursery opening hours.

A few staff worked unpaid. In two nurseries staff meetings were held in the evenings, in workers' own time: in one case staff working on an early shift had to return to work for the meeting at 7pm. Meetings were held every two or three weeks. Training days were also held in staff members' own time, at weekends. Some staff also took work home. Typically, this was writing work such as observation profiles on individual children. Michelle explained that: 'you do do it in your work time and you're given time but I must admit some of it does go home'. Stuart reported that he stayed later than he was paid on a Friday so that he could participate in planning and evaluation sessions with other members of staff. Other than this, workers thought that working hours were generally contained to the paid for, day time hours.

Membership of trades unions and professional organisations was low among this group of respondents. There were four members of UNISON (all public sector nursery and family centre employees); one member of the Association of Teachers and Lecturers; two members of the Montessori Teachers Association; and one member of the Social Care Association (a total of 8/21). None of the four private nursery employees was a member of an organisation representing staff; and only one of the five staff working in voluntary sector family centres was similarly a member of an employee body.

Staff Dynamics

We were concerned to explore whether the men and women workers we spoke to identified gendered differences in the styles of communication and the subjects of conversation when men and women were employed together in childcare centres. Moreover, we wanted to know how the workers interpreted these differences, and how they may contribute to shaping the working environment. We considered men's and women's experiences of staff dynamics in four aspects of working life in childcare centres: after-work social life, staff meetings, the staff room and working together with children and parents.

Gendered Ways of Talking

Two features of centre life that characterise gendered staff dynamics are subjects of conversation and styles of communication. Jensen (1996) reported that the Scandinavian experience of mixed gender childcare working is of differences between men and women in ways of communicating. The main difference was seen as men workers introducing a new directness and straightforwardness to communication that led to a faster resolution of problems than had hitherto been the case. Such differences were seen as adding to the strengths of childcare centres' staff dynamics particularly where more than one man was employed (Jensen, 1996: 25). Workers we spoke to reported that women's experiences, as mothers of children, and as workers, form subjects of conversation from which men are frequently excluded. Men and women were also seen as having different styles of communication. Terms used to describe women's ways of talking, by both men and women, were 'open', 'explicit', 'intimate', 'close', 'catty', 'het up', 'gossipy', 'beating around the bush', 'moan a lot', and 'emotional'. By contrast, men's ways of talking and being within the staff group were described as 'lively', 'exuberant', 'macho', 'competitive', 'more factual', 'more circumspect' and 'more laid back'. They were also described by women as being 'slightly ridiculed', 'more practical', they 'haven't formed a group by themselves' and they 'get stereotyped'.

Staff Social Life

The non-traditional working literature suggested that men who work mainly with women 'were usually included in informal socializing sessions . . . even though this frequently meant attending baby showers or Tupperware parties. Many said they declined the offers to attend these events because they were not interested in "women's things"' (Williams, 1992: 261). Among the workers we spoke to, there was some staff socialising in all the centres, but it was more often an occasional event for all staff, with a small group of staff meeting up more regularly. For the most part, the men in our study did not take part in social events, whether organised in advance or spontaneous.

Three men reported going out after work with colleagues more than once every two months. Stuart said the staff as a group periodically went out on the proceeds of staff syndicate lottery wins; John said he was part of small group of staff that went out for a drink now and again; and Yusuf worked in a centre where staff socialising was part of the everyday culture. A further two men saw colleagues after work occasionally, such as at Christmas events. All the men were aware that socialising among at least some of the women staff did take place on a more frequent basis.

Men gave the following reasons for their lack of involvement in work social life: family commitments; being older than those who do socialise; being the manager; being invited but not attending through living too far away, or the timing being inconvenient. William, newly in post, explained 'I personally haven't been able to go out, but they have asked me, I've just been unable to go . . .' Duncan said that he had been out with staff 'every now and again . . . 'cos I come from so far away, it takes me an hour and a half to get home, once or twice I've been out, but on the whole not.' Both Kieran and Trevor cited family commitments: Kieran said 'it's occasional . . . quite frankly, I'm not too upset about that. I like to spend as much time as I can with my family now because I didn't spend too much time when I was younger.' Trevor concurred on the matter of age: 'the staff who go out tend to be much younger than me . . . I've got family commitments, by 11 o'clock I'm tired, I want to go to bed.' Finally, Stuart reported that while it very much depended on the person, he realised he missed contact with male colleagues when a student on placement at his workplace left saying 'oh God, I don't know how you stick (working with all those women)'.

Only two centres, the Montessori school and Sheffield Children's Centre, explicitly encouraged staff socialising: the former at lunchtimes when everyone ate together; the latter by circulating all staff with home contact details of their colleagues and organising regular evening and weekend events for staff. As Yusuf explained: 'we know each other properly'.

None of the women's responses conveyed the sense that an after-work social life went on without them. Four of the women referred to having developed particular friendships within the staff group they valued after hours, the rest all mentioned arranging events such as meals out or visiting each others' houses. By contrast, there was a sense of isolation about the men's involvement in work social life. Whereas women referred to the links between the closeness of the working team and seeing each other socially, the men were more likely to emphasise social distance from their colleagues. What possible explanations are there for this difference between men and women? Is it less important for men to feel 'close' to their colleagues, and therefore they give it less priority? Are men less comfortable in staff rooms, where the social life begins? What are the men's and women's experiences of staff dynamics within centres?

Staff Meetings

The different settings gave differing emphases to staff discussion: in day nurseries, time to talk with colleagues was generally squeezed into quiet periods of the day and staggered meal breaks. Some of those who worked in nurseries said there was not really sufficient time during the day for discussion. In the family centres, on the other hand, there were no meal breaks, but there were daily and, sometimes, twice-daily meetings of the staff.

Most of the centres had regular staff meetings built into the working week. Seven of the ten centres had staff meetings once or more a week. Across the range of settings there were also room meetings, curriculum meetings, planning meetings and management group meetings at variable intervals. On top of this some centres held regular training days: in one case the centre was shut once a month to facilitate whole staff attendance.

Not all the meetings, however, were seen as productive or sufficiently reflective. Most were used for planning, practical arrangements and centre 'business', rather than critically appraising and then developing practice and team working. For example, Yusuf explained that every Friday they held 'a base meeting . . . we can discuss about structures, about next week, we sort out curriculums, we sort out about who is working, breaks and everything'.

Caroline reported that while discussion time existed, it was not necessarily enough time or structured well enough to argue out differences between staff over sensitive matters such as cultural practices. She said:

> I think we need more opportunities to actually sit down and get to the nitty gritty and the root of what's really going on . . . we may have a training day or we may have development time, which is like a morning, and just as you're kind of getting into something, it's time to finish and it's like 'well, we haven't really got to it . . .' and what you really need is more time out to actually get to what the root of the problem is. I mean it takes people time to kind of feel comfortable so that they can actually talk . . . you never get a chance to find out where people's strengths and weaknesses

actually lie and also . . . people have different working methods . . . different cultures have different ways . . . [and] people don't want to hurt other people's feelings.

The issue of the quality of staff communication through staff meetings was mentioned by Vera. She said:

> I think our communication has not been particularly as good as it could have been, we've had lots of staff changes . . . I think there's lots of feelings left over from that . . . it came to a head a few months ago . . . we've actually had opportunities to say things that perhaps can be quite hurtful out of the right setting . . . we've had a forum where we can actually talk about lack of communication.

Both these women raised the question of how staff meetings can incorporate discussion of sensitive matters of staff practice without appearing to slight individuals. Jensen (1996) argued that this concern to avoid 'hurting feelings' was a feature of women's methods of communication in Scandinavian child-care centres: where men were employed, especially where the staff group was composed of half men and half women, anxiety about conflict was handled differently and began to dissipate.

For Duncan, staff meetings were unproductive because not all staff used them to air their views, preferring to exchange views outside the meeting time. Some staff members, he said

> will say nothing in the meeting, but go back to their rooms and the door shuts . . . You think 'well, why don't they say it?' Some people, it's because they haven't got the confidence to say it, some it's because somebody else has just said it and there's other people who I'm sorry, but they're just bloody awkward . . . I think it can lead to bad atmospheres, it can lead to division.

This problem of not using staff meeting time to resolve problems can also be seen as indicative of an indirect method of communication. Not using the forums established but preferring informal exchanges within small groups would not appear to promote constructive, critical reflection or whole staff development.

If insufficient advantage of staff meeting time was reported by some workers, others felt there were too many meetings or they were sometimes held for their own sake. Lloyd, working in a family centre with daily, sometimes twice-daily, meetings, found they were often tedious or irrelevant. Other staff working in family centres reported that meetings, and therefore the discussions that might have been, were often cancelled when a crisis with a client arose. However, some workers did draw attention to productive use of staff meetings. Fred said that his centre was closed to children every Friday afternoon, and three hours were devoted to team working, discussing the children, the curriculum and other issues that arose. He described the staff as a 'close working team'. Kieran described time set aside in the centre's work as 'just for us'.

Formal opportunities for the staff to meet as a group are, we argue later in the book, essential for examining and reflecting upon practice and gendered practice in particular. The experience of these workers is that staff meetings are more often concerned with essential business, that they are subject to cancellation or deferral, and are open to being hijacked by minority interests within the staff group. However important the facility of staff meeting time and, even more important, the use to which it is put (Whalley, 1996), the focus of our discussion here is the effect of staff discussion on gendering staff dynamics. In this respect the use made of the staff room for conversation and the formation of gendered judgements seemed critical to the process of enabling exclusion or inclusion of staff.

The Staffroom

Staffrooms as a site of gendered discussions was highlighted by four men and two women. These discussions were described as 'women's talk' or 'intimate conversations', from which men were generally excluded. William said 'in the staffroom they'll forget I'm there and carry on talking. Sometimes I simply can't grasp what they are talking about.' Nick found staffroom discussions so uncomfortable he had excluded himself from the room altogether. As a consequence, he said, 'I don't really know what goes on in the staffroom'. Two women recognised the role of the staffroom for intimate conversations among women. One, Michelle, said: 'you get less personal with a man sitting there'. Being excluded from conversation is a powerful means of dividing staff; and being excluded on the grounds of gender is a powerful means of dividing men and women, and isolating the minority group. Recognition by centres of the potential of exclusion for dividing staff groups would be a first step towards recognising that differences in style of communication can offer new methods of working together (Jensen, 1996).

Working Together

Working closely with children provides further opportunities for gendered staff dynamics to emerge. Men workers reported ways in which women staff acted in front of children and parents which effectively excluded them, sometimes because they were men, sometimes because they were new and unusual recruits. John, for example, reported being 'cut off' by a woman member of staff when he was talking to parents. She would interrupt him and repeat what he had said, and he would be left feeling embarrassed. Duncan had the further complication of working in a nursery where the fact that he was white, working among a group of black staff, caused resentment, as well as being new and a man. He reported feeling uncomfortable working in a room where the 'door seemed to be closed all day . . . it was very secluded'. Nick similarly felt under suspicion from staff, but this time it was because he was a male manager, and felt to have access to information about the future of the centre that other staff (all women) did not have.

Two men reported that they felt their women colleagues were needlessly overprotective to begin with. They would 'jump in before a possible problem could occur' in Oliver's dealings with children's mothers, or would assume that because

Stuart was a man, he wouldn't be able to do some things with children properly. Interestingly enough, Stuart reported that there were no staff discussions about his role when he was appointed, despite the ample opportunities for discussion structured into the working week, but, through a process of becoming familiar with each other's styles, mutual trust was gradually won.

Some centres had recognised the gender difference of employing men and had allowed for the difference in their approach. Kieran said that his colleagues had 'all been understanding and allowed me to make my own mistakes' which he saw as supportive. Two men in senior positions, Trevor and Fred, both reported a lot of attention being paid to staff communication, as did Yusuf, who had experienced much positive encouragement as a new recruit. This attention had had benefits in enabling the men workers to feel comfortable working with the whole staff group.

To some extent, the incidents of exclusion reported during interviews are related to being new recruits, and given added significance through inhabiting the minority, or other, gender by being a man. Being Other in terms of seniority or ethnicity also held the potential to trigger feelings of exclusion, as the above reports show. The significant finding here, however, is that no woman interviewed reported feeling anything other than at home in her childcare centre: there were no reports at all of feeling excluded, or, for that matter, included, by the practices of colleagues. Women respondents, in fact, were more likely to say there were no differences between men and women in the ways they communicated or acted with children on the basis of gender, and any differences they had identified were more to do with individual personalities.

In terms of staff dynamics, therefore, we can see emerging a different, gendered, set of understandings about the work and the way the work is discussed and enacted according to whether a member of staff finds themselves categorised as Other or not. The process of working together and establishing trust and respect appears to diminish the significance of being Other, but the remnants of the experience linger.

Support

Managers

A key factor in the success of working together is the support role of the manager, as well as that of the staff team (Pugh, 1996). Nearly all the respondents felt their working environment offered them support through their managers (19/21). For example, Hannah said: the 'manager is always there if you want a chat . . . her door is always open'. Stuart described his centre and its manager thus: 'one of the best things . . . I know if I had a problem then I could talk . . . any problem, even if it was personal or work I could talk to (the manager).' Three of the men had taken problems over specific issues, such as with children's parents or with colleagues, to managers in the past and had found them to be supportive.

Most respondents did not mind whether their source of managerial support was male or female, although nearly all had, and had always had, women managers. The most important characteristic of support was being able to solve problems taken to managers: for most, therefore, gender was not so salient. Two men and three women, however, said they preferred to have a woman manager for discussing problems at work. In general, it was not clear why they preferred women managers, although one woman in this group, Erica, provided a clue when she said 'I know I'm generalising but . . . I feel like I flow more easily when I'm talking with women'. In this case it seemed to be an affinity with styles of communication born from gendered life experiences that could be assumed between women, but not across genders, that Erica found helpful.

The two respondents who did not feel supported in their work both came from the same centre and both were managers themselves. Their position was characterised by unstable and unclear managerial arrangements both within the centre and, as it was publicly funded, at the level of the local authority. One of them explained that she was unsure

> where the support was supposed to come from. I find sometimes that it feels like we're very much on our own and you're kind of left to get on with things . . . and you're always sort of thinking 'well, what's going on?'. You know there's always talk about we're becoming the Under 5s Centre, well, when's this happening? And there's some things just kind of dropped on you . . . I think support should be there from the staff group, it should be from the management and then I think it should be from the outside (local authority).

Staff Teams

As well as support from managers, most workers found support was available from staff teams. Lloyd, working in a family centre, said 'the work you do you can't do alone and so you . . . you've got to be working as a team and that means being supported and giving support'. Fred added to this when he said 'we are a close working team . . . It doesn't feel hierarchical.' Michelle agreed that 'most of the staff are supportive when you need them'. Fozia, the worker from Sheffield Children's Centre, said 'this is a very supportive place to work'.

Among this group of male and female workers there were no expressed differences between the genders about the extent to which they felt supported by managers or staff teams, nor strong preferences about whether the person providing support was a man or woman, although nearly all had women managers and were reasonably happy with them. All the respondents recognised support as an issue and knew there were times when they would use managerial or staff support: it was integrated into everyday life in childcare centres.

Two points about the managers referred to here need to be made. First, our study relied on access to our respondents through the permission of their managers; in two cases the respondents were the managers. It may be that our managers are comparatively or unusually competent at their jobs or, alternatively, interested in research. Second, the near-universality of women managers in childcare means that workers, whether women or men, have limited experience on which to found their preferred choice of gender of manager. They do not know what working for a man would be like, but they hope men managers would have the same skills as women managers.

Workers' (Dis) Satisfaction

How satisfied were men and women with their working environment? The main source of satisfaction, for both women and men, was the sense of participation in children's achievements and progress. Seventeen of the 21 respondents thought of childcare as intrinsically rewarding work. The staff's delight in, and reward from, children's responsiveness, excitement about learning and creating a positive environment for them to learn, were all mentioned as sources of satisfaction. Those who worked in family centres also mentioned the satisfaction of seeing families and children effect change in their lives, often in difficult circumstances. A second source of satisfaction was found from working in staff teams. Five women and two men cited the staff groups as rewarding. All but one of these staff were working in the children's centre and in family centres. In these centres, considerable emphasis was put on staff relations and working together. The remaining woman, a manager in an educational nursery, said she drew satisfaction from seeing a range of staff skills and techniques being used with children.

Sources of dissatisfaction were numerous and evenly spread across the genders. The low pay and feeling undervalued were mentioned by six workers, three men and three women. A further three, two men and a woman, said it was hard and/or tiring work, at times repetitive and boring with insufficient challenge. Four of the five workers in senior posts mentioned difficulties, mostly staffing difficulties, arising out of their managerial roles. One person disliked the immense amount of paperwork, detracting from her work with children. Four of the five family centre workers cited their work with parents as potentially stressful, but four workers could think of nothing bad to say about their jobs at all.

What do the sources of staff satisfaction tell us about staff dynamics? The near unanimity of reward through working with children and witnessing their progress means that, as one respondent, Trevor, put it, the work attracts 'a certain type of person, that's fairly caring, that kind of ethos'. In other words, childcare employs people with certain characteristics, such as those interested in caring, who value support and team work. Regardless of gender and gendered prior experiences, it would appear men and women childcare workers have similar mental and professional frameworks for their work satisfaction.

Discussion

What is the case, then, for arguing that gender differences exist between childcare staff in the ways they work together, relate to and support each other?

Moreover, are they significant? What does the issue of gender in staff dynamics tell us about childcare institutions themselves?

If we return to the different styles of communication, or ways of talking, identified by over half the respondents, they suggest that 'gendered beings' exist within the dynamics of childcare work. Women, it is suggested, have an open communication style, they hold conversations about intimate and personal subjects, they develop close working relations and they are emotional about work issues. Women's style was also seen as indirect and possibly over-involved and potentially hurtful. Men, on the other hand, were seen as more circumspect and factual in their subjects of conversation, more relaxed and lively in their style, but more prone to being isolated, ridiculed and stereotyped in the staff group. They were also seen as potentially more competitive. Pushed to extremes, an image is gained of garrulous women and tight-lipped men. Some of the men's ways of being in centres were clearly related to being Other. The scope for stereotyping and ridiculing men, for example, would presumably diminish should the staff group become more equally divided between men and women. Indeed, at the children's centre with half men and half women staff, both Fozia and Yusuf said that because the staff group was 'truly mixed' and 'so friendly', they didn't notice any gender differences in conversation styles or in subjects of conversation.

But these gendered beings can be valued within staff dynamics or dismissed and undermined. A critical factor in mitigating how gendered differences are internalised into the culture of the centre appears to be that of a climate of staff support. Support from managers, for these workers, was in effect a combination of advocacy at critical moments and problem solving, and from the staff group as a whole, the development of mutual appreciation and trust. Well developed supportive practices and strategies should enable both women and men to 'feel at home' both with their own and other gendered beings.

The model of support employed here relies on two features of work in childcare centres. First, a hierarchy of responsibility and seniority exists, so that solutions to problems can and should be sought in the authority of managers. Support is viewed as part accountability (or supervision) and part personal help or therapy. Second, the work is an individual performance and responsibility for performance thus rests on a sole worker. Support is thus viewed as helping individuals to do their work better. There is relatively little emphasis on the group working together, or group discussions reflecting on the experience of being a (man or woman) childcare worker that could provide mutual support in the sense of the development of the skills and the team of workers. This activity, if it takes place at all, is done during socialising, which as we have seen is limited to a small section of the staff group, and few of the men workers, in particular, took part.

Penn (1997) observed nurseries in Spain, Italy and the UK. She argued that the UK is embedded in an Anglo-American tradition where hierarchical arrangements for management and support of staff are unquestioned, whereas in Spain and Italy there is a strong tradition of staff working together on a co-operative basis, with less of a sense of a hierarchy. In both the latter countries, some support, such as professional development, was provided by outside bodies, such as regional nursery co-ordinators, but there was a clear emphasis in day-to-day nursery practice on peer support. Penn argued that staff relationships that offered peer support were seen by staff in Spanish and Italian nurseries as integral to their work with children. She states: 'relationships between staff were an important model for children's relationships with each other, and (it was believed that) the more egalitarian the relationships between staff, the more the children would develop reciprocal friendships and co-operation amongst themselves' (Penn, 1997: 37). Thus, different models of organisation of support produce different ways of conceptualising the work with children, and, according to Penn, the collective way of working produced childcare institutions where the activities and professional development were considered as a whole, and where the whole was 'viewed as a functioning organism, as opposed to a collection of individuals in the same place' (ibid.).

In our study, some staff could not identify differences between the support by their peers on the basis of gender, but preferred to do so on the basis of individuality. Hannah put it as 'it's who I relate to, who I can trust and build up a relationship with . . . I don't see it as men and women, it's just an individual person, and how close you are to people . . . I like working with men, have a laugh with them.' Hannah used the characteristics of women's gendered being reported above to describe how she saw emerging staff dynamics: she relied on notions of personal relationship, trust and even friendship to describe good working relations between colleagues, and the basis on which she liked working with men, 'having a laugh', was because they were not women, but were Other. She also raised the individual character of staff support in her institution: for Hannah, support from the peer group was something she worked at: she built up relationships that were modelled on the style of friendships she knew from outside the work environment.

The point about gender differences between staff is not to divide men and women on the basis of gender into irreconcilable camps, for such a division may falsely categorise gender as homogenous, and obscure other differences such as ethnicity. As we argued in Chapter 1, differences between men, for example, may be as, or more, critical than the differences between men and women (Connell, 1987). Nick, with long experience of working in centres where men are in a small minority, demonstrated the significance of differences between (or perceptions of differences between) men. He said that

> I think men get stereotyped quite easily in these settings and I think if you're seen as being quite sort of attractive, then it does sometimes create a bit of a buzz at . . . and if you're not I think it's sort of, it's almost as if . . . you know, you're a useless man, . . . you know, 'what does he know' . . .

In this situation, men are open to scrutiny because of their novelty, scrutiny on women's terms, as well as scrutiny in terms of their performance as childcare workers.

But the exploration of aspects of gendered beings can provide new or different dimensions to working in the physically close environment of childcare. Lloyd put this point well:

I think that there are people . . . women are given a set of things . . . they grow into a way of looking at things and men have done the same thing and it's about what shapes a person . . . so I suppose there is a female way of . . . and a male way of looking at things . . . we've all got bits of each and that sometimes comes out more strongly in certain situations.

He went on to give an example of how employing men makes a difference to staff dynamics: if a child has had a negative experience of men before arriving, then having a man employed to care for them has 'got to evoke a response. I would hope to give a different picture' of being a man, and that different picture is then open to discussion among the staff group. In this way men provide an added dimension to staff dynamics. Their very Otherness and difference evokes, or can evoke, appreciation of new ways of working with children and thinking about childcare. This difference is not confined to 'difficult' issues such as abuse or divorce in a child's experience, but is also relevant to play issues, as we shall see in the next section.

Difference as Other

Before we move on to discuss gender and the children's day, we want to highlight two important and enduring themes which have emerged from this chapter so far. Through the discussion of working conditions, of staff dynamics as seen in the use of staff meetings, socialising and working together with children, and in the sources of staff support, the first theme to emerge is that of the production of difference as Other. The experiences of men workers suggest that it is common for gender difference to be marked out as Other, and open to exclusionary or, in some cases, inclusionary practices. Men's sense of Otherness can remain or dissipate according to the management and staff team practices of support and awareness of the potential impact of difference. It is not a structural Other as men are able to progress to managerial roles themselves with relative ease, but it is a temporary, and easily invoked Other experienced as isolation and social distance from colleagues.

Making Use of the Staff Group

The second theme is that of how institutions value, and make use of, the staff group as a whole. This was raised in the context of discussions of how staff are supported, and support each other, in their work. Women's experiences, as staff, and as women, and women's ways of communicating, constituted the norm. Their models of support, or friendship, prevailed, but also existed in the context of the institutional organisation. Nearly all the institutions operated on a hierarchical model, in which support was viewed as something given individually, by seniors, sometimes through supervision sessions. Peer group support was something that happened through individual effort rather than being integral to the way the institution worked. The exception was Sheffield Children's Centre, which, as a workers' co-operative, recognised the importance of staff support through peer groups, although it also employed hierarchical positions of responsibility. Support provides a chief avenue for workers to express their views about childcare practice, to develop their skills and to reflect on their practice. It provides the potential to value workers' views and contributions towards the institution. But we argue that support is important because it also provides for the possibility to make visible the genderedness of childcare practice, where opportunities exist to recognise, discuss, and reflect upon men's (and women's) experiences of working with staff, children and parents. This, we argue throughout the book, is an essential step in not only recognising what difference(s) gender makes to childcare practice, but in recognising the purpose and ethos of the childcare on offer.

The Children's Day

Men and women childcare workers work with children who are also gendered. To date, most consideration of gender in childcare settings has been linked to the pursuit of an anti-sexist curriculum (e.g., Vernon and Smith, 1994). This means there has been a concern to ensure that equipment is equally available to girls and boys, and that the language used does not attribute certain characteristics to one gender or the other (*ibid.*, 1994: 101). However, far less attention has been given to gender than to, for example, developing a multi-cultural curriculum and framework for early years work (*cf*, DoH, 1991; Siraj-Blatchford, 1996). Concerns with the childcare curriculum, however, overshadow the gendering of the staff-child dynamic. Where the role of men staff as carers of gendered children has been considered, it has been seen in a fairly homogenous way: men workers can provide role models of 'being men' to boys, or, alternatively, can provide role models of fathering to children from lone mother families (Burgess and Ruxton, 1996; Jensen, 1996). Being a man by itself is held to offer distinctive experiences to children. But how do men and women workers identify and so render significant these supposedly distinctive experiences? Do they see children as girls and boys with different qualities and forms of expression, or as individuals with needs to be ascertained and met, for which men and women are equipped in the same ways?

A starting point for our work in this area was the work of Jensen and colleagues in Denmark on the concept of 'gender pedagogy', as we noted in Chapter 2. Danish early childhood services combine notions of 'care' and 'education': in developing gender pedagogy some workers and services have drawn on ideas about what happens in the childcare centres (or, broadly speaking, the curriculum) as critically interrelated with the (gendered) self that pedagogues bring to their work. Jensen (1996) argued that gender pedagogy 'emphasised that specific gender behaviour (of children) must be reflected in pedagogic work' and that while these considerations apply 'irrespective of the gender mix of the staff group', they are probably more readily fulfilled where men are employed (Jensen, 1996: 20–21). The development of ideas of working with the gendered choices of children builds on work identifying gendered differences among girls and boys in education more generally such as that by Arnot (1983) who identified policies and practices which shaped school paths and choices for girls and boys at secondary school level. While Arnot's work developed in a rather different direction from that of Jensen and the Danes, there are parallels, in that Arnot also argued that gender differences, and so opportunities for gender equality, were built into the structural and social fabric of educational institutions and dominant ideologies which inform educational practice.

So gender pedagogy is the articulation of differences between young girls and boys, which, Jensen argued, need to be acknowledged, examined and consciously worked with in childcare centres. This is not just a matter of eliminating prejudice within the curriculum, for this method works to conceal and not celebrate differences between girls and boys (as Arnot (1983) also found when comparing the organisation of secondary age schooling). Rather, practising gender pedagogy entails revealing differences, 'in order to create equality' (Jensen, 1996: 20). For Jensen, the idea of difference recognises men within childcare centres as Other, in a general sense, but not in an individual sense which would open the way to exclusionary practices.

This sense of positive, conscious, difference has implications for childcare workers, for the institutional experience of girls and boys is enhanced in different ways by the employment of men and women. For example, Jensen reported that 'men influence children towards spatial accomplishments' more than women staff do (ibid., 1996: 18). The concept of gender pedagogy is, however, particular to Scandinavian countries: we were not expecting to find it being practised to any great extent in England. The central tenet of the concept we wanted to explore with our workers was whether the idea of gender difference among the children was promoted in any way, or whether the idea of 'difference' was reserved for describing individuality.

Gendered Jobs, Gendered Skills

Men and women workers had different perceptions of the division of labour in childcare centres. All except one of the women workers, for example, believed that jobs were shared out equally. The exception said that while differences existed in practice, in theory there were no differences between what men and women did in the centre. Men, on the other hand, knew that they were asked, and, in some cases, expected, to do practical jobs around the building such as fixing things and changing light bulbs. This was one area of men's experience in childcare that some men and some managers considered their 'natural' role. It is also reminiscent of some domestic divisions of labour (Brannen and Moss, 1991; Jowell et al., 1991). The discrepancy between women workers' belief about the division of labour and men's experience of it tells us something about the gendered construction of childcare work. It may be that women are not aware of men doing these practical jobs because the role is 'naturally' one for men, in an environment where caring for children has traditionally been a 'natural' role for women. The ascriptions of 'natural' roles to men and women replicate traditional notions of parenting, and, in childcare work, are an extension of the conception of childcare as 'women's work' because it is 'like mothering' (Penn and McQuail, 1996).

The element of gender differences in the everyday organisation of the institutions was rendered more or less invisible by the assumption, conscious or unconscious, of a natural division of labour between men and women workers. It is interesting to compare this approach with the conscious articulation of gender difference in Norway described by Nilsen and Manum (1998) as 'masculine caring'. For these two kindergarten leaders, masculine caring meant developing new dimensions of childcare work based on, but not exclusive to, men's use of the outdoors as a learning environment. They argued that childcare institutions rely too heavily on emulating domestic life. Masculine caring involves extending the work of childcare institutions to include traditional ways of life, both using and learning from the outdoors (by which they mean rural outdoors), ways which they argued are being lost to children in childcare institutions, but which are deeply familiar to men workers from their (outdoor) childhoods. Describing such work as masculine caring, however, runs the risk of ascribing essentialist features of gender to childcare work (e.g., that all men would work in this way). It is also in danger of employing stereotypes about men workers that appear similar to those that state that men workers 'should' do the practical jobs in English childcare institutions. But with a debate framed as masculine caring, at least the gendered contribution of care is made visible, and the debate picks up on the differences in working with children that some of our workers noted.

Beyond gendered divisions of the practical jobs, some men workers interviewed said there was an almost implicit expectation that they would enjoy particular types of play, such as ball games and playing with cars and trucks. Men's responses to these somewhat stereotypical 'masculine' activities varied. One response was to revel in the opportunity for loud or rough play. William said:

> I've never been asked to do those things . . . I sometimes find myself doing them . . . getting myself engaged in rough play with them . . . that's sometimes simply because I'm always down . . . I sometimes put myself on the floor and that's like an open invitation to anybody to jump on you . . . or if I'm out in the garden and there are footballs out there . . . I think sometimes the children have a tendency of coming to me to play those things . . . they invariably draw me into their game with them.

Other men resisted the temptation to be portrayed as 'a man's man'. Nick said:

> If it has been suggested, I have counteracted it . . . I have certainly been aware of situations where men have functioned in a completely different way with children . . . when they're out in the garden, it's the men that are kicking the ball about and running up and down with it . . . and I've consciously tried to prevent myself getting sucked into that.

These expectations and responses indicate that despite the widespread belief among the workers that 'we all share out the jobs equally', there are underlying and unarticulated gender divisions in childcare work. These gender divisions follow fairly predictable lines and stem from a 'traditional' organisation of labour within parenting, the only other model for mixed gender caring for young children available. The men workers we interviewed could either integrate themselves into this model: Kieran even said 'we all do the same' and in the same breath said 'I do change the light bulbs'; or they could resist the culture of defining men, and therefore themselves, as 'masculine' in a 'traditional' sense.

One method of avoiding the imposition of gender stereotypical expectations onto men (or women) was through discussion, planning, and making 'gender consciousness' a visible issue. This was practised at Sheffield Children's Centre, where Fozia explained that:

> we have a structure in each unit and we plan it every week when we have the meetings, we have the planning meetings as well, so we plan a structure, and then, you know, at the end of . . . on the planning sheet we do put down who's going to do what, who's going to bring what, and what their responsibility was.

The childcare centres we visited all had a theoretical commitment to gender equality, which the workers believed was at least partly demonstrated through the elimination of differences between men's and women's jobs. For example, Anne, a manager, said when she first recruited a man, she considered carefully whether he should do the same jobs as the women or whether there should be different expectations of him. She decided that 'equality was important for the children to witness and there should be no differences between the men and the women workers'.

Applying the concept of gender pedagogy to the approach of these centres, we can see that the idea of 'difference' becomes problematic. For the centres, difference is the problem in the quest for gender equality, and the aim is to at least formally eliminate differences between men's and women's jobs. An approach informed by gender pedagogy, on the other hand, would see difference as an avenue to be exploited. Recognising and valuing differences between men and women would be seen not necessarily as regressive, or as engaging solely in stereotypes, but as helping to diversify and improve what is already on offer during the children's day.

Recognising differences between men and women could lead to a better appreciation of gendered skills. For the most part, though, there was a concern among the workers interviewed to see individual skills as more important than gendered skills. For example, Nick said 'I think it all boils down to how good the person is as a person really . . . I've worked with some great men who've [been], you know, really good with children and some men who've been useless, and similarly with women.' Similarly, Hannah said, 'I'm very much into an individual person and their individual needs . . . I think men and women should be treated equally.' Lloyd saw this attention to individual skills as beneficial to him as a worker. He said 'I think it's quite good here in that I think people . . . tend to be able to work with their strengths . . . I think I'm steered in a particular direction because of the skills I have rather than due to being a man.' Erica thought it was 'dangerous to generalise' about gendered skills, if that meant preventing men from doing something with children, as each child has 'very specific needs' some of which are 'more to do with their gender or their gender in that particular family'.

Where workers' skills were recognised as divided along gendered lines, men were described (by women staff) in comparison to women as 'calmer', 'more disciplinarian' and 'not having as many inhibitions – more willing to get down and play'. These descriptions gave an impression of men as on the one hand standing back, conveying authority with their style, and on the other, being more playful and spontaneous. Some men, particularly those working in family centres, also described themselves as having more direct methods with, or influence over, children, such as holding them physically if they are out of control, or being more verbally directive, whereas their women colleagues were more likely to be patient and to resolve difficulties by talking them through.

Anne said that men could identify with boys and provide for their needs much better than women ever could. This comment was the only one from this group of workers to claim there were gendered differences between girls and boys, differences which require both men and women to work with children with an awareness of their gender as a positive contribution to the work.

Women workers' skills were seen by men workers to differ from their own chiefly around relationships with the children. Men staff said that women were better, or more experienced than themselves, at 'reading children's thoughts', at 'being patient' with children, and at providing 'a matriarchal figure' which children respond to. These were attributes and skills which the men thought did not rely on being a mother, but on practice at being around children, being able to empathise with, and be attuned to, their varying and often indirect methods of communication.

Women's skill with child-adult relationships apart, two women thought women workers were 'better at concentrating, they will stay at an activity for longer' and were 'more easy going' than men. The ability of women and men to attribute gendered skills to one another is of course coloured by their perception of the specific men and women they work with in a very particular setting. In general, gender was seen as a facet of character that was rarely generalisable, and should be suppressed in favour of individual methods and skills.

Girls and Boys – Individuals or Gendered Categories?

Despite the extensive literature on differences between girls' and boys' behaviour and use of space when in primary school (Thorne, 1993; Mayall et al., 1996), for the most part, childcare workers in this study claimed 'each child has different needs – it's impossible to generalise', in the words of William. Thirteen of the 21 workers, five men and eight women, believed that individual needs were more important than gender based ones. However, two men and one woman did identify boys as having particular needs based on their gender: they said that even by the age of 2, for the most part boys demand more attention than girls, they have a greater need for physical space and to use physical space actively and creatively, whereas girls need to be able to work quietly. These three workers were all experienced teachers. Two men saw boys from lone mother households as having particular needs within the centre – to be able to identify with and relate to men who worked in centres as a form of compensation.

Why this focus on individuality at the expense of gender? Is it possible to identify both philosophical and policy explanations for the focus on children as individuals rather than members of groups? Singer (1993) argued that an 'attachment pedagogy' underlies Anglo-American ideas about children's up-bringing in both domestic and institution based settings. This pedagogy asserts that mother-care for young children is the ideal in order for them to develop securely and, when looking at childcare out of the home, the child has similar needs for a dyadic adult-child relationship. Penn (1997) argued, by way of contrast, that nurseries in Italy and Spain have a different set of ideas underlying the way children are cared for in childcare institutions. For example, these nurseries invest in the group of children, or 'peer culture' and 'peer routines', as a method of creating a stable and predictable caring environment.

Attachment pedagogy helps explain both workers' focus on individuality, and the male workers' attribution to female workers of greater skill in develop-ing relationships with children. First, the model for 'good care' is attention to each individual child's relationships with adults. Second, women, as substitute mothers, offer the closest match to the prescriptions of attachment pedagogy. There is little scope within attachment pedagogy for focus on the peer group as a form of security, nor is there much scope for men workers to develop dis-tinctively masculine ways of caring for young children. While not the explicit focus of our study, it would appear likely from our group of workers that attachment pedagogy informed daily practice in childcare.

Moreover, recent policy initiatives in childcare have encouraged a focus on individuals rather than as members of gendered groups. First, the Children Act 1989 gave emphasis to the principles of assessment of children 'in need' through their individual health and development (s.17); it also recognised children's diverse backgrounds (Sch 2, para 11) and stated that services should meet their differing and individual needs (DoH, 1991: 6.10). In the field of early education, the introduction of Desirable Learning Outcomes for 4 year-olds across childcare and education settings has encouraged the introduction of assessments and learning profiles for young children (Owen and McQuail, 1997). All the centres we visited had some form of record keeping about children's progress and reporting to parents at events such as parent clinics, parent evenings or review meetings (see Chapter 5). With these policy mea-sures, and pedagogic reliance on the adult-child relationship in mind, as well as a concern to demonstrate gender equality, it is not surprising that workers viewed children as individuals and resisted the category of gender as a means of defining differences between children.

Men and Women Meeting Children's Needs

If men and women childcare workers see their skills and their jobs as essentially indistinguishable from each other, are there any differences between them in how they meet the needs of girls and boys? If not, what significance do workers attach to the idea and practice of men working with young children? There was no consensus among our group about how men and women childcare workers might make distinctive contributions towards young children's lives. On the other hand, many reasons why it is important for men to work with young children were given. Some workers, both men and women, said each gender worked in the same way and therefore it made no difference to the children whether men or women looked after them. This 'no difference' view was further qualified by a few workers who said that the employment of men probably represented an unspecific but added bonus in children's experience of childcare institutions. For example, William said that the other staff 'all give a cuddle just the same way I can give a cuddle'.

The remainder saw more specific reasons for the employment of men working alongside women. First, as a challenge to children, providing them with alternative models of men's work roles, and of men's caring capacity. In this sense employing men challenged gender stereotypes. It was also seen as offering children a choice of establishing relationships with men and women within their centres. Second, the employment of men in childcare was seen as replicating wider institutions (such as the family) and society at large. Lloyd said, 'the world's inhabited by men and women and both offer valuable lessons . . . I think it's got to be a healthier group if it's mixed . . . Children need to see men and women working together.' Similarly, Anne expressed it as: 'it's about closing the circle, children in families have men and women looking after them and the same should be the case outside the home. I like the nursery to be like a family.'

The third response was to see men in childcare as a form of compensation for 'deficient' parenting, as offering something distinctive to those children whose fathers were absent or who had had negative or abusive representations of men in their lives. Vera said 'it's good to have men to have the role model for single parent families, to see that men aren't necessarily awful, that they can be genuine positive roles as such'. Oliver reported that a lot of their children had had 'bad experiences . . . quite often through a male,' and coming to the centre showed them 'that men . . . are not all the same . . . they can be just ordinary people'.

The range of responses to this question suggests that 'men' as a category has attained a symbolic significance for childcare work. Men working with young children represent idealised family forms (the nuclear family); they are employed to help put right the wrongs of family life (such as child abuse or father desertion); but they are also there to challenge stereotypes of gender divisions in wider society. Chief among these is that men are able to show children they are able to be caring and to undertake caring work. Taken together, these various representations for men are somewhat daunting. How can a single man working among a group of women achieve these objectives in anything other than a token and piecemeal fashion? But the range of responses also indicates, as reported above, a lack of consensus about the meaning of 'men' working with young children. Given the evidence cited earlier in the chapter about the lack of time devoted to discussion about gender issues, it may be that a lack of consensus reflects a lack of debate about gender within childcare institutions and childcare generally. When we examined whether men working in different kinds of settings attracted different kinds of responses, we found that men working in family centres were more likely to be associated with compensatory type roles, but certainly not exclusively so.

Role Models

The idea of adults providing role models to children in order to transmit desirable values and ways of being has captured the popular imagination, particularly when discussing the benefits of men working with children (e.g., DfEE, 1998; Lepkowska, 1998). Men workers providing male role models for young children is a familiar theme in the literature on men and childcare work. Ruxton (1992) reported that 'the vast majority of [family centre] staff recognised the importance of positive male role models which help to challenge stereotypical views of men as "breadwinners" alone, and to validate their role as "carers" ' (Ruxton, 1992: 25). Men's work showing them to be 'sensitive and caring', as 'taking part in play activities and in cooking meals', and 'changing nappies', were all cited as evidence of role modelling. While these workers were modelling alternatives to the predominant male stereotype, other studies have seen modelling as providing examples of stereotyped male behaviour. When Murray (1996) interviewed and observed childcare staff including men, she argued that 'in the childcare environment men are often sought after as workers because of the perceived need to have male role models for children,' models which were seen as doing 'truck play with the boys' (1996: 374). In both cases, a single man was seen as able to represent 'men' as a category, and the principle of male role models was seen as a unique dimension of employing men.

What Kind of Role Model?

Providing 'positive role models' was seen as important to all the workers in our study. But there were differences in how this was understood. Some workers saw modelling in professional terms, setting standards (through language, interaction with children and parents and so on) to which they would like others (children and/or parents) to aspire – a sort of living example of best practice, integral to the childcare job. Across the different settings, this type of modelling was differently emphasised. For example, in family centres, modelling was seen as relevant to the mothers as well as the children. Brenda saw her modelling as 'I think sort of positive in the sense that where mums are lacking . . . you know, maybe parenting skills, or you know, sort of stimulation for the children . . . along those lines . . . to encourage, yes, you know that if they're not able to do . . . you know they can learn to do these things'. Working in a day nursery, Rachel described being a role model as a taken-for-granted part of the work. She said:

> I mean I think it's something quite natural, the way we are . . . I mean all the boundaries and things that we've set, the way we work here . . . [we show them how] to be with each other . . . one of them might bite another child . . . [we] explain to them that's wrong . . . always give them a reason why . . . I wouldn't be a, like a mother or anything like that.

For both these workers, role modelling is a professional task, part of being a worker, rather than being a part of their selves.

Others, however, saw modelling in more personal terms. Some thought that upholding values was the key element of role modelling. Fred said: 'the most important thing is to be yourself and to be truthful to the child'. Duncan said 'I'm a very positive role model . . . I hold good moral values and beliefs . . . morals that would be good for a child to learn and to see and I try to bring those into the workplace.' Anne said 'we are role models, of nice decent people, adults the children want to be with'. Some men saw aspects of their personal character being modelled. Trevor said 'I like the outdoor environment, I like the rough and tumble, I'm quite a loud person . . . I hope they think I'm an affectionate person . . . there are things I do with them which . . . like cooking . . . which maybe they see as traditionally female.' Kieran simply saw himself as a man: he said 'I'm not trying to fill a gap, I'm just a nice man who works in the family centre'.

Some men also saw their role modelling as distinctively gendered. All the women, but only five men, saw themselves as offering professional childcare in their modelling. But six men saw aspects of being a man as constituting their role modelling, in other words viewing the task of modelling being given to them *because* of their gender. John said that on some occasions he had been asked to chat with boys from lone mother households. He explained this as: 'I mean obviously it was just more of that role model pulling through'. He reported having 'built up a really good strong relationship' with two boys whose mothers were 'really pleased, because of the fact that there was no male at home'. Still other men saw their role modelling as demonstrating that 'men can conduct themselves better than those men [children had] seen before' (Oliver) or showing children how to 'be a man without being a bully or using physical strength – I may be the first man a child can trust' (Lloyd). Being a male role model was evidently an additional part of the job, an element of being a childcare worker that women could not perform.

Role Models as Problematic

Men and women in this study showed that while the principle of role modelling is accepted by both alike, the implications of being a role model differ for men and women. For the latter group, the issue of professionalism dominates: their role modelling can be described in terms of setting standards of adult behaviour which they would like children (and in some cases, mothers) to follow. For the men, however, their gender constitutes a novel dimension to children's experience, certainly within children's institutions, sometimes in their families as well. If investigating the meaning of role models for both men and women workers shows a confused picture, the situation appears more problematic for men.

What type of role model do men working with young children provide? Are they a substitute father, or a good friend, or a playmate, or a more specific source of ethnic or familial identification? But even if an answer can be found to this question, how should men workers 'model', for example, being fathers? As Williams (1998) points out, fatherhood remains a problematic status and activity in Britain. Men in families can be both physically absent, and emotionally distant, from their children. Such distance can take the form of relatively poorly developed relationships with children, perhaps through not living in the same household, or physical or sexual abuse of their children. These features of men's behaviour in children's domestic lives create a particular environment for men who work with young children, one where the images of men are not neutral or consensual, where men as fathers are seen to have shortcomings. We 'know' how we want fathers to behave, and as expectations are not always realised, there is an impetus to reinforce a construction of a 'good' father through services where children spend time with adults. Men workers may be modelling presence, reliability and trust for children in contrast to their other experiences of men.

Are men workers being asked, instead or as well as modelling these specific roles, to offer a more general model of masculinity? If so, the same questions arise. What does being 'masculine' mean? Should they be offering a dominant or stereotypical view, or instead challenging preconceptions of 'what men do'? Only one worker, Stuart, raised some of the dilemmas that these questions about role models as a task for men working with young children can pose. We will quote his interview at length, because the extract shows clearly the difficulties of defining men's tasks in childcare as being 'role models' without any further reflection on the precise character or purpose of the model.

Stuart accepted that male role models are an important part of the work, and one expected by his employers:

> That's one of the things when they wanted a man to work here [but] I don't know if it's important what sort of role model you are . . . often I don't come across as a role model that some of the children, boys in particular, would . . . 'cos if I wear pink or something . . . my clothes are sometimes quite bright . . . and . . . their mothers wouldn't put them in that and they'll say 'Oh you can't wear that 'cos you're . . . boys can't wear that' sort of thing.
> [So what kind of role model do you think you are and what kind of role model do you think they expect you to be?]
> I'd like to think that I'm a role model that questions the way men have to be . . . but I don't consciously go out to do that, maybe I'm rejecting the old sort of stereotypes

and role models that I had . . . by default that means I'm something else . . . and their role models sometimes . . . they might want a guy to play football.
[So you think they, the children, families, perhaps other staff, are looking for a kind of fairly traditional male role model?]
I think that's their expectation when they come here, but then they don't find that . . . they see me cooking and washing, then that's their role model and . . . so many times they say 'oh men can't . . .' and talk about men and things . . .
[They talk about men as having a restricted role with children, you mean?]
Yeah and they can't do this and can't do that and I'll say 'well, that's just your experience of a man, you can't say all men are like that' and they think about it . . . I challenge them every time they say it.

Stuart's role modelling challenges children, families and colleagues alike. His masculinity, in the particular context of his work setting, is a constant challenge to predominant ideas about 'what men do' and how men behave. He accepts that merely on grounds of his gender, he has a particular role to play with children and families, but what role is that? He finds the role apparently expected of him is to embody notions of masculinity that were not in character for him and to reinforce features of masculinity, such as choice of clothes and sports, that the children (and possibly other members of staff) may have seen in their own families, but features which Stuart has consciously rejected as a part of his self. Consequently, his working life was punctuated by regular challenges to his sense of self, through the preconceived ideas of families and children about 'what men do'. The degree of discomfort Stuart experiences in reconciling his own masculinity with the gendered expectations of him is tangible. His report indicates that the issue of role models is not underpinned by any consensus about 'men' working in childcare, or perhaps, the role of men with children in general.

As Stuart's experience reveals, the whole issue of what roles to play and how to play them is becoming increasingly complex and uncertain. This can be understood in relation to discussion about the changing nature of identity. It is argued, for example, that identity, of which roles are a part, is becoming increasingly diverse, contingent and fluid, and that this is a feature of living in what some describe as postmodern times:

[In the modern project] identity was to be erected systematically, level by level, brick by brick, following a blueprint completed before the work started. The construction called for a clear vision of the final shape, careful calculation of the steps leading towards it, long-term planning and seeing through the consequences of every move. . . . [But] in the life-game of postmodern men and women the rules of the game keep changing in the course of playing . . . The snag is no more how to discover, invent, construct, assemble (even buy) an identity, but how to prevent it from being too tight – and from sticking too fast to the body. Well-sewn and durable identity is no more an asset . . . The hub of postmodern strategy is not making identity stand – but the avoidance of being fixed.

(Bauman, 1997: 20, 89)

Even if the issue of which roles to model and how to do so was uncontested, a further problem arises from men workers usually being employed in a setting where they are virtually the sole representatives of their sex. The man worker is faced with a nearly impossible task. This one person may be regarded as symbolising all men, and may be expected in some way to serve as a universal, all-purpose and comprehensive model. Were more men to be employed in children's lives, argued Williams (1995), 'boys would not have to define masculinity as the negation of femininity: they would have 'real life' male role models with whom to identify' (1995: 188). However, even in a report evaluating a Swedish equal rights childcare centre, the staff of which were equally composed of men and women, the value of men workers was also seen, in a fashion reminiscent of the claims given by workers in our study, as 'positive male models', and 'good for the children who do not have fathers' (Jensen, 1996: 11).

The last issue concerns the theory of how role models 'work'. The unproblematised discussion of role modelling, as it often relates to childcare work, takes as a given that role models 'work' through demonstrating 'how to be' to others, in this case, children. A sort of process of transmission or reproduction is envisaged by which children assume roles. In the case of men working with children, role modelling transmits to boys how to be male. Implicit in this idea of role models is a passive view of the child, the empty vessel ready to receive knowledge and identity from the adult world, an exact equivalence between what the adult models and what the child becomes.

However, role modelling can be understood otherwise, an active process of negotiation, rather than a passive process of transmission, in which the workers provide the resource which children can work with in co-constructing their individual identity, for example, boys finding their own way of being masculine. Viewed in this way, role modelling works not through transmitting some norm to be assumed, but through providing one set of resources and perspectives which children use, with others, to 'make' their own, rather than 'take' others' roles. But understood in this way, 'role modelling' is both more complex in process and less predictable in outcome.

This examination of role models in practice suggests that a number of ambivalences and potential conflicts exist for workers that undermine the attractive simplicity of the idea. What roles should be modelled? How do we understand these roles? Are they unitary or diverse, universal or particular, essential or contingent? If diverse, particular and contingent, then whose roles are being modelled? For example, are men workers to challenge stereotypes of men's roles in families, replacing the absent, distant or disciplinarian father figure with a man who is more physically and emotionally involved in caring for children – more like a woman cares, in fact? Are they to replicate men's roles, and be a strong, 'firm', caring figure to demonstrate 'balance' with women? Or are they to compensate for 'deficient' fathers, by introducing to children new ways of trusting and believing adults? What does the term 'modelling' imply and how does it relate to understandings of children, learning and identity? Is role modelling the exercise of disciplinary power, the shaping of children's subjectivity or does it stand for a less governing and more emancipatory process – in which case is the term 'modelling' appropriate?

Although the issue of role modelling appears more prominent and problematic for men workers, partly at least because the perceived 'unnaturalness' of men as carers makes the subject of role very visible, there seems no reason why it should not be increasingly prominent and problematic for women workers, as part of a general process in which role and identity are becoming more complex. In both cases, men and women, what is at stake is our understanding of the childcare institution, and, indeed, of caring. Is there one right way to be with children, to understand children, to be men and women, one correct body of knowledge, behaviour and identity to be transmitted, in part at least by role modelling understood as a process of normative re-production? Or are there many possibilities, whose meaning and value are always open to dialogue, disputation and reflection, and in which role modelling, very differently understood, also makes an equally important but very different kind of contribution? Is the purpose of childcare institutions to contribute to a process of normalisation for children? Or is it to provide children with a diversity of resources, relationships and experiences, to which men and women workers make a major contribution and which enables children to construct their own knowledge and identity?

Discussion

The findings presented here about the gendered environment of childcare work suggest that the genderedness of the work is difficult to articulate for men and women workers, who tended to refer instead to individuality as a source of difference. This can be seen when we asked staff how having men childcare workers makes a difference to the work with children. There was a range of responses from no difference to unspecific differences such as an 'added bonus' and then more specific ideas of men workers offering a challenge to, a replication of, and a compensation for, children's experiences of gendered behaviour in families and gendered divisions in wider society. Such a lack of consensus about describing gender differences may suggest a genuinely wide range of reasons for employing men.

Two further suggestions occur to us: first, that the purpose of employing men and mixed-gender childcare workforces more generally has perhaps not been widely debated among staff groups. We saw earlier in the chapter how staff meetings were held at variable intervals, but were mainly used for business and administration purposes, rather than reflecting on practice issues such as gender or gendered ways of working. Such reflection might be a precondition for becoming a 'gender-conscious' childcare institution. The second conclusion we came to was that one of the reasons for not identifying differences based on gender is a perceived link between being 'different' and being Other and/or being marginalised as a source of experience which may contribute to understandings of gender in the centre as a whole. Staff may have been reluctant to identify difference because they did not want to mark out male colleagues – as reported earlier there is sometimes a reluctance to discuss sensitive matters in order to avoid hurting feelings – but when we talked to men workers, their reports illustrated subjective differences of experiences, suggesting that they may already be marked out, marginalised or Other. This is not to suggest that men workers are not welcomed by their women colleagues, but that the defining culture of childcare centres is woman-centred, and men's contributions have yet to be articulated and consciously integrated into how we understand childcare as a workplace and as a way of working with children.

So childcare work is organised around women workers. This in itself is not surprising as it is traditionally 'women's work', but the depth of the construction of the work as women's work did come as a surprise. Various exclusionary practices existed which women did not notice but men workers were required to respond to. These practices took place in the staff room, or in front of the children, parents or colleagues. The men workers responded by casting themselves as a joker, or by avoiding awkward discussions, or by informing management (in quite an authoritative manner) that they will leave if an uncomfortable situation persists. Staff dynamics, then, are riven with understandings of gender difference. The point is not that gender differences exist, but that childcare may be organised with little discussion of, or reflection upon, the impact of gender differences (or similarities). There are many similarities between men and women, just as there are many differences among men. One similarity is the chief reward from childcare work: both men and women enjoy working with children. But often men workers experienced working in childcare as Other. Men tended to be isolated in staff social life inside and outside the centre; they were asked or expected to do the practical jobs; any 'masculine' (i.e., not women's) ways of doing things were marked out as different.

Women workers appear to see men workers as seamlessly integrating, or assimilating, into the woman-centred organisation of childcare. But at the same time, men workers are seen as having a unique dimension of maleness to offer: that of a male role model. The role model can be interpreted as demonstrating that men workers can be like men, or, alternatively, like women. Men workers know themselves and their working environment to be different from that of women: usually as a function of being a 'token' male presence. If the numbers were to even up, would the genderedness of childcare start to fade? Only if simultaneously, the distinction of men and women was recognised and discussed and valued.

Summary

The childcare institution produces and incorporates gendered practice. Such gendered practice may be visible or invisible in that workers may or may not recognise and 'work the tensions' between theory and practice that gendered work involves. This chapter began by setting out the conditions of work in the institutions we visited: both men and women workers felt their salary was low compared to the worth of the childcare job, and few staff were members of trades unions or professional bodies who might exert pressure to raise expectations of salaries for childcare workers.

We then considered aspects of staff dynamics, and explored how men and women workers reported differing experiences of after-work social life, of staff meetings, of the staff room and of working together with children. Perhaps because the men in the study were nearly all employed as a single representative of their sex, their experiences tended to be different from the mainstream, or Other, suggesting their experience could be marginalised compared to women's experiences of work. Simultaneously, both men and women were reluctant to identify gender based differences, preferring to emphasise individuality, both between men and women workers, and between girls and boys. This led to two conclusions. First, that the woman-centred environment in the childcare institutions both overtly welcomed men and at the same time did not recognise, suppressed and rendered invisible their distinctive experiences and potential contribution to the way childcare work is thought about and discussed. Second, that an absence of reflexive discussion of gender among the staff group further suggests an 'invisibility' of a discourse of gender in childcare work.

The analysis of the children's day continued the themes of individuality and Other in workers' views and experiences. We argued that the range of representations of 'men' and male figures by staff suggests that there may be difficulties for a single male worker in achieving such a wide range of objectives. Finally, we discussed the issue of staff being role models and argued that whereas women workers interpreted their modelling behaviour as a 'professional' role model, for men workers role modelling was less straightforward and potentially problematic. The problems surrounded a confusion around the purpose and style of role model men workers should be with children, the extent to which men workers were challenging male behaviour, replicating men's roles in families, or compensating for men's behaviour in particular families.

5

Practice with Parents

I think that the parents, and bear in mind that the vast majority of parents are usually mothers . . . I think are receptive to women who are mothers and have children . . . they say to me 'at least you have a family'. . . (Male worker)

This chapter, and the next two, shifts the focus of study from what happens within the childcare institution to the interaction between the institution and the outside world. Such interaction refers primarily to communication between childcare workers and parents of children attending the centre. This chapter will consider the development of the policy and practice of parental involvement in early childhood services overall before examining the data from this study. The chief objective in work with parents was building up a relationship: we consider the differing experiences of men and women workers in doing this. We also explore the issue of fathers and childcare centres and whether men workers make a difference to fathers' involvement, using both the reports of workers and the work of two exceptional early childhood services.

Although ostensibly workers and parents have a clear common interest – their children – in practice, social, religious, and cultural (among other) differences between the two groups can emerge which can cut across any consensus about this common interest. In this chapter, the analysis of practice with parents through the lens of gender illustrates well the potential for conflicts of understanding as well as that for mutual support. The issue of parent-staff communication is invariably dependent on other factors, on the purpose and ethos of the centre, on the personal style and skills of the manager, and on the staff themselves. Such contingency does not, however, reduce all communication to individual behaviour. Reframing communication as discourse allows us to view the interaction 'outside and inside' the institution as structured, and so subject to predominant ideologies that provide both a common language about childcare, and differing interpretations within that language.

Parental Involvement: Policy and Practice

The policy principle of parental involvement or 'partnership' is now widespread in early childhood services. In nurseries and pre-school education, the

92

principle of parental involvement is endorsed by the Guidance to the Children Act (DoH, 1991: 6.12). Parents, it is said, have the greatest knowledge about their children, should be kept fully informed about children's activities, and should be offered opportunities to discuss children's progress. Moreover, institutions should have a policy on parental involvement, and opportunities for parents to be involved in the management and in the day to day activities in the centres should be provided. This guidance built on previous government reports which identified the value to services, to children, and to parents, of involving parents in their children's services.

In the early 1980s, Smith (1980) suggested that the then growing debate about preschools and parent involvement stemmed from two main sources: ideas about educational intervention and the environment, with parents' involvement being a key to improving a child's chance of educational success; and ideas about consumer participation. The Plowden Report 1967 examined primary education. It became the 'manual for policies of compensatory education, positive discrimination and parental involvement,' so that what Smith calls 'post-Plowden orthodoxy' accepted without question that better communication between teachers and parents was a 'good thing' (Smith, 1980: 23). Subsequent to Plowden, the Brimblecombe Report 1980, with the broader remit of addressing the needs of the under 5s in the family, emphasised the importance of ' better understanding' between parents and professionals as the 'only sound basis' for developing services for young children (DHSS, 1980: 19). The central aim in the development of parental involvement policies was 'building a relationship' between the home and the institutions young children attend for their health, care and education. The emphasis throughout has been on persuading parents to support the objectives of schools and other institutions as a key to children's success.

Extending 'Involvement' to 'Partnership'

Work by the National Children's Bureau in the 1980s further developed the debate on parental involvement in services for young children. This work extended the idea of 'involvement' to 'partnership', and argued that the success of initiatives to promote parental involvement depended upon all early childhood services incorporating parents into the services through staff training and development, a process of rethinking and perhaps diversifying the appropriate roles for professional workers (Pugh, 1985: 6). Rethinking roles and changing staff attitudes towards parents could help staff to see parents as partners in a joint enterprise with an emphasis on reciprocity and joint responsibility rather than inviting 'parents to join them on their terms' (ibid., 1985: 4).

Later, particularly under the Conservative administrations of the 1980s and 1990s, the policy of involving parents in children's services was drawn into a political project to further the principles of the market-place in the provision of services. Ideas of the market-place came to define the relationship between parents and services, so the chief aim was to get the 'market', or free enterprise, to generate 'choice' by opening up services wherever they appeared viable (Cameron and Moss, 1995). Subsequent to the Children Act, there was an appeal by government to the idea of parents directly influencing the supply of preschool care and education. For example, the Education Minister respons-ible for expanding preschool education, Gillian Shephard, described the launch of the Nursery Voucher scheme as putting 'purchasing power in the hands of parents,' implying that parents' judicious use of vouchers would affect the demand for, and success of, childcare services (Sherriff, 1995/6).

An Ideology of Parent Involvement

Such is the consensus that parents should be involved in the services their preschool children attend, that the belief could be referred to as an ideology of parental involvement. So far as day nurseries and other childcare services are concerned, this ideology refers in essence to two levels of parent involvement: first, sharing information relating to particular children; and, second, encour-aging parents to make a contribution to the 'total nursery environment' (Ver-non and Smith, 1994: 120). The data from this study mostly concerns the first level of parental involvement.

The ideology of parent involvement has been a consistent theme for decades but what do understandings of parent involvement mean for childcare institu-tions and workers, and for their relations with parents? While parent involve-ment referred to interventions to improve a child's chances of educational success, the shift to partnership emphasised sharing information and a joint enterprise. Underlying both these methods of involving parents is the idea that parents know their children best. This idea can be found in public policy documents. For example, in *Meeting the Childcare Challenge* (DfEE, 1998), the government states that: 'parents are the first and often the greatest influ-ence on their children's development and education. They will always have the primary responsibility for the care and wellbeing of children' (DfEE, 1998: 1.1). The implication is that because parents know their children best, the care or education services they attend will not have primary responsibility for chil-dren's well-being, but will follow the lead given by parents. The best care, for young children in particular, is where childcare workers' care replicates par-ents' care. This is the 'mother-substitute' idea and can be seen in the idea of keyworkers to ensure continuity of care between home and childcare centres (Penn, 1997), and in the dyadic adult-child relationship we noted in the last chapter.

Alongside the 'parents are the experts, childcare follows' ideology is the notion that children are dependent on adults and the family to define their place and their access to services. They require parental 'permission' (and resources) to attend services, they are not entitled to attend as a citizenship right, for example. Childcare workers, for their part, decide what is important to communicate to parents in the knowledge that the parent as expert ideology is predominant. For example, workers may draw on knowledge of 'child development' and 'parenting' to convey certain behaviours or language as worthy of mention: these may represent an objective attained or, conversely, be socially undesirable and require parental acquiesence to the institution's viewpoint. Working with parents, then, draws on understandings of children's needs and parents' responsibilities, but also draws on the social boundaries or expectations of the childcare institutions, such as rules or conventions about acceptable behaviour. Worker-parent relations may be designed around 'sharing information', but the selection of information for particular purposes, and drawing on particular bodies of knowledge or expertise, means that mere 'information' is situated in a code of common understandings and practices about 'good' childcare, in which the child is largely seen as a passive recipient of 'expertise'.

Differing Interpretations of Parent Involvement

The different services represented in this study have differing origins, and consequently differing interpretations, of parent involvement. As noted in Chapter 2, all the family centres we visited were of the therapeutic type. The main aim was to engage parents both as individuals and in groups in order to improve their parenting skills. Involving parents, then, was the *raison d'être* of the work. The discourse of parental involvement was about helping vulnerable adults as much as sharing the care of the children. The nurseries, both public and private, endorsed the principle of parent involvement, and had formal and informal methods of communicating with parents, such as parent evenings and observation records, and 'handover' times at the beginning and end of the day. The discourse here was one of discussion and consultation with, and accountability to, parents.

Sheffield Children's Centre had the most extensive parent involvement, and, of all the services, was nearest to a genuine 'partnership'. Parents were involved in the running of the centre through advisory groups, and were encouraged to use the premises to run support groups of various kinds, and could ask for a meeting to discuss any concerns about their children's care. Moreover, the parents evidently did use these avenues to become involved in the centre's life. The discourse here was one of extending consultation to democratic participation. Studies of partnership and parent involvement in the field of child welfare services have referred to a continuum of involvement, from information giving to participation (Thoburn *et al.*, 1995). The striking thing about the services in our study, though, is that what varied was not just the extent, and methods, of involvement, but the meanings invested in this involvement by the workers.

Parent Involvement in Practice

But the orthodoxy of policy and principle does not compare well to the reality of parental involvement. In numerous published studies of both early education and playgroups, the practice of parent involvement was less widespread than approval of the principle (Tizard *et al.*, 1981; Pugh, 1985; Brophy *et al.*, 1992). In a recent study of day nurseries, for example, three approaches to parent involvement were found, ranging from 'proactive', through to 'inactive' and 'discouraging' parental involvement: most nurseries were described as inactive, relying, for example, on parents to ask to see records about their children (Vernon and Smith, 1994: 134). With increasing levels of mothers' employment (Holtermann *et al.*, 1998), one of the reasons for the difficulty of realising parent involvement may be a lack of time and availability of parents in general, and mothers in particular, during the working day (Brophy, 1994).

A further problem with the implementation of the parent involvement philosophy, and one particularly relevant here, is that 'parent' tends to be a euphemism for 'mother'. It is well known that mothers take responsibility for childcare arrangements, and so it is by and large to mothers that childcare centres appeal when involving parents (Brophy *et al.*, 1992; Brannen and Moss, 1991; Meltzer, 1994). As nearly all childcare workers are women, the discourse of 'outside-inside' childcare has been almost entirely woman, and mother, centred. For example, a discussion of preschool home visiting schemes focused on mothers' responses, pointing out that it is mothers who receive the service, and at whom the service is directed (Edwards, 1989). When examining practice with parents in our study we were looking at practice with both fathers as well as mothers, and with men and women workers. By doing so we became aware of introducing a new, complex, and contingent gendered discourse between childcare centres and the wider world.

Not only are worker-parent relations structured by gender, they are also structured by the worker's position in the workplace hierarchy. All of the childcare centres we visited operated with a hierarchy of seniority. As men are more regularly found in positions of seniority in the caring professions in general (O'Grady, 1998; Budge, 1995), there is the potential for men in childcare workplaces to be 'expected' to be managers in the eyes of parents at least.

To summarise, then, we conceptualise practice with parents as part of the way in which childcare institutions are represented to the wider society. The discourse with parents leads the childcare worker out into a world where the shared interest in a child is intersected with a range of other assumptions and beliefs about childcare, about parenting expertise, about gender and caring and about the gendered division of labour in both domestic arrangements and in childcare institutions. Underpinning the practice is an ideology of parental involvement in preschool services which has informed policy, but has not necessarily been translated into practice by either nurseries or parents.

In this chapter we will separate out the data from mothers and fathers where possible. It will become evident in the reporting of the data that workers themselves elide the terms 'parent' and 'mother' and where it follows sensibly, we will use the term parent also. Our primary aim in investigating staff practice with parents was to identify how employing men made a difference to staff-parent relations. For example, do fathers come into childcare centres more often as suggested by Burgess and Ruxton (1996)? Do parents assume any men workers are the managers? Are men workers seen as equally suitable by parents, a point noted by Jensen (1996)? Do men staff feel the conditions for men and women workers in their practice with parents are identical or not? If not, in what way are they different? Finally, what does the experience of our group of workers suggest for the contribution of childcare centres towards enabling a more equal sharing of family responsibilities, an argument put forward by Ghedini et al. (undated) for the increased employment of men in childcare.

When do Staff see Parents?

Bearing in mind the differences between the types of childcare centre discussed above, Tables 5.1 and 5.2 illustrate the formal and informal opportunities for staff to see parents.

Merely listing methods of communication, however, obscures the extent of opportunities for communication, as formal structures can exist and not necessarily be used or useful. More significant for shaping the staff-parent discourse is the purpose, and the interpretation, of communication.

Table 5.1 *Staff and parents: formal points of contact*

Childcare type	Formal points of contact with parents
Private nursery	Quarterly parent clinics/evenings
Children's centre + private nursery school	Annual parent evenings
Public nursery	Arrange to see manager
Private nursery school	Send home notes
Public nursery	Child review meetings
Public nursery	Parent carer's committee
Family centre	Group work
Children's centre	Meetings arranged after observations on children completed and when requested by parents
Children's centre	Advisory support group run by parents
Children's centre	Support groups run by parents

Table 5.2 *Staff and parents: informal points of contact*

Childcare type	Informal points of contact with parents
Private/public nursery	Morning and evening handover
Private nursery	Lunchtime visits to feed babies
Public nursery	In passing in the corridors
Public nursery	At the beginning and end of morning/afternoon sessions
Private nursery school	Try to telephone parents we don't see for a while
Family centre	Drive parents into/home from the centre
Family centre	Eat lunch together

Across all the settings it appeared that the main purpose of communication with parents was to develop a relationship with parents in order to get to know their parenting style, their habits and behaviours. This knowledge would help workers to replicate, complement or improve the childcare given by parents, according to the ethos and purpose of the type of childcare centre. In a private nursery, for example, Hannah said they were trying 'to build up a relationship' with parents. To do this, they would 'talk about everything, [including] holidays, how their weekend's been'. In a public nursery, similarly, Caroline reported that they would discuss the child's day and night at home, 'what sort of moods they're in, have they had breakfast, . . . anything that you can actually share . . . you try and find out more about the parents, what do they do, do they go out . . .' In these nurseries, the aim, particularly with babies, was to replicate parental care, using the resource of parental knowledge. It was critical to develop and maintain a relationship characterised by mutual trust and respect so the workers could take over the care of young children while their parents-mothers were not present.

In the nurseries with an educational remit and in the school, the relationship with parents was also consciously developed, but workers were less dependent on the details of family life in order to do their job of complementing parental care. One manager, Nick, said conversations could be about career advice to parents, as well as the child's development. Another teacher, Trevor, said he had built up a relationship with parents over some years, and parents sometimes sought to extend the subjects of conversation beyond the children's progress to other, more personal matters. As an example, Trevor reported that one of the mothers had talked the day of the interview about legal matters emanating from her divorce.

At the family centres, the relationship with parents took on a different quality. The aim of the work was to improve parenting in families where there had been serious difficulties, and the relationship with parents was the key tool for achieving change. Kieran illustrated the depth and intimacy of worker-parent relations in family centres when he described the kinds of things discussed with parents:

> We discuss . . . nappy rashes, the proper way to bath children who are afraid of the bath, how do you get a young girl's hair brushed when she hates the hair brush . . . 'how much should I buy my child? I keep buying him all the toys and he wants more, is that good, is that bad,' how do you deal with bad behaviour, . . . everything . . . right to 'where should I start to clean my house, in the kitchen or the top?' . . . and separations, if somebody's gone for a long time, . . . and they come back into the family house, who does what to make it work . . . and that I am familiar with and that can be very painful.

This relationship goes beyond assisting the worker to care for the child, towards a confiding relationship with the mother (or, in theory, the father) in order to improve her methods of parenting. Kieran readily confessed that he did not have a lot of experience of some of the items he listed in the quote above, and the point was not to tell the mother how best to clean the house, for example, but to develop her trust so she would carry on confiding her problems.

To summarise, childcare workers see parents both informally at either end of the child's day, or during the day in the case of family centres, and formally, at pre-arranged meetings. Childcare workers use the opportunity of seeing parents to develop a relationship with them, the significance and style of which varies according to the purpose of the centre and the ages of the children concerned. The workers we interviewed, particularly those longer in post, also reported that mothers will draw on this relationship to discuss other personal matters, which workers may or may not feel is relevant to their primary role.

In some settings, such as family centres, discussing personal matters was key to the work with parents. Across all the settings we visited, the boundaries of the relationship could be fluid and perhaps ill-defined. Caroline reported, for instance, that 'you tend to find that you build up not just a professional relationship, but also more as a friend'. The emerging picture, then, begins to unveil the contingent character of worker-parent relations. While it is about, at the outset, obtaining and sharing information relating to the care of the child, the methods of doing so rely on developing individual relationships between workers and parents, and this in turn can translate into a far more intimate relationship characterised by confiding personal troubles, and modelled on social relations experienced outside the centre, such as friendship. Such an individual-based style also opens the way for parents to make judgements about workers, as we will see in the next section.

What Difference does a Man Make?

Parental Curiosity

So far we have referred to workers and parents. We now want to explore the distinctions between men and women workers, and between mothers and fathers. The main difference between the men and the women workers was that while some men reported difficulties in their relations with parents, usually mothers, no woman worker did so. The difficulties surround being male not just in a hitherto all-female environment, but also one where the cultural expectations are woman (or mother)-centred. For example, William reported that at times parents had given him the impression, by their questioning, that 'they didn't want me to work there'. He continued: 'it's been a world of extremes . . . you've had those that totally and utterly just did not want me working in nurseries and did not want men having any contact with [their] child at all . . . to those who have been almost ecstatic that they've found a man working in a nursery.'

Persistent inquisitiveness was also reported by John, who said 'you always get parents asking why you're doing it', and who are initially 'shocked' to see a man working with children. Nick found that parents come into the childcare centre with preconceived ideas about who looks after children and reported that 'some parents assume that some men are not really competent or qualified enough yet . . . don't expect that they're going to be as competent as the women staff.' The reluctance of parents to communicate with Duncan became apparent when he found that parents would ask for other, women, members of staff and not accept him as a substitute. Duncan described himself as a foreigner in the midst of women, marked out not only because he was male, but also a migrant from the north, and a relatively new recruit. He saw the key to solving the scepticism of parents as 'building up trust and building up relationships'.

The reports of these men suggest that the experiences of men workers cut across the predominant ideologies of who cares for children and on what premise. Men constitute an unexpected Other in the childcare workforce, and their gender presence is open to challenge by parents, who, of course, are constructed as the 'experts' on their children's care. The men workers thus start out at something of a disadvantage in their relations with parents. This is caused by, first, the unexpectedness of their gender, and second, the dependence on individual effort put into building individual relationships as the means of resolving difficulties. In other words, men recruits find that their very gender presence is, or can be, a barrier in the key to success in their job: sharing information relating to children, as the information can easily be withheld until a member of staff with more 'acceptable' characteristics arrives.

Different Relationships with Parents

If men start out at a disadvantage, the experience of difficulties continues when we examine the workers' efforts to overcome problems in relations with parents. Kieran reported that mothers 'are receptive to women who are mothers and have children', and gave him the impression that they 'would quite naturally feel safer and open the door more readily to a woman who's had a family and understands children, than a man . . . sometimes I get the perception that they're thinking "here comes this guy who's going to tell me how to run my own house and he hasn't got a clue" . . . I have to be very careful how I establish a relationship and what I say.' Although Kieran works in a *family* centre, the emphasis is interestingly on *mothers* and their mothering skills. He has therefore to cross the gender divide with each new mother relationship, where his gender presence reveals his apparent inadequacies: not only is he a man, he is also not-a-mother.

Stuart also had to make more of an effort to win credibility with parents-mothers. His personal style, he reported, was to incorporate humour into the relationship, which some parents-mothers liked and others did not. Brenda reported that the parents-mothers 'feel they can relate more to female members of staff, and they will go to them straight away . . . [the man] has to make the effort you know, . . . but although like with the younger parents he has established a good relationship, but in groups . . . mums have said "oh you know, we can't discuss certain issues with the group" because he's a man.'

The issue of subjects of conversation that are perceived to be outside men's sphere was raised in other childcare centres. Lloyd thinks that 'some of the mums find it hard to broach certain topics with me because I'm male . . . it's quite hard sometimes for them to actually accept me as a counsellor.' Oliver has also found that mothers could be much less forthcoming, and more selective, to him than to his women colleagues. There are times, he said, when 'I've had a conversation with a mother and she's said this and that to do with her children . . . and then they've had a conversation with female staff and it's a completely different story!'

As a long standing member of staff, and a senior teacher, Trevor has built up relationships and overcome the initial difficulties of being a gender-out-of-place. But he too reported difficulties, this time around offering appropriate comfort to mothers who approached him with their personal problems. He said 'I do find it difficult if parents get very upset, if they burst into tears. I feel quite restricted, I really don't feel I can put my arm around a woman and hug her, I think that's wholly inappropriate.' Trevor's difficulty is that, as a consequence of his long service and his place in the hierarchy, parents' perception of his role has expanded to take in their own, as well as their children's, lives. This aspect of worker-parent relations may be completely appropriate in family centre work, but is outside Trevor's training and area of expertise, and would appear to be a consequence of an emphasis on individual relations with parents. Fred, also a senior member of staff, has found that his gender has perhaps lent him an unintentional authority in his relations with parents. He said 'sometimes I've felt that parents take what I've said with too much weight. Perhaps it's because I'm head, or because I'm a man, or perhaps because I'm confident about what I say. Or perhaps it's the aura of school and teachers as authority figures.'

Many of the men workers prefaced their comments with the remark that they had good relations with the majority of parents-mothers who came to the childcare centres. Nevertheless all the men, except for Yusuf at Sheffield Children's Centre, could think of examples when they felt the circumstances of their relations with parents, the vast majority of whom were mothers, were different to those of their women colleagues. The men, entering a woman and mother centred world, found that establishing relations with mothers encountered, on occasion, shock, hostility or doubts about their competence. There were also those who were terribly enthusiastic, 'almost ecstatic', said William, to find a man childcare worker. Men have to make more of an effort to achieve the relations needed, or expected, for the work. When they do, they find parents-mothers can push the boundaries of the relations with their own needs, in turn potentially causing further difficulties for the men.

So for men practice with parents is, far from being a straightforward process of involvement in sharing information, problematic. Turning from this small scale study to childcare centres at large, the problems may be largely hidden in individual experiences scattered across a great many childcare centres, precisely because there are so few men. We have argued that the key tool in practice with parents is the use of the relationship, the development of which is seen as critical in the ideology of parental involvement. The development of relationships is where men feel at a particular disadvantage. But what is the alternative? Before discussing how childcare's practice with parents might adjust to the recruitment of men, it is worth examining the question of practice with fathers. Are there not advantages in being a man when it comes to working with fathers?

Fathers and Childcare Centres

Ruxton's (1992) study found a widespread belief that the employment of men family centre workers would encourage fathers to use their services more readily than where only women were employed. Similarly, Jensen's (1996) discussion paper on men and childcare claims that 'a male presence can be influential in getting fathers more involved in the centre' (Jensen, 1996: 27). Burgess and Ruxton (1996) in their policy report on fathers, argued that men need to 'feel comfortable about using childhood services' through the presence of men as workers inside childcare institutions (Burgess and Ruxton, 1996: vi). A consensus exists, then, that men workers can bring fathers into centres as they can identify with the 'maleness', the gender presence of people who are like themselves.

Our study confirms that fathers do not visit childcare centres as often as mothers, even where men workers are employed. For example, in the survey of mothers and fathers, three-quarters of mothers, but only just over half of fathers, said they visited the centre their child attended every day or most days (see Chapter 6).

Contrary to the arguments in the literature given above, workers in this study were unsure whether fathers were encouraged to attend by the presence of men, and several of the respondents could think of incidents where fathers had raised suspicions about, or objections to, men workers. We want to suggest here that, as with the idea of role models documented in Chapter 4, the expectation that men workers will attract fathers into centres requires a recognition of the diversity of 'men', of heterogenous masculinities, and of the multiple elements of identity, such as religion, ethnicity, sexuality, class and so on that will shape the gendered experience (e.g., being a Muslim man combines gender and ethnicity).

Four women workers and one man worker had either not seen any fathers in their centre or could not think of any examples where the response of fathers and mothers appeared to differ according to whether a man or woman member of staff was present. One man had found that mothers were, on the whole, more accepting of his presence than fathers, and one man had only ever seen two fathers, one of whom was 'extremely receptive' to the male worker and the other was largely absent and disengaged from his family life. Two of the very experienced men workers were not sure whether their gender presence had encouraged fathers to come into the centre. Trevor said 'we get very few

fathers [who] come into these environments, that's always been my experience
. . . we could possibly target fathers more.'

The remaining workers were evenly divided into those who felt fathers were
happier to come into the centre with men workers present (6/21), and those
who thought some fathers were wary of men workers (6/21). Comments from
the former group included John, who said 'a couple of fathers seem to approach me first', and Brenda, who said that having men staff was a 'definite
attraction for men' to come into the centre. Of the latter more circumspect
group, four workers had had experience of incidents where fathers had raised
objections to men workers or had been suspicious of them.

Two of these incidents surrounded religious or cultural beliefs about the
gender of childcare. Georgia recognised that religious and cultural beliefs affected some fathers' receptiveness to men workers. She cited an example where
'one father wouldn't let his child come to the [centre] because there was a man
working there. He said in his culture it just wasn't right for a man to be looking
after a child that young.' Duncan also had had experience of a father who
wasn't happy for him to be looking after his daughter. Once, he said, 'a
Muslim man, and a lot of it was based around religion . . . he just said "I don't
want [him] changing my daughter".' Duncan stressed that such an objection
had only happened once in his five years of working in childcare, but also said
that fathers rarely came into the centre, although a mother whose husband
never came in had told Duncan her husband disapproved of him working
there.

A third incident occurred in the children's centre. Fozia reported that a
father, far from staying away from the centre, repeatedly visited to do 'spot
checks' on who was looking after his daughter, and more specifically, their
gender. A meeting was called and the father finally confessed that he didn't like
the fact that the staff group was half men and half women, and he felt his
daughter was being abused there. Abuse as an issue will be discussed in Chapter 7, but the point about this incident here is that the mixed-gender of the
workforce evoked considerable hostility and suspicion from a father. Not only
was he uncomfortable within the centre, he was also able to wreak havoc
among the staff group through his discomfort with consciously gendered
childcare.

Stuart had also encountered suspicion from fathers. This time the fathers
were partners of women attending the family centre who would sometimes
visit the centre to 'check me out . . . if their partner is going to be at a centre
where there is a man, they come down and see who I am . . . and make sure I'm
not going to make a pass at their woman.' The suspicion here is one of old
fashioned sexual politics. Lastly, both Anne and Lloyd thought that some
fathers were wary of men workers. For example, Lloyd thought that his maleness acted as a catalyst for some men's violence and anger – they recognised
themselves in him in a negative way.

These incidents suggest that diverse masculinities exist among fathers in
relation to childcare: many sources of identity contribute to fathers'

enthusiasm for visiting and/or taking an interest in the activities of childcare centres. Moreover, each worker who could recall an incident where fathers had been hostile to men working in childcare also claimed that such incidents were an absolute minority. For the most part, where fathers do come into centres, they do so accepting that men work there.

The conclusion from this discussion of fathers and childcare must be that these workers had not noticed an increase in the numbers of men coming into their childcare centres through the employment of men. In fact, the response of fathers to men's employment was on occasion quite adverse rather than welcoming. In addition, one woman made the point that while they saw a lot of fathers, they could be, and often were, intimidating to women staff, and used the fact that there was a hierarchy, and a man manager, to go above the women's heads. It is clear that it is problematic to assume any particular response from a heterogenous category such as 'fathers'.

Discussion

Men's Place in Parental Involvement

Examining staff practice with parents through a gendered lens reveals the heterogeneity of categories such as 'staff' and 'parent'. Critically, the term parent is often used to refer, in fact, to mothers. As we pointed out earlier, workers at times referred to 'parent' and 'mother' in the same sentence when referring to the same person. The term 'parent' conceals the gendered characteristics of parenting. This is not just an equality issue for mothers, although this is important. When introducing fathers into the debate about parents and childcare, it is clear they do not have a place, even in the terminology used to refer to carers of children, except perhaps to sit on the sidelines and proffer comment.

Moreover, staff in this study were drawn from a range of different childcare settings with differing discourses on parent involvement, from helping and improving parenting, through to a relationship based on consultation with, and accountability to, parents, and ultimately to participation in the management and the support work of the centre. Despite this wide range of meanings attached to parent involvement, there is a common premise in the centres' practice with parents, and this is the centrality of 'the relationship' as the key tool in caring for parents' children.

The exploration of gender in worker-parent relations has revealed the implicitly gendered notion underpinning the parent involvement discourse. It is not just that workers and parents are heterogenous beings within which differing interpretations of the unexpected Other, man worker, occur. It is also that the idea of parent involvement is interpreted in the light of the wider notion of care as a replacement for 'mother' whose expertise with her children is assumed to be indisputable. This renders men's involvement in the care of very young children problematic, as his gender precludes, or renders suspicious, being a substitute mother.

Towards Gender-Conscious Practice with Parents

There are ways to resolve this problem for childcare worker-parent relations, and to open up childcare for mixed-gender working and receptiveness to fathers. They depend upon a conscious articulation of gender within the centre, through staff discussion, reflection and debate. The work of two childcare centres in England demonstrates that gender-awareness can challenge the way childcare is thought about and constructed as gendered work.

Ghedini *et al.*'s (undated) report about fathers, nurseries and childcare documents the work of Pen Green Centre. Here, the proportion of men employed compared to women has historically been low, but the proportion of fathers involved in the activities of the centre has grown considerably. The scope and scale of the work at Pen Green is impressive, as it offers not just childcare but aims to develop the strengths of the local community through the skills and empowerment of the parents of children who attend the centre. The chief ingredient in their success appeared to be the development of a broad strategy to challenge prevailing ideas that identified the centre as a place for women and children, and not men. The strategy included making the centre more 'men friendly' both through use of visual images displayed around the centre, and through debate, reflection and training among the mainly female staff group about their gender consciousness. For example, the workers examined their gendered communication with parents when they videoed themselves greeting mothers and fathers. Whereas mothers were welcomed in a straightforward fashion, fathers were seen skirting the edges of the room, looking distinctly uncomfortable (Ghedini *et al.*, undated).

Further work included running support groups focusing on the particular experience of fathers: a men's group for fathers, and a separated parents' group for fathers and mothers. Ghedini *et al.* argue that 'developing a strategy to involve fathers has been a continuous and interactive process – analysis of the issues, development and implementation of action, review and further development' (*ibid.*, 17). As a result of this strategy of empowering the parents of children, the centre concluded that children themselves are 'entitled to access to male workers' (*ibid.*).

A second example of a childcare centre involving fathers is offered by the Sheffield Children's Centre. Rather than start out from the point of empowering parents in the local community, this centre recognised that its objective was to demonstrate equality by providing choice and diversity to the children. The Co-ordinator recalled the development of the mixed-gender policy as:

> To work towards equality and in order to actively seek equality . . . it doesn't just fall on you and it's a working process . . . So once we were talking in terms of equality, in terms of ensuring diversity in terms of race, gender couldn't be left out of that equation. What was important was to affirm children and to affirm their identity first and foremost and to give them opportunities to have access to a range of diverse and positive role models and clearly gender had to be one of those, and so we actively sought to encourage men to participate in the work.
>
> (additional interview material)

The policy to recruit men involved an extensive and multi-faceted campaign of advertising jobs and volunteer opportunities in the centre at a time of high unemployment and challenge to traditional conceptions of men's work in heavy industry. The response was good from the housing estates where fathers were caring for children in a context of poverty and low self-esteem. The centre selected, recruited and trained suitable fathers and within two or three years, the policy had translated into a mixed gender workforce, with about equal proportions of men and women. The Co-ordinator put the success of the strategy down to 'a working process, it hadn't been imposed on anybody and everyone had been in agreement and everybody had understood from the beginning that if they were talking about equality, which all of them felt committed to, then, you know, you can't pick and choose who you want to be equal to' (*ibid.*). In time, the scope of the centre grew beyond childcare to incorporate family support work which included groups for parents, such as a fathers' group, a gay parents' group, an Asian men's group, a lone parents' fathers' group as well as a similar range of groups for women.

These two centres have succeeded in making gender a visible issue in their daily childcare practice. They had different starting out points which led to differences in their strategies. While Pen Green put their emphasis on empowerment of all community members, including men and children, and identified the recruitment of male workers as an element of that, Sheffield Children's Centre saw the recruitment of men as the essential ingredient in demonstrating equality and providing choice to children, and saw fathers as the immediate target in their campaign of recruitment. The greater visibility of gender, through recognising it as embedded in a discourse of childcare practice, and then consciously challenging it, had the effect of bringing fathers into the childcare centres.

Importantly for this discussion, both strategies involved a process of staff debate and reflection on the subject of gender, and a recognition that the centre had to become visibly more 'men friendly' in order to welcome fathers onto the premises. In addition, the success of both strategies may have been influenced by the prevailing social and economic circumstances in their local communities. In both cases, recent closures of heavy industry had meant high levels of male unemployment, and consequent financial and social difficulties for families. In other words, the local cultural climate may have been receptive to change in predominant ideas about caring for children. In terms of the present study, the lesson from both centres is that increasing the number of fathers visiting and participating in childcare centres depends on much more than a token male presence on the staff. It depends on a clear, consensual idea of why it is important, backed up by a comprehensive strategy and a system of review and reflection on progress, a process which needs to be undertaken by the whole staff group, women and men.

There are a number of differences, then, that mark out these two centres from most childcare centres we visited. First, these two centres were comparatively large scale; they offered a wide range of services (for the under and over 5s) and spanned specialist welfare services as well as education and care. This breadth meant that a wide range of staff backgrounds was represented, and perhaps offered more opportunities for men workers to come in with one area of expertise and transfer gradually to other areas, when suitably qualified (e.g., playwork to infant care). Second, there was a clear focus on building up team working, with opportunities for debate structured into the working week. Whalley (1996) describes how Pen Green closed on one day a week to facilitate training and discussion. This focus provided a forum for discussion of gender issues as an element of diversity in parallel with other issues such as race and ethnicity. Having a high proportion of men staff is not, it appears, a prerequisite for being 'men (or father) friendly'; the generation of 'gender consciousness' within childcare can take place regardless of men's presence.

A Different Place for Childcare Institutions?

Moving beyond this discussion of alternative methods of making visible gender practice, we return to conclude with what might be the implications of the predominant pattern of worker–parent relations. In Chapter 4 we drew on Singer's (1993) theory of attachment pedagogy as it seemed to fit the focus on individuality seen in the workers' approach to children and gender. We suggest that workers also absorb this theory in their approach to relations with parents-mothers, as explored earlier in this chapter. If the mother is seen as the ideal and pivotal carer, and childcare institutions have the core aim of replicating mother-care either through taking over in the absence of mothers or through improving mothering, then understanding how the mother constitutes her caring role will be key information for the childcare workers.

As argued in this chapter, men workers have particular difficulties in obtaining this information, and in developing a relationship, because childcare work is constructed as principally woman and mother-centred. Crossing the gender divide with parents-mothers is, despite the assertions of workers that they are the 'same' as their women colleagues, always a difficult task and one uniquely so for men joining a mostly women staff team. Moreover, the situation is not easily reconciled when considering men workers and fathers. For although most workers could see that fathers accepted men workers as part of the centre's workforce, a significant minority had witnessed incidents when parents-fathers have judged men workers to be unsuitable to look after their children, or believed their own gender had evoked strong and negative emotions in fathers.

Following this line of argument, our data suggests that the constitution of childcare as it stands militates against men's practice with parents on an equal basis to women's, mostly because of a reliance on viewing childcare as a one-to-one nurturing relationship for which the parent-mother is the best informant. Changes may come about in various ways. Some men workers may have or develop qualities and skills that enable them to cross the gender divide. Changes in the family, with fathers assuming caring responsibilities in their own right and being holders of information, may also contribute, albeit this seems a slow process. Then there are changes in the way childcare services – indeed early childhood services – are understood.

There is still a widespread understanding of these services, especially those included under the heading of 'childcare for working parents', as substitute homes, and their workers as substitute parents-mothers. The young child is an 'empty vessel', needing to be 'made ready to learn' and then filled with knowledge by adults, both parents and workers. Emphasis in both cases is placed on adult-child relations, intensive and shaped by predetermined outcomes – a didactic and developmental model.

But there are, as already indicated, alternative understandings: the early childhood institution offering something qualitatively different to the home, with different experiences and relationships, in particular the group of children and its powerful pedagogical role; the child understood as a 'co-constructor' of her own knowledge and identity in relationship with other children and adults; the worker no longer seen as substitute parent-mother or technician, but as pedagogue or early childhood teacher and researcher, seeking to make sense of children and their learning processes. Were this to be the case, one could imagine the relationship between worker and parent could take on a different significance to that currently held. According to Dahlberg *et al.* (1999), under the new construction of childcare 'working with parents does not mean pedagogues giving to parents uncontextualised and unproblematised information about what they (the pedagogues) are doing, or "educating" parents in "good" practice – but both parents and pedagogues (and others) entering into a reflexive and analytic relationship involving meaning making about pedagogical work'. For example, a question that parents and workers might hold in common might be 'how do we understand early childhood?' (*ibid.*, 1999: 68).

In many ways we have sketched two extremes here, with all the distortions that such dualism produces. We do not wish to convey that all early childhood centres in Britain are like the former and none like the latter. The situation is, in practice, much more complex. Many early childhood services do work with ideas of children as active learners and recognise the potential of a 'pedagogy of relationships', and many workers would reject the idea of being substitute parents. However, we would also contend that other understandings of young children, early childhood centres and workers, produced by wider discourses about gender, parenting and childcare, remain widespread and deeply embedded, and continue to cast their shadow over practice and relationships, not least between mothers and men workers.

This alternative, then, demands an altogether different place for childcare institutions within wider society. The institutions are subject to debate and scrutiny, they are open to all regardless of income, or parents' employment status. They occupy a central and contested place in civil society. This seems a considerable distance from the current position of childcare within British society, and a long way to travel in order to ease the recruitment of men into childcare work and welcome fathers into childcare centres. But the central tenet of the argument is one already largely achieved at Pen Green and Sheffield Children's Centre: that of opening up the childcare institution to debate and scrutiny concerning the project and meaning of childcare work.

Summary

The analysis of practice with parents in this chapter began with a framework for viewing the subject as a discourse of 'outside and inside'. The 'outside' referred to wider society and its views and expectations of childcare institutions as represented through the parents of children who attend the centre. The 'inside' referred to the internal workings of the institution as having its own representation of what childcare was about and what practice with parents constitutes. This framework sought to move away from the traditional analyses of parental involvement which construct the mother as 'parent' and conceal or ignore the potential or actual contribution of fathers to the term 'parent'. Such analyses also accept that the principal method of parental involvement is building a relationship with parents, and concern themselves with how this might be achieved. Our framework sought to reframe the relationship between the centre and the parents, as the comparative analysis of women and men workers showed how the emphasis on relationship was problematic for men workers in particular, mostly because the relationship was constructed around the experience of mothering and caring on a motherhood model.

6

Parents' Response to Men Childcare Workers

When he turned up I was a bit surprised but I thought 'good, why not?'. It's great that a guy should want to work with children, to see that it's not just women looking after children, to see that men have a caring side and to see both sides of the population. The one fleeting thought I had was you hear so many horrible things, you know, the sexual things. But I trust the nursery and once I met him I trusted him. I don't think I've thought about it since.

(Mother)

In this chapter we consider material from a new data source, a telephone survey of a sample of parents, both mothers and fathers, whose children attended the centres we visited. Although, as we discussed in the last chapter, there is a significant body of literature devoted to the subject of parental involvement in preschool services, it is much more rare for parents, rather than professionals, to be asked their views about childcare services, and what goes on within them (*cf.* Edwards, 1989). Here we consider parents' views about early childhood services more widely and some problems noted by researchers about interpreting parents' views in surveys. We examine to what extent mothers and fathers support the principle and practice of men childcare workers and how parents described and interpreted their relations with men and women members of staff. Towards the end we outline the parents' reports of disadvantages and advantages of men workers. Throughout the analysis certain themes recur. Examples of these include issues of equality, of the relationship between domestic life and childcare services, of role models and of trust in the childcare centres the parents know.

Parents' Views about Childcare

Owen's (1997) secondary analysis of the existing surveys of parents' needs for childcare points out that where parents, both users and non users of services, are consulted, their demands are clear: demand for care and education services far outstrips supply, and in particular parents would like to see more nursery education, more day nurseries, longer hours in playgroups and less expensive childcare costs. Elfer's (1994) analysis of parents' views contained in local authority reviews of early childhood services in 1992 broadly supports these conclusions, as does Meltzer's (1994) study of parents' views. It is clear that parents want a service for preschool aged children, a service that is accessible, meets the varying needs of working and non-working parents and combines care with promoting educational goals.

Moving away from the general picture of childcare provision, and towards parental views about the gender of the workforce and what happens within childcare centres, very little is known. Ruxton's (1992) study of men in family centres, for example, only surveyed the views of workers, not parents. Jensen's (1996) discussion paper refers to an interview with a father, but gives no details of how many other interviews were undertaken. Hill (1990) refers to a parent management group debating and recruiting a male worker, but is a very local example. Ghedini et al. (undated) used questionnaires to gather the views of parent users of childcare centres, but do not describe systematic results, only a selection of comments from parents about their experience of participation in a project to develop mixed gender working.

Our aim here in surveying the views of parents was to assess the level of parental support for what is undeniably a very unusual childcare staffing situation: the employment of men childcare workers. Conscious that in Britain at least, two somewhat divergent views about men childcare workers are represented – that men workers contribute towards equality for children and workers, and that men working with young children are potentially dangerous and should be discouraged (Cameron and Moss, 1998) – we set out to ascertain the prevalence of these views among a group of parents with some experience of men childcare workers.

In Chapter 2, we set out the procedure we adopted for recruiting parents and some characteristics of the parents we interviewed are given in Appendix 3. Briefly, we interviewed 77 parents from across the ten centres where we interviewed workers, composed of 52 mothers/co-mothers and 25 fathers. Although this method of reaching parents had the advantage of parental experience of men workers, it also posed the disadvantage that, where there was only a sole man worker, the views expressed would in effect be a judgement of the particular man employed (see Chapter 2 for more details).

Expressing Views about Childcare

Studies of parents of young children attending childcare services and studies of childcare services agree on two points: first, that on the whole, parents are satisfied with the services their children attend, and second, that it is mothers rather than fathers whose opinion is asked, because the use of childcare services is generally constructed by families in relation to the mothers' employment (rather than mothers' and fathers' employment), and it is normally mothers who organise childcare, and who deliver children to, and collect them from, childcare services (Brannen and Moss, 1988; Meltzer, 1994).

Brannen and Moss (1988) discuss some possible reasons why mothers are reluctant to express adverse views about childcare services, and so why there is likely to be a high degree of apparent satisfaction with the services offered (*ibid.*, p. 108). There are implications here for assessing parents' views. If, as Brannen and Moss found in the 1980s, it is the case that mothers find the search for childcare difficult, the arrangements sometimes less than ideal, and sometimes difficult to maintain, 'you have a recipe for women . . . not taking too critical a look at the actual arrangements. As long as there is no blatant cause for concern, there is little point in scrutinising the arrangement too closely' (*ibid.*, p. 108). A second finding by Brannen and Moss of relevance here is that, in this climate of expressed satisfaction with childcare, those whose children attended nurseries, rather than being looked after by a child-minder or a relative, were more likely to voice some dissatisfaction with the service (*ibid.*, p. 106–7).

So, when examining the response of parents to the issue of men workers, it is important to bear in mind that there is a limited culture of complaint, or reflection and debate, about childcare services in general, and that it is, and has been, a mother's rather than a father's area of domestic responsibility. One implication of this is that one might find that mothers had better developed views about childcare services than fathers on account of their greater contact with services, and their higher level of 'worry' about, or responsibility for, children (Clarke and Popay, 1998). On the other hand, we felt it was import-ant to move away from the assumption that fathers were *uninterested* in their children's services, an assumption that might be inferred from a decision not to attempt to talk to fathers, particularly in the light of assertions in the literature that fathers would be encouraged to go into childcare services more often where men were employed, and also in the light of debate about the risk men working with young children might pose (see Chapters 5 and 7; Owen *et al*, 1998; Pringle, 1995; Pringle, 1998).

In interpreting the parents' views and opinions, then, we were prepared for a degree of hesitation. We were aware that it is rare for parents to question or critically reflect on what happens inside childcare centres, and expected this to be reflected in the responses to open-ended questions. For example, quite often parents' views became more critical, or were refined, *during* their response to a question. In analysing responses that seemed to evolve during the space of a few sentences, we attempted to interpret the 'essence' of their position. This was not an attempt to deny complexity or contested views within the respond-ent, but to represent that complexity as best we could.

Our group of parents was relatively new to the childcare centres, as one would expect where two-thirds of the total group of all their children were under school age (see Appendix 3). Over 80 per cent of parents had been using the centre for two years or less, and 37 per cent of the total had been users for under a year. In keeping with the research reported above, mothers visited the childcare centres more frequently than fathers. Forty, or 78 per cent, of mothers went to the childcare centre every day or most days a week. This pattern of visiting was the case for only 15, or 58 per cent of fathers[1]. Equally telling was the high proportion of fathers who never visited the centre. Eight (31 per cent) fathers, but only four (8 per cent) mothers said they never went to the centre to drop off or collect children, or for any other reason. Mothers were asked who, beside themselves, took the children to the centre: 17 (35 per cent) said no one else did. For a third of mothers, contact with the childcare centre was a sole responsibility.

Awareness and Support of Men Workers

Most parents, both mothers/co-mothers[2] and fathers, noticed a male worker was employed when they first visited the centres, and were broadly in favour of the practice of employing men, as Table 6.1. shows.

Table 6.1. *Parents' support for male workers: numbers (and percentages)*

| n = 77 | Noticed a man at first visit | Principle of male workers | | | Other | Missing |
		In favour	Not in favour or mixed views	No view/ can't remember		
Mothers/ co-mothers (n = 52)	36 (69)	26 (62)	6 (14)	10 (24)	-	10
Fathers (n = 25)	14 (56)	9 (56)	1 (6)	5 (31)	1 (6)	9

With the advantage of some experience of their children attending centres where men were employed, by far the majority of parents said they were still in favour of men workers: 44 mothers (86 per cent) and 21 fathers (85 per cent) agreed that they supported men childcare workers. This broad picture conceals a diverse range of views about why parents supported men workers, however, and how parental support fitted into their views about other aspects of the institution and its staff.

Concern for Boys

A clear reason why parents supported men working with young children was concern for their boys (16 mentions). One mother said when her baby was six months old she 'was keen for there to be a male role model' at the nursery he attended. She continued: 'I felt strongly there should be male contact for him as he got older'. Similarly, another mother said 'my child is a boy. I thought it was good for a male to be looking after him as well as being surrounded by female adults all day.' Two more mothers gave some detail about how it would be good for their sons. One said 'my son has hearing difficulties – a male voice is easier to hear because it is deeper. [In general] it adds something different, very positive.' The other extended her argument to the relationship between the nursery and the outside world: 'I personally think it's a more realistic reflection of the situation outside the nursery and to see men in caring roles. I have a son and I'm a single parent. It makes a balanced staff gender group.' A father picked up on the issue of images of men caring: 'it can help with certain stereotypes about men and childcare. And boys think men shouldn't do that work.' Finally, a mother of three boys said 'I like my boys to have male role models. They don't get men in nursery or primary usually until comprehensive and that's a bit late. It was one of the positive things about the nursery, for my boys to be able to interact with men and women.'

Although ten parents mentioned their daughters, there was much less certainty about the beneficial impact of men workers on their daughters than on their sons. Only three parents, two mothers and a father, referred to their daughters' positive experience of being cared for by men workers. For example, one said 'she's always really liked the men'. Four parents mentioned in passing that they had daughters while saying they thought it 'natural' or 'normal' for men to care for children. One father referred to his daughter as the person who had told him a man worked at the centre. 'My daughter just mentioned it and said he's our best friend, this man at the nursery . . . I thought it was just normal.' The remaining three parents, all mothers, expressed some caution about men in the light of having daughters. One said 'I was worried about a man with my daughter because of my [childhood] experience'. The children of the other two mothers attended centres where the man worker was the manager, and didn't work directly with the children. Both mothers thought they would revise their views about men workers should they work more closely with the children. One said 'a man dealing with my daughter, I would rather know him more personally'.

Concern for Girls?

The caution expressed above is explored more fully later. The interesting point here is that in contrast to the clear enthusiasm for boys to be cared for by men workers, the presence of men workers was not seen as so relevant for girls. The implication from these parents' views is that the benefits of men workers are expressed in terms of the benefits of same sex identification, as an added dimension to boys' childcare experience. What does this mean for girls' needs for same sex identification? That they are 'naturally' catered for by the women staff? As we saw in Chapter 4, staff on the whole did not like to differentiate on the grounds of gender, but preferred to see children as having individual needs. This may mean that girls' needs as a gendered group within childcare institutions are not conceptualised and are comparatively neglected: if boys are identified as benefiting from the added dimension of men workers, but girls are considered only as individuals and not as a group, which adults, parents or staff, will be conscious of, or articulate, girls' needs as a whole? As we have already argued that childcare is 'woman-and-mother-centric' from the workers' point of view (see Chapter 4), it may be that girls' needs for adult identification are assumed to be met by the embeddedness of the female experience within the construction of childcare. The parents' use of the gender of their children in their responses to the question of support for men workers is a good example of how gender is, for the most part, invisible within childcare institutions until it is consciously evoked.

Men Workers as Role Models

Linked to the issue of the benefits for boys, a second reason why parents were in favour of men workers was that they were seen as good for children (10). The dimensions of this mentioned by parents were the ability of men workers to provide a role model of 'being male', and to provide some compensatory 'male contact' or a role model for children of lone mothers or in other circumstances where fathers are absent from home. As we saw in Chapter 4, being a role model can be interpreted in various ways. It can mean demonstrating perceptions of essential 'maleness', in a traditional authoritarian, paternalistic sense, or it can mean challenging gender stereotypes and showing alternative, caring, ways of 'being male'.

Parents had no more consensus on this than did workers, but they tended towards the latter interpretation of being male. One mother, for example, said 'when he turned up I was a bit surprised, but I thought "good, why not?" It's great that a guy should want to work with children and see that it's not just women looking after children, to see that men have a caring side.' Another mother thought it was not just the example of men caring for children within centres that was important, but caring activity in the home as well: 'It's important to get a male role model for children outside the home. Men should do everything. My husband does not necessarily agree. I see that my husband does meals and nappy changing, children should see it's the same in both worlds.' A third mother extended the argument to gendered work spheres: '[it's] important for men to be there as a role model and that it is seen as an acceptable career for men and important as children get older. An all female environment is not representative of the world. There needs to be a balance.'

The remainder of the group who favoured men for their ability to provide role models saw them operating in a much more general sense: being 'a man' around children, itself seen as novel and of positive benefit to children. A father at the mixed gender children's centre said: 'there are very few positive role models of men around. They have fostered this here and it's a big plus.'

Evolving Views about Male Workers

A large group of parents was more neutral in their support of the principle of men workers. This is not to say they opposed the idea, but that they were less forthright in expressing their support than those reported above. Typically, this group began their comments by saying 'I hadn't thought about it' or 'I have no problem with it'. Typically, also, when they elaborated on their thoughts, their response became more supportive, but in addition introduced other factors which they thought of relevance to the characteristics of the staff group. One example of this evolving viewpoint is this father: '[there's] nothing wrong with it. I was surprised to see a man working there . . . I have no problems with it. Some people might say never trust a man. You can't stereotype men like that. It's a good thing. He seems a pleasant bloke.' Here we have a slightly defensive beginning, as if the question assumes there is a problem, an acknowledgement of personal surprise, a dealing with perceptions of the outside world, and a personal interpretation, drawing on what the father knows about the man worker in question.

A second father who reconciled his perception of the outside world's view of men and his own experience voiced it like this: 'I have no personal problem with it myself. It's more the preconceived ideas about men working in childcare. I've got to admit when [he] first started working there I raised an eyebrow seeing a man working with such small children. It's a stereotype of the job. You don't expect to see a bloke doing a nursery nurse's job. It's a good decision he is there. It's not a good thing or a bad thing.'

The Role of the Institution

One of the ways parent respondents expressed their indifference to or lukewarm reception of the principle of men workers was to draw on other aspects of the institution which they thought of more, or equal, relevance. Trust in the management to have checked and supervised workers was one method parents used to assess whether workers were suitable, regardless of their gender. It was also important that workers were qualified to do the job, and that they appeared competent. This mother emphasised trust in the management and a professional approach when she said: 'it makes no difference to me one way or the other. The only thing that concerns me is that the person is qualified and enjoys being with children all day and I know [the manager] will employ such people. Their sex does not matter one way or the other.' A second mother in this group concurred: 'no problem. No, I hadn't thought about it. The moment I went to the nursery he was there. It was nothing strange. It's just like men in nursing, you have men nurses and women nurses. I knew he was qualified.' A third mother said simply '[it's] not a problem. He's a very nice man, always pleasant. If he's good at looking after my son it's no problem.'

The reference in the last quote to being 'nice' was another method parents used to assess whether a worker had suitable personal characteristics to care for their children. One father said 'it never occurred to me one way or the other if I should be for or against a man working here. If he was unpleasant I might have thought about it but I would if a woman was unpleasant too.' Being able to sense a good atmosphere through the characteristics of the workers was important to this mother, who had witnessed a man worker being promoted:

> When he became head, I was relieved the change in personnel did not lead me to revising my opinion about the nursery. I didn't have any negative feelings about him. It didn't matter except about my son going into a nursery with a happy atmosphere. He did nothing to change my view of the efficiency and ability of the nursery.

Some parents had not had cause to think about whether they supported the principle of men workers because the men workers in the institutions they visited were long-standing members of staff and thoroughly integrated into the culture of the centre. Describing her support of men workers, this mother drew on her relationship with an individual:

> [I'm] not against it. There was a users' meeting and someone brought up the issue of whether it was alright for a man to be changing nappies. It just made me think about it. Maybe because my son had gone past the nappy stage and was no longer in the room where the male worker was. However he has a male worker now. He is the closest teacher to me. I've got so used to it.

Cautious Support of Men

A small group of parents either did not support the principle of men workers or only did in specific environments. One mother, whose profession was in social work, and in particular child protection, explained her caution about men workers like this:

> I have a general concern about men working in nurseries . . . I have worked through the academic and emotional issues . . . if men are employed in nurseries [the] whole issue of men has to be open, discussed, debated, and the possibility [of abuse] minimised. You can't remove it entirely. This nursery is trying to put it on the agenda. Their practice is so that it is much more open and minimises the opportunity for abuse. I now feel quite comfortable here. I would not automatically feel comfortable somewhere else.

This mother's very specialist knowledge of a particular group of men, those who have abused children and who have deceived employers about their intentions, led her to believe that men childcare workers were potential abusers unless the institution addressed the issue of possible abuse by a process of constant debate and awareness. For two other parents, personal experience of child abuse was the reason for not supporting the principle of men workers at all. Both referred to difficult experiences with men in their own, or in the case of a father, his wife's, childhoods, and the difficulties of reconciling that history with men working with children. The father referred to the publicity given to men abusing children and said he'd be more inclined to leave children with women rather than men. (The issue of abuse is explored more fully in Chapter 7.)

To summarise, mothers and fathers were, for the most part, supportive of the principle of men workers, and they based their support on their experience of the workers they knew. But the gender of the worker was not the overriding consideration in assessing the suitability of staff, and parents were often aware that the presence of men workers was unusual in childcare, and had to reconcile their own position (sending a child to childcare where a man was employed) with perhaps disapproval 'out there'. On the whole, parents had not thought extensively about the issue. Some referred to it being 'natural' for men to care for children, others to men caring as an extension of home. Those who were more enthusiastic referred to the benefits of the added dimension of masculinity-as-caring that men workers represented, especially for boys. However, this section has shown that not having thought about the issue did not mean that parents did not have any views. It is perhaps the case that parents had had few opportunities to contribute to debates about matters such as gender in their childcare services, and that they therefore had little practice in articulating their views on the matter. Only at Sheffield Children's Centre did it appear that parents were involved in discussing matters of practice such as gender. Reasons for not supporting the principle of employing men as childcare workers centred around the possibility of men abusing children, and the difficulty of knowing which men might, or might not, abuse children.

Working with a Mixed Gender Workforce

Time Mothers and Fathers Spend in Centres

We have already noted that among the group of parents we sought to interview, fewer fathers than mothers were available (see Chapter 2) and, among the group we did interview, fewer fathers than mothers participated in the daily, or nearly daily, childcare run. Fewer fathers than mothers, therefore, have experience of working with the men and women childcare workers. Among those who did regularly visit the childcare centre, 88 per cent said they had 'much contact' with the staff. Typically, this contact was like that of this mother: 'I chat a bit when I take her and when I collect her. I know them through my work . . . so sometimes I talk to them about that.' In Chapter 5, we outlined various methods identified by workers for communicating with parents. In the survey of parents, however, very few such methods were mentioned. Beyond the informal chats at the beginning and end of the day, it was only parents who attended family centres who spoke of other kinds of contact such as groups they attended with workers, and the personal counselling they might receive.

Some parents evidently barely went inside childcare centres. One father said: 'I've not spent a lot of time, just ten or 15 minutes there', and another father: '[I've] not been there to see him working with them'. Mothers also said they saw very little of what went on inside the centres: 'I have only seen him in public for the first five minutes . . . haven't really seen him on a one-to-one' and '[the] maximum time I have spent in the nursery is one hour'. Other parents, when asked to comment on the issue of differences between men and women staff, drew comparisons from their own domestic life. One father reported that 'male and female are different species. I know I would handle things differently but I am not trained in the work. I can only talk about myself', and a mother said: 'I'm not very knowledgeable about the workers. I say this more from seeing fathers than carers. It's another role model. Men do more of the rough and tumble.' Clearly, parents have relatively little opportunity to form opinions based on personal experience of observing staff with their children. Questions which asked parents for details of their views of centre life illustrated that the claim of widespread contact with workers is probably limited to morning and evening 'handovers' as in the quote given above.

Our evidence suggests that parents as a group are relatively uninvolved in the childcare centres, and that this is even more the case for fathers than for mothers. For mothers, some of the contact is around building 'therapeutic' relationships with members of staff, particularly for those attending family centres. For most mothers, though, working with the staff is about ensuring the smooth passage of information about the child's day in the centre or time at home.

Parents' Views of Gendered Staff

In Chapter 4 we discussed the issue of gender difference among the staff group and among the children. We noted how difficult and novel the subject of gender difference was to the workers, who preferred to see children, and to some extent each other, as individuals. For parents, who, by and large, as we have argued above, accept uncritically the models of childcare they are presented with, there are similar difficulties of identifying differences between men and women staff. Table 6.2 shows that in response to a question about gender difference and the staffs' behaviour with the children, most parents could not identify any differences or had no opinion on the matter. Among those with no opinion, fathers outnumbered mothers by two to one. Mothers were more likely to see no differences.

Table 6.2 *Parents' perception of differences between the way men staff and women staff are with the children*

n = 77	Mothers (% of mothers)	Fathers (% of fathers)	Total (%)
Yes	14 (27)	7 (30)	21 (28)
No	27 (52)	5 (21)	32 (42)
No opinion	11 (22)	12 (50)	23 (30)
Total	52	24 (1 missing)	76

Where differences between men and women staff were noted by parents, their descriptions tended to follow fairly stereotypical gendered lines. The terms used to describe men were 'enthusiastic', 'relaxed', 'playful', 'fun', 'authoritative', 'rule bound', 'physical' and 'someone special'. Men, it was said, were more likely to play football, to do things outside, and to 'muck about'. They 'let the kids get on with it', and 'are not inhibited by risk'. One mother remarked that when the man worker first started 'I saw him cuddling the babies [and] I thought that was different. It was nice. I wouldn't have noticed it if a woman had been doing it.' Another mother said 'the men staff are less likely to be sympathetic. If the children are hurt they say pick yourself up . . . they are more directive, more bossy with the children, louder, too.' Finally, one mother neatly summarised the gender divide thus: '[the] women look after the young children. The men look after those in the garden but will come in and help the women when they need it.' These comments clearly position the man worker as outside the 'expected' within childcare, or Other. None of the activities or characteristics described is necessarily gendered, but the fact that they are mentioned by parents, despite having relatively few opportunities for observation, suggests that they stood out for the parents as peculiar to men's presence within the centres.

By comparison, the characteristics of women workers observed by parents cast them as providing the substantive, consistent parts of caring, even as dull. Women workers were referred to as 'giving guidance', providing a 'maternal role' or 'instincts', as 'taking fewer risks', providing 'more in-depth caring and nurturing' and doing more 'planning' for the children. Women were seen as 'more natural', 'open-minded' and making 'more compromises' than men. Women were also described as 'traditional carers [who] are more aware of the consequences of actions, more concerned about danger'.

In a sense these differences parallel the differences noted by family researchers about divisions of labour within heterosexual families: the men do the 'fun' childcare, and the women do the routine nurturing (Oakley and Rigby, 1998). Again, the question is posed about the conceptualisation of childcare work as replicating, or being modelled on, idealised versions of mother-care: comparing the descriptions given above, the women are seen as providing the core elements of childcare, while the men are seen as providing the additional extras, the bonus. One father illustrated how women are seen as central to the work of childcare, while men are constructed as more peripheral: 'Women spend more time and are more in-depth in caring. They do more planned work. Men are just messing about. I say this from two nurseries that I have used for my sons. Men are used in different roles as well. They didn't seem to change nappies much. It's more physical things and going out and playing football.' From this father's observation, men are not just differently caring stemming from their masculinity, but the institution constructs their role differently so they are kept on the periphery. As the mother quoted above put it, the men come inside to 'work' when they are needed. The depiction given by another mother quoted above of a man cuddling babies as 'different' is a striking evocation of just how gendered baby care is: we just do not expect men to do this and we have to consciously adjust our expectations to accommodate men carers.

No Difference?

As with the analysis of the worker data, our task is to make sense of the finding that many parents could not identify any differences between men and women staff. Parents who commented on their observation that there was no difference fell into two groups. First, there were those parents who argued that childcare workers were merely 'different people working in different ways'. For these parents, gender was irrelevant to the job of childcare. As one father put it: 'a voice is a voice telling the kids to do something. It's just the same whether it's a man or a woman.' Some of these comments came from the same parents who admitted that they rarely saw the inside of the childcare centre, so their opportunities to observe workers were limited. In addition, other parents thought that one of the key differences between men and women was the depth or tone of their respective voices, making the last comment above at the least subject to question. On both counts, it would appear valid to consider these comments as arising from parents, particularly fathers, who had thought little about what goes on within childcare centre work.

The second group of parents was those who felt factors such as individuality and conscious team working played a large part in assessing differences and similarities between staff. Largely represented by the parents of children attending Sheffield Children's Centre, this group made comments such as 'maybe men are more active, but then women are active too. It evens up really, there are quiet men too' and 'in a co-operative, the left hand knows what the right hand is doing. There are regular staff meetings where issues are discussed.' One mother saw that 'one worker is probably more of an entertainer, it's part of his role. He is funny and making up songs. His approach is less cuddly and caring but very beneficial. I wouldn't want to generalise. It's down to the individual. The men are as interested in the children, it's not necessarily a matter of gender.'

Another mother from the centre confirmed that differences between men and women are not evident 'in how much they care for the children. I have an impression men do interesting things and may be more dynamic, but it's hard to tell. It seems fairly well balanced in the rooms.' These parents, compared with the parents of children attending other centres, were at a relative advantage in that they were able to observe staff groups composed of more or less equal numbers of men and women. This meant they saw a range of 'masculine' and 'feminine' behaviour. Their assessment of 'no difference' was not, then, an assumption of 'sameness', but a consideration of many facets of gendered characters. In Connell's (1987) terms, these 'individuals' were in fact representations of *masculinities* and *femininities*, in other words gender identities constructed in the particular context of childcare, and of consciousness about gender, and cross gender team working. Issues of gender in this children's centre have been constructed as worthy of debate, measures have been adopted to address the issue, and through this gender has become institutionalised: it is part of the way of being of the centre and parents take men and masculinities for granted within the centre's work.

Parent-Staff Communication

Parents' observation of differences between men and women staff was parallelled by their comments on staff-parent communication. On the whole, mothers and fathers did not mind whether they spoke to men or women staff when they visited their children's centres. Table 6.3 shows that two-thirds of parents felt equally happy with a man or woman worker. Among the group of parents who did express a preference, there was some preference among mothers for women workers, and a small group of mothers and fathers who felt the choice of the gender of a worker would become more important when discussing certain issues.

Table 6.3 *Parents' gender preferences when talking to members of staff*

n = 77	Mothers (% of mothers)	Fathers (% of fathers)	Total (%)
Man	2 (4)	1 (4)	3 (4)
Woman	11 (21)	3 (12)	14 (18)
Either	33 (64)	18 (72)	51 (66)
Depends on the issue	6 (12)	3 (12)	9 (12)
Total	52	25	77

We explained above that the key aim of parents in their discourse with staff was to ensure the smooth passage of information about their children. In their preferences about the gender of staff, it was clear that key workers, people who knew the children best and 'whoever was around' were important factors in obtaining this information. Typically, parents would want to talk to 'just someone who had spent time with my daughter in the day'.

We argued in Chapter 5 that a key aim of staff in their practice with parents was the development of relationships: but this was important to only a few parents in our study. Four mothers and a father said they preferred women, or in the case of one mother, a man, because they knew those staff better, over a longer period of time, and felt more comfortable with them. The mother who preferred a man worker explained that

> With this male teacher I do go to him because he's extremely nice and friendly and interested in my son. He's not my son's allocated worker. When we went back in September, there was a new female teacher allocated to him but because she is new she tells me to go and see him and talk to him. So I do, I go to him directly. It saves time. And he cracks jokes, he teases me.

In effect, this mother was subverting the system of allocated workers by going to the worker she knew, albeit with the blessing of the new woman worker.

The strength of the relationship with the man, established over some time, was evidently important to the mother for herself, as much as for the information about her child.

The father who preferred to talk to women staff alluded to a personal history of confiding in women rather than men: 'I personally prefer to talk to a woman only because I have always got on well with women. I'm not into that buddy stuff. It's lost on me.' Alongside knowing the women staff better, another reason for choosing women workers was having more confidence in them, perhaps from the familiarity of seeing women as confidants or as experts in childcare. A mother commented on this: 'probably a woman. No, I can't say why. It would depend on what I wanted to discuss . . . if it was an emotional worry I would be more inclined to go for a female worker.' Another mother said 'if another child is fondling my child I would talk to a woman, I would want the woman to empathise, I would want someone to be in my shoes.' Finally, one mother said she preferred a woman because 'my daughter is a girl', suggesting that there were issues about being a girl that women staff could better identify with.

To summarise, parents are aware of, and respect, the organisational hierarchies of childcare centres. They want good quality information about their child from the person who is best placed to give it: the worker caring for her or him. They are less concerned about relationships with members of staff than about ensuring a smooth transition for the child(ren) between home and centre. Parents frequently differentiated between types of problems, and would take issues relevant to the whole centre to the manager. For example, one mother said 'if it's something relating to a particular person's practice or if he had wet himself I would talk to the person who had changed him. If it was serious or a care issue that had not been addressed fully or something I did not agree with, I would talk to a manager.'

Although some parents thought if they had problems with a member of staff they would discuss them directly, one father thought there were circumstances in which he would not: 'if it was about my child's relation with a male worker I would talk to a woman worker. Men are not being impartial about policing themselves. It's a question of utilising that polarisation between men and women and using it to make sure issues are explored thoroughly.' This father saw gender as a dynamic between staff members that he could potentially use to resolve issues on behalf of his child. This father also referred to the issue of men and self-control or 'policing themselves'. This picks up on the references above to parents' caution about men workers *per se*, and will be explored in the next section on parents' views about men workers.

Views about Men Workers

So far we have focused our analysis on men and women workers, and seen it as equally important to analyse the work of women as that of men. In this last section using the parents' data, we have adopted the more traditional mode of analysis of viewing the men as a statistical and cultural anomaly and asked the mothers and fathers to comment on the problems and advantages they perceived of employing men in childcare services in general.

Two-thirds of the parents in this study could not think of any problems with employing men childcare workers (67 per cent of mothers and 60 per cent of fathers). Viewed from the other way round, all the fathers and 87 per cent of the mothers could see advantages in men childcare workers. Overall, 91 per cent of parents with experience of men workers saw advantages in having them employed in childcare centres. However, these global figures conceal an array of comments about the advantages and (potential) disadvantages of men workers.

Disadvantages

Virtually all the potential disadvantages with employing men workers that parents could identify revolved around the issue of regulating men (and women workers) in view of parents' recognition of men's association with child abuse. Overall, however, parents were sanguine about the issue of abuse. They were aware that child abuse existed 'out there', but saw two main ways in which their personal experience of it through childcare centres would be minimised. First, there was a group of parents who referred to wider society's construction of men as dangerous for children. This group referred to the 'bad publicity' men childcare workers got in the press. One mother said '[the] only [problems arise] because of what you perceive because of what you read. If you didn't read it you wouldn't think about it like about men in children's homes. Fathers or most fathers don't abuse their children. It wouldn't occur to you. It's the bad publicity.'

A father commented 'I'm a realist. It's a bad world out there. A male worker could be as white as the driven snow. But there is always the fear he could be accused of something. But there are bad women as well as blokes.' Another mother said 'we have our own personal prejudice some of which is fed by the media . . . It's only a problem if we allow it to be. If the vetting is done properly. Saying that paedophiles are very devious and good at getting into places where children are. We have to be constantly vigilant.' A third mother referred to 'other' people who 'have feelings about it because of abuse . . . Just because most perpetrators are men doesn't mean you can exclude them. Men in dirty macs are a figment of *our* imagination' (original emphasis).

These parents were acutely aware that the world 'out there', of which they were also a part, disapproved of men working with children because of incidents of reported abuse of children and the difficulty of spotting in advance which men would abuse children. Nevertheless, they justified their own position of sending a child into a childcare service where a man was employed by calling for a sense of perspective. For example, one mother said 'men is a huge concept. It's a problem of personality and character and sensitivity as well as training . . . paedophiles are less likely with women at the extreme end of the range. There are female harridans you wouldn't want for your child. It's not about all women and all men.' One father summarised this position by saying 'I just think there is a fear of men in any profession that involves young children. We are in a fear period. I personally am not afraid.' These parents wanted to position themselves outside what they recognised as a fairly hysterical response to men workers (seeing them as paedophiles, for instance), whilst simultaneously not entirely disregarding the notion of risk.

Similarly, the second main way parents thought their children's risk of exposure to child abuse could be minimised was through steps to regulate the workforce. Many parents referred to the importance of screening, checking and vetting workers, and of close supervision. For some parents this applied equally to men and women workers: '[there are no problems with men] given adequate screening of both male and female workers. I have no concerns if there are proper safeguards. The concerns about abuse are especially in relation to men but can apply to women too' argued one father. Another father concurred: '[there are no problems] in this nursery, I have every trust in them. Anybody who works with children has to be vetted, man or woman.'

But for other parents, being a man worker merited additional supervision compared to the women workers. One mother said '[men] have to be vetted properly. There is a natural tendency to watch them more closely when changing nappies and things. It's unfair but it's the reality.' A second mother agreed that there should be no problems with men workers 'so long as they are well supervised. I am worried about abuse.' A third mother thought the supervision extended to constant vigilance by staff and parents alike: 'men have to be aware of their problems. They have to be vigilant about their colleagues as well . . . [they] should involve parents in raising awareness, and of the grooming and what steps to take to reduce it.'

Particular activities in the childcare centre were seen as perhaps requiring close supervision of men workers. In the main, these were taking children to the toilet and nappy changing. Five parents mentioned intimate personal care as an area that posed particular difficulties for men staff. A mother who saw toileting as an occasion for extra care said: 'you have to watch out that children won't say funny things' and another mother, responding to the policy in her centre, said 'men can't take children to the toilet'. Lastly, a father from the children's centre where there was a policy of members of staff witnessing nappy changing said 'we took the nursery as a whole. If a child had to have a nappy changed the male worker was accompanied by a female as a precaution. That's how it is.'

It should be stressed that parents, both mothers and fathers, saw abuse as a potential disadvantage of men workers and not a reason for excluding men as a whole. They put considerable trust in the management to recruit suitable workers, and assumed that adequate screening of new workers would reveal any unsuitable candidates. As one mother said 'you need to take care in making the appointment and then monitoring afterwards'. The majority of this group of parents voiced their concern about possible abuse of children by workers as a problem they personally were distanced from. Two fathers summed up this sense of distance: one said 'maybe there is a potential problem. It's a theoretical issue. Men are more prone but it's theoretical' and the other said simply 'it's an issue but not a problem'.

Advantages

Moving away from the disadvantages of men workers, what did parents think were the advantages of men in childcare? In contrast with the clear focus on abuse and the regulation of the workforce in the previous section, there were many reasons why men were an advantage in childcare work. As one would expect from a group of parents whose responsibility for their children mainly lies outside the centre, within families, the most commonly mentioned advantages were those that linked the role of the men workers with children's lives within the family and wider community. A broad group of parents saw the employment of men as modelling or reflecting domestic family life or life in the community.

We use the term 'modelling' here in the sense of 'educating', or providing an example from which children can learn. Parents thought it was 'good for children to see that men can have a share in the responsibility of caring for children'. A second mother thought it important for 'children to see both men and women in roles that are caring. Like cleaning the floor and washing up.' Through men's employment in childcare children would learn 'that those jobs are for men as well as women'. These parents wanted to broaden the definition of caring away from a traditional association with mothering to be more inclusive of men, and, in doing so, both to have men adopt some of the more routine aspects of caring, such as cleaning, and have men encouraged to be employed in caring work. Closely related to educating boys and girls to expect caring from men and women, several parents raised the point that through the employment of men, children could witness men and women relating to each other. One father said 'society is made of men and women in intimate relations. We need to have men and women doing [the work] and for children to see men and women getting on with each other and to see models of good practice. Children may then get the messages and the opportunity to relate to men.'

Parents saw the employment of men alongside women as a way of reducing children's prejudice about men's and women's roles at home and in work. They thought it would create a 'better balance' in children's views of the world and it would be 'good for their socialisation'. Providing 'diversity', a 'different perspective' and a 'mixture' of people from 'both sexes' caring for children was thought important by a swathe of parents from across the different types of childcare institutions. Some parents saw it as important to differentiate between 'men'. One mother thought 'the opportunity of meeting a gentle, caring man is broadening of a child's early experience. Nurseries can be a cosy experience and that can be limiting of children's early education.' A co-mother expressed this from the other side: 'it depends on the men. If they are big and brusque it wouldn't do, but it wouldn't for women either.'

As well as modelling aspects of mixed gender relations elsewhere, some parents saw the employment of men in childcare institutions as reflecting family or community life. In these circumstances, children could identify with men childcare workers as similar to those men seen in other spheres of their lives. One mother saw men child care workers 'just being there, it's a more natural environment'. A second mother saw the benefits of men as making childcare a 'more normal environment' and a third said 'that's the way the world is. Both men and women . . . it [childcare] should reflect what goes on at home.' Finally, a father argued that 'children have contact with both sexes outside the nursery. It's natural to make that continuity in the nursery.' Clearly, these parents thought 'normal' constituted a nuclear, heterosexual family, where both sexes contributed to children's upbringing. Whether this actually is 'normality' is somewhat contested (Williams, 1998), but, evidently, an idealised form of the family is uppermost in these parents' thinking.

A further way in which the employment of men was seen as reflecting family life was the ability of men to be 'masculine' with the children, particularly the boys. For example, a father and a mother both commented on football, men workers and boys. The father said 'for boys the man can take them to play football. It's better to have that masculine thing rather than all females' and the mother said 'when it comes to sports activities, boys like kicking a football. Women are not likely to know the rules of football.' Three mothers continued this theme of children playing with men: 'children have got a father. Children like to play with men as well as women'; 'some kids prefer playing with their dads. So why shouldn't they have the same thing when they go to nursery'; and, finally, 'it gives them a chance to know that men can play with them and join in games and be fun.'

The importance of the man worker was also seen as an opportunity to compensate for deficiencies in the household structure and organisation. Men childcare workers were seen as especially beneficial for children living in single parent, or rather, lone mother, households, where it was assumed that children would not have access to fathers or father figures. Twelve parents, four of whom were lone mothers themselves, identified the benefits of men workers in this way. The lone mothers' comments were about children having contact with men, about having a man's perspective on the upbringing of children and about having a change from 'women all the time'. One said 'with my daughter just being me in the house, it gives her a chance to be around men' and another said 'it is beneficial having things said from a man's point of view'. Lastly, the fourth lone mother said 'it enables traditional role stereotypes to be countered particularly for children who don't have access to men in the family'.

Nuclear family parents saw similar advantages for children from lone mother households. One mother said 'children with no dads are not likely to see men caring. The men taking children to school and in the park are very isolated. People look at men caring for children', and a father said 'the child will have more of a sense of a male. Especially in the case of a single mother and where the child had never seen a man.' This mother underlined the idealisation of nuclear family formation when she said 'my son has a *normal* family but if it's a single parent and no male around [men childcare workers] would be particularly good' (emphasis added). A mother with a mixed race child stressed the advantages for

> young males who do not have a father around. And black males tend to get excluded from schools and nurseries. I read a report where they brought in young males to work with boys in danger of being excluded and had problems. Having the men there worked. Being a black child tips the balance towards exclusion. Boys aren't encouraged educationally as well as they might.

The compensatory role of men workers, for 'missing' fathers in the case of family structure, was also emphasised by those parents who saw men workers as being able to offer a 'male bond' to boys in childcare centres. One mother said 'especially me having a boy. It's the male bonding that's important when so many females surround him.' A father thought a boy could 'look up to a man in the nursery' and a mother reported that her boy 'goes for [the man worker] more. He's a daddy's boy at home. It's good for him to have a man at the nursery as well.' A third mother thought it would be 'good for a boy to have a man to talk to. Also he might look up to him a bit more, and respond better to a man.' Finally, a mother whose son attended the children's centre reported that her son had had an 'extra dimension' to his experience of childcare through a relationship with one particular man worker that the son had appreciated immensely. She said 'there was a different atmosphere at the children's centre because of the men'.

The main advantages of men workers, then, was their ability to offer a demonstration of what is, or what should be, going on in children's domestic lives. Men workers were seen as being able to educate the next generation of children in reorganising the gender distribution of domestic and paid work. Links between gender roles in family life and childcare institutions were also made by parents. Men workers were seen as being able to offer some compensation to families where it was assumed fathers, or father figures, were not present. Both single and couple parents' comments illustrated the continuing predominant ideology of the heterosexual nuclear family. This could be seen through their emphasis on the 'normality' of two, male and female, parents, and some perceived deficiencies where children live with mothers alone.

Before leaving this section, it is worth including the comments of a few parents who did not refer to the child's life in the family in the context of the benefits of the man worker. Four parents thought the 'security' and 'strength' of the childcare institution were better served by the employment of men 'who will take responsibility for security' 'in case of danger', mainly from 'strange people'. These parents were thus feeding into notions of 'masculine strength' and the protection of women and children through versions of 'masculinity', again, arguably, part of the predominant model of men's role within families.

Table 6.4 summarises the range of views of mothers and fathers about the advantages of men childcare workers.

Table 6.4 *Advantages of men workers: mothers' and fathers' views*

Advantages of men childcare workers	Mothers	Fathers
Modelling domestic life		
Good for children to see men sharing the care of children	7	1
routine caring work e.g., cleaning		
reversal of gender work roles		
witness constructive gender relations		
Reducing prejudice	9	9
diversity and a different perspective		
a gentle, caring man		
Reflecting domestic life		
Men in families, men in nurseries	4	1
Men can be 'masculine': sport, play and boys	4	1
Compensation for deficient family structure		
Beneficial for children of lone mothers	8	4
role model of fathers		
a change from women		
a man's point of view		
stereotypes of men countered		
Male bond for boys	1	4
Security offered by men to childcare institution	1	3

Note: not all parents made comments in answer to the question; some made more than one comment.

Discussion

Among this group of parents there was near universal agreement that more men should be employed to work with young children: 43 or 83 per cent of mothers, and 21 or 84 per cent of fathers. On the basis of experience of having their children cared for in institutions where at least one man was employed, men childcare workers were broadly welcomed. We referred at the beginning of the chapter to the paucity of research addressing parents' views about the childcare workforce, and on the issue of gender in childcare institutions. We also recorded the finding of other more general studies that parents (mothers) are satisfied with their services. This puts our findings in a somewhat unique position. Not only have we obtained the views of fathers as well as mothers, we have obtained them about a largely unresearched, and possibly under-discussed, issue: gender, or men working alongside women in childcare.

However, the group of parents we spoke to was small, and skewed from the norm in that their children all had some experience of men workers. In addition, making sense of parents' views has to take into account the culture of childcare services in Britain: hard to come by, expensive for those who have to buy it, subject to ongoing debates about whether it is 'good' for children (or mothering) for childcare to exist at all (*cf*, Mooney and Munton, 1997). For those who do not purchase it, such as those in local authority or voluntary sector childcare or family centres, there are often conditions attached, such as it being time limited or reviewable care, or there being requirements for parents/mothers to have counselling, or attend group work sessions on parenting skills and so on.

One could argue, then, that pressures exist on parents to not articulate views about childcare practice, or certainly, to formulate and articulate views only when there is pressure to do so. Parents of young children in Newcastle Upon Tyne, for example, could arguably have been under pressure to formulate their views about childcare services and/or men workers in the light of two cases of child abuse in childcare centres occurring in their city in recent years and the consequent publicity attached to the cases (Hunt, 1994; Barker *et al.*, 1998). Despite these pressures not to articulate views, the parents we spoke to came up with a wealth of data to amplify their broad welcome of a mixed gender workforce in childcare services.

An interesting feature of the commentary from parents was the different way parents linked the care of their boys and girls to men workers. While some referred to benefits for children, others consciously articulated the benefits to boys of having men workers. The gender alliance of boys and men workers may be coincidental: the parents we spoke to had more boys than girls (57 boys and 40 girls). It could also have picked up on public debates about differentiating boys' and girls' experiences in schools and the perceived 'under-achievement' of boys and the place of male role models (Lepkowska, 1998).

Summary

This chapter has been concerned to give a voice to the views of parents about the presence of men workers in childcare centres. We began the chapter by examining national research on parents' views about childcare and discussed some possible difficulties with expressing views about childcare services in Britain. We found that the majority of parents interviewed supported the principle of men working alongside women in childcare. The main reasons for this support were given as advantages for boys to be cared for by men as well as women, and advantages to children of being in the presence of male role models. Various kinds of role model were noted, but parents tended towards supporting a role model that demonstrated gender equality and challenging gender stereotypes of men's and women's roles with children.

Reservations about men workers were mentioned by parents, but were largely thought to be dealt with by entrusting the management of childcare centres to recruit suitable workers. However supportive of men workers, parents were relatively unable to specify how men's and women's working styles differ. In part this was accounted for by a lack of time spent by parents inside the childcare centres, but some parents wanted to stress the individual identities of men workers beyond any essential 'male' character. Parents were open minded about the gender identity of staff members they spoke to in connection with their children: for most the quality of information was more important than the gender of the worker. Finally, we discussed the advantages and disadvantages that parents saw in recruiting a mixed-gender workforce: while few disadvantages were noted – principally the possibility of recruiting a worker who then abused children – many advantages were cited, mainly around the relationship between demonstrating adult behaviour in centres and what goes on, or may be missed out on, in family lives.

Notes

1. It should be remembered that the family centres did not offer full-time, every day attendance, so parents could not visit these centres every day.
2. There was one co-mother among the parent sample. For ease of reading we will include her within the 'mother' category.

7

Child Protection and Equality: Dilemmas and Solutions

One parent made it quite clear, with me there, to my boss, that . . . men do not work in nurseries . . . and if they do, they work in nurseries because they are in it for one thing and one thing only . . . because they are paedophiles . . . That was her opinion and she stated it straight out . . .

(Male worker)

This chapter addresses the issues of child abuse in childcare centres and the relationship of such issues with men workers. Almost invariably when discussing men childcare workers, doubts and suspicions are raised about the men's motivations for working with children. This is not just because the pay is lower than that men workers might expect, or that the work is considered 'women's work'. Men have entered other low paid, so-called women's work without attracting such specific attention to their moral character. There is something about the combination of children and men and a caring environment which is seen, by some, and particularly in Britain and North America (possibly also in Australia and New Zealand (Smith, personal communication)), as outlandish to the point of being 'a risk' or even dangerous to children's health and wellbeing. Men childcare workers have had their sexuality and their sexual morals questioned (Kelley, 1998; King, 1994). This construction of men in relation to children is not restricted to young children's childcare institutions: an analysis of newspaper reports on men and children in 1996 showed that by far the majority of relevant newspaper stories were about men's violence towards children across a range of settings (Cameron and Moss, 1998).

Simultaneously, as we saw in Chapter 6, men workers' positive contribution to childcare has been welcomed by parents, both in itself, and for its contribution towards gender equality and diversity in the workplace and in the home. In Chapter 1 we set out the idea of twin, competing discourses that frame discussion of men in childcare work and referred to these as discourses of equality and risk. The emphasis given to these discourses is not universally found: while they appear to run in parallel in Britain, in Scandinavia the discourse of equality is clearly paramount (Jensen, 1996). So our aim in this

132

chapter is not to take 'risk' for granted, but to explore the discourse of risk as a way of giving meaning to men working in childcare. We have repeatedly argued that this book is about making gender visible in childcare work: in a sense, the risk discourse makes gender highly visible, if somewhat uni-dimensional.

How do we make sense of the reaction to men workers as 'dangerous' when in the vicinity of paid work with children? This chapter will draw together the known research about men early childhood workers as abusers of children, together with our data from childcare college lecturers, a survey of local authorities, and workers and parents. The chapter will summarise the perspectives adopted in the literature on this issue and consider how the debate about men childcare workers might move forward in the light of the competing discourses of equality and risk (Cameron and Moss, 1998).

What do we Know about the Risk of Abuse to Children by Workers?

What do we Mean by 'Abuse'?

The first point about establishing definitions of risk and abuse is that much has been written (DoH, 1995). The chief conclusion is that definitions of abuse are subject to changing societal values, just as the 'acceptable' discipline of children by parents that is not 'abuse' changes over time and in differing cultural contexts. For example, Nobes and Smith (1997) found that in the UK hitting even very young children remains a normative part of parental discipline. Another example of varying standards is that Britain, unlike other European countries, retains the parental right to smack children as a form of discipline. The definition of abuse is set by the Children Act 1989 as likely harm to a child through ill-treatment and impairment of health and development (s.43 (1), Children Act 1989) and professional definitions of abuse refer to 'physically harmful action directed against a child' and 'the involvement of dependent, developmentally immature children and adolescents in sexual activities that they do not fully comprehend' (cited in DoH, 1995). Legal and professional definitions proscribe the limits of state intervention in children's lives, and imply there is a gap or threshold between normative parenting and deliberate actions to harm children which require official attention and are defined as abuse.

Moving away from abuse committed by parents to that committed while children attend care and education services, there may be broader definitions of abuse in use (e.g., that employed by the UN Convention on Rights of the Child). It may be that a complaint about practice of whatever kind is regarded by parents as a complaint about 'abuse'. In the case of abuse within registered childcare services for children under 8, Elfer and Beasley (1997) detailed the arguments heard in cases where local authorities have tried to enforce standards by prosecuting childminders and other day care providers where they appeared to be in breach of the relevant regulations in the Children Act 1989. In many of these cases, the arguments were about what constituted abuse, and the court was upon to decide between the versions put forward by providers and local authorities. In this chapter, however, we only look at sexual abuse, since it is the fear that men workers will sexually abuse young children that is the major concern, not that they will be hit or neglected by them.

The Extent of Risk

What do we know about the risk of abuse to young children attending childcare institutions? There are no reliable indicators about the risk workers pose to children. If risk is assessed on the basis of *known* cases of workers abusing children relative to the number of children attending services, then on the basis of current British data the risk to children in childcare centres is very low. A careful study of press cuttings at the NSPCC and the National Children's Bureau and law reports to find cases of alleged sexual abuse in childcare centres that had come to trial was conducted (Owen and Josephs, 1996). Only two such cases were uncovered, and this finding was confirmed by the regulatory body responsible, the Social Services Inspectorate.

One of the cases involved a male nursery nursing student who was accused of sexually abusing children whilst on placement in two nursery classes (Hunt, 1994). When the case came to court, the student pleaded guilty and was convicted of sexually abusing over 60 children. The other case involved two workers in a public day nursery, a man and a woman (Barker *et al.*, 1998). These two denied the charges against them and when the case came to court, the children's evidence against the pair was deemed inadmissable and they were consequently found not guilty. Nevertheless, the independent inquiry into the case concluded that the these two workers were probably part of a paedophile ring (*ibid.*).

This situation contrasts with that in residential care for children. Here, a series of cases involving hundreds of children have been exposed and numerous residential care workers have been prosecuted. For example, in 1993, the Kirkwood inquiry reported on the case of Frank Beck who was jailed for abusing children in residential care in the 1970s and 1980s; and inquiries in north Wales and Cheshire have investigated the complaints of abuse by over 300 children who had previously been in residential care. The lack of substantiated cases of sexual abuse in early childhood services, while reassuring, gives no grounds for complacency: sexual abuse in residential children's homes has only recently come to light and it may be that cases of sexual abuse in childcare centres go, or have gone, unreported.

The independent inquiries into both these cases of alleged sexual abuse in early childhood services (Hunt, 1994; Barker *et al.*, 1998 respectively) each stated that these cases should not be used as grounds for not employing men early years workers. Moreover, in the second case, the report was extremely critical of the management and supervision in the nursery. However, more extensive research from the USA suggests that both gender and organisational factors are significant.

Risk from Men and from Women

Finkelhor *et al.* (1988) contacted day care licensing offices and child protection services across the USA. Information was received from 40 states and from these replies the study team enumerated 270 substantiated cases of sexual abuse in centres and family day care (childminders licensed to care for at least six children) in a three-year period in the 1980s[1]. These cases involved 1,639 victims and 382 perpetrators. Not all the perpetrators were childcare workers: janitors, drivers and relatives of family day care providers were also involved.

Finkelhor's research also showed that not all the abusers were men. In fact, 36 per cent of all cases involved a woman and more children were abused by a woman than by a man. This raises the question of whether women were themselves victims, coerced into the abuse by men. While 60 per cent of cases involving a woman did not involve a man (Finkelhor *et al.*, 1988:Table 2.11), the small number of men workers overall committed a disproportionate amount of the abuse. However, this very complicated issue of women as sexual abusers of young children is only just beginning to be documented (Saradjían, 1996). Nevertheless, the research does show that removing men from early childhood services does not remove the threat of sexual abuse.

Margolin (1993), in a study of all cases of sexual abuse in childcare services in one US state, found that although men were far more likely than women to have been abusive towards children, no cases of sexual abuse were found in childcare centres: it was conducted in childcarers' homes by adolescents and adults known to the children, particularly when children stayed overnight. Thus the organisational context of informal care arrangements seemed a risk factor. All the US studies reviewed by Kelley (1998) showed that men did commit abuse more often than women within childcare settings. However, this is not to say that men pose an exclusive risk to young children in services, for women constituted an unexpectedly large proportion of the abusers in each study. Kelley argued that 'parents and employers must keep an open mind with regard to females as perpetrators' (*ibid.*, 1998: 140).

Risk in Early Childhood Services

Finkelhor's research shows that children are probably more likely to be abused in their own homes than in early childhood services. The research concluded:

> the risk of abuse a child in day care faces cannot be termed 'higher' than the risk that a child faces in his or her own family. The risk in day care may possibly be lower . . . the impression that day care constitutes some especially risky environment is probably an illusion.
>
> (Finkelhor *et al.*, 1988: 24–25).

This is a fairly basic requirement for services, for, as Pringle (1995) pointed out, parents who purchase care or attend public services have a right to know that that care is 'as safe as is humanly possible' (Pringle, 1995: 183). Research from the USA also suggests that the organisation of childcare in centres for young children, such as those described in this book, offer less risk (in that there are very few known cases) than other kinds of childcare, such as child-minding, informal care arrangements, or, perhaps, residential care (Margolin, 1993).

It would appear, on the basis of research evidence to date, that men do pose a greater risk to children for sexual abuse than do women, but that risk is relative to the organisational context in which the worker and children are situated. For example, men working in childcare centres for preschool aged children do not pose a special risk for sexual abuse. There are, of course, other types of abuse possible in childcare services, such as neglect or emotional abuse, or simply poor standards of care, for which both men and women may be responsible (Elfer and Beasley, 1997). But these types of abuse are not so closely associated with men workers and are not seen as a reason for excluding or restricting men's employment in childcare centres.

What do we do about the Perceived Risk of Men?

A Risk Indicators Approach

We referred earlier to discourses of equality and risk that run in parallel in Britain. The literature follows these discourses and suggests three ways of addressing this question. The US literature (largely from the risk discourse perspective) has focused on providing indicators which will diminish the likeli-hood of sexual abuse occurring regardless of the gender of the adult. Kelley's review of this literature suggested that unlimited parental access to centres is one key indicator of reduced levels of sexual abuse, so parents should be encouraged to visit childcare centres at any time (Kelley, 1998). Other import-ant factors are effective and thorough screening of new recruits, both through police checks, and of employment history and emotional background. Atten-tion should also be paid, argued Kelley, to prevention programmes for chil-dren, which are viewed as more useful in revealing past or ongoing abuse than in preventing abuse, and to the structural layout of centres as allegations of sexual abuse typically take place around toileting activities. The removal of opportunities for adult privacy with children, it is argued, should diminish the risk of abuse occurring (Kelley, 1998).

Men's Preventative Work Approach

An alternative method of addressing the 'risk of men' has been put forward by Pringle (1995; 1998). Rather than recommending methods of reducing the risk of abuse by altering institutions, Pringle argued that the object of change should be men workers. As men are responsible for the majority of sexual violence not only in welfare services, but across society as a whole, Pringle argued that all men are potential abusers of children in whatever setting, although only a minority will actually abuse children. Pringle proposed that men workers should examine and change the way they relate to children (conducting 'preventative work on themselves', Pringle, 1995: p. 185). Alongside this work, training of staff and parents in welfare services should be undertaken to alert them to the 'significant minority' of men who are sexual abusers in their midst, and the impossibility of telling them apart from the majority, non-abusing, group. Men, Pringle argued, should also receive awareness training, to 'help them choose not to abuse' (*ibid.*, 1995: p. 186).

Finally, Pringle argued that the behaviour of men workers should be 'adapted' or, in some cases 'restricted', to 'help protect children from being sexually abused' and to help prevent 'men workers from having their actions misinterpreted as being abusive' (*ibid.*: p. 186). Examples of adaptation are given as men's use of touch, especially where children have been previously subjected to violent behaviour (*ibid.*: p. 188), and the use of men as co-workers with women rather than sole workers in cases where considerable intimate physical or emotional care of children is necessary (*ibid.*: p. 189). Examples of possible restriction of men's access to children's services are given as 'work with very young children in nursery care and day care' (*ibid.*: p. 189) as well as those with severe disabilities or learning difficulties and work with a specific focus on sexual abuse.

Reconstructing Care to Include Men

The third way the literature deals with the issue of 'men as risk' is to reconstruct the issue as one that caring men as childcare workers can be part of the solution, not the problem. This follows the 'equality' discourse. Norwegian policy makers and practitioners have addressed the issue of 'men as risk' by downplaying it in favour of a focus on the problem of violence in society as a whole. Men childcare workers are thereby seen as a valuable part of the 'recruitment of men into children's everyday lives' (Sataøen, 1998: 137). The profession is seen as 'quite the opposite' of 'violence and destructiveness', and the recruitment of men offered an opportunity for children to see men as 'people you could trust' (*ibid.*: p. 137). In Norway more men, not fewer, playing a fuller, caring, part in children's lives, is a move towards the solution. Sataøen believes that:

> the Norwegian nursery school organization and culture is a preventive measure in itself. [They] are small, with few children, few adults and a large number of staff members; there are open areas and playgrounds; and parents have a say in the daily life of the nursery school. From the outset it seems almost impossible to commit sexual abuse in a nursery school environment. (*ibid.*: p. 137)

However, even in Norway, it is not unknown for the possibility of sexual abuse in services for young children to arise: they have had a large investigation into a case which began with allegations against a male school assistant who indecently exposed himself in 1992 (the Bjugn case). Eventually, the man was acquitted, but in response to the case, and the consequent discussion, new laws were passed to require all childcare workers to have a Police Certificate verifying their history as free from allegations or convictions for sexual abuse. But, critically, the issue of sexual abuse is not seen as challenging the validity of men as childcare workers. The issues are separate, and challenging for all. A similar approach was adopted by a Danish local authority. A case of sexual abuse in a public children's centre was investigated and this drew a lot of publicity. The response of the local authority was to call together its male workers and assure them of their support as employers (Jensen, personal communication). Both Pen Green and Sheffield, two children's centres whose practice with fathers was discussed in Chapter 5 have also devoted considerable resources to the issue of how to deal with the risk of abuse, this time in the more critical climate of Britain.

Two Practice Examples from Britain

At the two British centres whose work we drew attention to in earlier chapters, the key to successful protective practice is discussion, reflection and consensual policy making. For example, Bateman, reflecting on the work of one of these centres, the Sheffield Children's Centre, argued that 'the protection of workers and the protection of children is rarely contradictory and usually goes hand in hand' (Bateman, 1998: 173). The aim of the work is to endeavour to ensure that children remain the prime focus, and the 'rights of all are being upheld' (*ibid.*).

The policy making process is seen by the mixed-gender staff at Sheffield as a method of challenging implicit and explicit assumptions about gender and thereby shifting the philosophical underpinnings of the work away from being intrinsically 'female' to a new form of care for young children, incorporating both masculinities and femininities. This project is much more wide ranging than introducing specific measures to limit sexual abuse, such as those suggested by the US research, and, although there are probably overlaps with Pringle's proposals, it addresses gender, and men, much more positively than Pringle does.

A similar holistic approach is also adopted at another centre whose work we have highlighted. Workers from the Pen Green Centre, Chandler and Dennison (1994), summarised a conference workshop entitled 'Should men work with young children?' and argued that 'the whole ethos, philosophy, policy and practice [of childcare institutions] had to be right if children were to be protected'. In particular, they saw the hierarchical organisation of childcare institutions as significant: 'as long as our institutions are built upon hierarchical systems where worker, parents and children are disempowered, the potential for abuse is possible'. They continued:

> the power of abuse lies in secrecy. If the culture of an institution is based upon empowerment and openness where adults and children are encouraged to speak up for themselves then the potential for abuse is minimised. When the structure, philosophy and practice of an institution proactively addresses issues of free communication where people of all ages and status are encouraged to listen to each other with

respect, the abuse of power in relationships between adults; children; men; women; management and workers; service users and service providers will be avoided. This is clearly a complex and ongoing task.

(Chandler and Dennison, 1994: 44).

Pen Green, then, addresses protection as an issue of individual self-expression and assertiveness and organisational openness demonstrated through staff, indeed whole-centre, reflection and debate. This approach sees rights, citizenship and responsibility as being at the heart of protection strategies.

The three methods of approaching risk vary in their emphasis on men's employment in childcare as a factor. The view from the US research sees risk as an issue regardless of gender in the workforce, but men as an additional risk. Pringle's view is that men are the most significant risk factor associated with sexual abuse and it is primarily men's behaviour which has to be changed or restricted. The implication here is that men are not able to control their sexuality when employed to do caring work. The third argument, representing the equality discourse, rejects this view of men and argues instead that men's caring work can help to address, and reduce, wider problems of violence if it is conducted in a 'gender-conscious' environment, where assumptions about gender behaviour are continually debated and unpicked as a staff group, and joint decisions about ways forward are translated into policies.

Other British Evidence

The survey we conducted of childcare college lecturers on the issue of gender and childcare revealed that for the most part, lecturers supported an equality discourse on the childcare workforce. Nearly all (86 per cent) would prefer to see a mixed-gender workforce working in childcare services, in order that children could see men and women working together (95 per cent) and as role models (98 per cent). A few lecturers (13 per cent) thought a disadvantage of men workers was the possibility of an increase in allegations of sexual abuse and there were isolated cases (12) where lecturers had been worried that a student had been abusing a child while on placement, although not all of these were men.

Our survey of local authority policies on protection, however, suggested that while the issue of child protection is well established, that of worker protection, or that of awareness of the possiblity of children being abused while attending centres, is not incorporated into local authority policies. More than three-quarters of responding local authorities had child protection policies for public and registered childcare centres. But almost all of these focused on procedures for staff to follow in the event of a child bringing signs and symptoms of abuse into the centre, rather than focusing on the protection of children from abuse while in the centre, or for the protection of workers in the event of allegations of abuse being made against them. This is not to say that local authorities as employers do not, and do not advise others to, support staff, but it contrasts with the approach in Denmark cited earlier.

To summarise, this discussion of abuse in childcare settings has tried to steer an even course through (admittedly somewhat limited) research and popular impressions concerning the relationship between men childcare workers and workers' sexual abuse of young children. Despite the paucity of reliable information, and the difficulties of assessing risk, it would appear that although men are responsible for more sexual abuse of children than are women, both in families and in services for young children, men are by no means exclusively responsible and the links between men workers and sexual abuse should perhaps be dismantled. In the next sections, we will examine the contribution of the men and women workers we interviewed to this debate.

Physical Contact with Children: Limitations on the Use of Touch

In this section we will examine how workers deployed themselves in their personal care of children, how they and others interpreted the use of touch, and how they devised both individual and institutional strategies to ensure that they were offered some protection and that children's rights to privacy in the area of personal care could be upheld.

Personal Care

One of the most sensitive areas of caring for young children is their personal, physical care and comfort. Physical care includes nappy changing, taking children to the toilet, comforting children when they are hurt and sitting them on a lap. These activities provide a clear opportunity for demonstrating intimacy and affection with young children. One of the reasons for the sensitivity of this area of care is that in some extreme cases it was just these activities that were misused in order to abuse children (Hunt, 1994). Another reason is that while childcare is already sensitive to the charge of replacing mother-care and 'disrupting' the mother-child bond, close physical care and affection is a vivid sign of a child's new, independent and non-mother relationships.

Comparing the men and women workers in our study, it would appear that close physical care is a particularly sensitive area for men workers. Building on the analysis in previous chapters of men workers as Other, their experience in physical care seems to suggest that a reason for men workers' extra sensitive position may be that they are both 'not-mothers', and not 'father-like' either. Recall the mother in Chapter 5 who was struck by how 'different' it was for a man to be cuddling babies. Not only was the man different because he was a childcare worker, it may be that he was also different through not behaving like a father might in public.

Using the example of workers' practice when a child is accidentally hurt while at childcare centres, it was clear that both men and women saw both first aid and physical comfort, such as cuddling a child on a knee and talking through the incident, as essential ingredients of good practice. The most common first reaction was to cuddle a child, and this was the case for seven men and six women. A smaller group saw first aid as their first reaction, and then physical comfort, but the message from nearly all the workers was that the natural, taken-for-granted approach to children's injuries involved the combination of physical and emotional care. Only two workers distanced themselves from this method: Kieran thought his personal style meant he did not 'naturally' cuddle children. He said 'I'm attentive and caring but not excessively demonstrative'. The other worker, Georgia, said she would use physical comfort 'only if they think they want it', practice which followed a policy in her childcare centre of asking children's permission to pick them up or cuddle them, and not assuming they wanted it.

These workers, then, were not afraid to use touch. Indeed, some of them saw it as essential to their work. Erica, working in a family centre, frequently with traumatised children, said she had heard about a

> ruling about nursery workers not being allowed to have physical contact with the children and I was furious about that, 'cos I think that's abusive, because . . . the children [are] separating for the first time from their parents, coming into a group and they're projecting their mother's and father's role . . . and to withdraw that kind of essential physical . . . I mean not just if they fall over and hurt themselves . . . I mean you know I cuddle a child if they come up to me or if they come and try to give me a kiss . . . I feel fine about that.

Brenda, also a family centre worker, similarly felt physical contact was fundamental to the job. She said 'there's a lot of physical contact . . . children build that relationship and they just come up . . . there's no way you can avoid that, and I don't think that we could do the work that we do if we, you know, there were certain restrictions' placed on workers.

Interpreting the Use of Touch: a Code of Caution

But workers' confident use of physical contact in their work with children is different from their feelings about its use. Some men workers had experience of being told not to use touch or felt their position was vulnerable to accusations of misusing touch. John had worked in a nursery where the deputy had interrupted his work with a child making a difficult transition between rooms, work that required, in his view, plenty of cuddling as reassurance, to say that she did not want him to cuddle the children. The reason given was that it was not 'expected' of a man. John said 'the other carers, it wasn't a problem, they'd all cuddle and that sort of thing . . . I kicked up quite a stink about it . . . and in the end they changed the whole ruling and they just said they didn't want anybody to cuddle the children.'

Also in a previous job, Duncan had had experience of trying to implement a policy of staff not being allowed to take children to the bathroom on their own. 'Nothing happened . . . it was just to cover yourself, it was nursery policy that you were not allowed in the bathroom on your own with a child.' This policy, however, created problems in itself. 'How practical,' Duncan queried, 'is it for two members of staff to go to the bathroom? So you'd end up taking big groups of children to the bathroom, which again creates issues, taking 15 children to the bathroom at times is not the easiest of things to do . . . because you've got . . . you tend to have one member of staff in the room waiting for the children to come back, you've got one member of staff stood by the toilet and the sinks, going backwards and forwards, backwards and forwards, and another member of staff trying to sit with the other 13 children.' It would seem that in these circumstances the protection of members of staff begins to take precedence over other issues, such as the rights of children to enjoy privacy or self-determination about going to the toilet, and the organisation of the centre's day around group toileting arrangements.

Ironically, Duncan reported that in the same nursery the staff as a group had been told that they were not being sufficiently affectionate with the children. As an example, Duncan said they would pat a child on the head when they cried rather than cuddle them. Duncan had not agreed with the practice and had picked up and held children when they were upset as a 'natural instinct' although he was conscious that he could be open to criticism by doing so, both as a man and for challenging the accepted practice. It would seem that some childcare institutions have become absorbed by questions of the appropriate boundaries of touch and intimacy to the point of disrupting what may come 'naturally' to those who care for children.

Trevor's career as a teacher began with a colleague's advice: 'you musn't be in a class alone with a girl'. It was clear to him from the beginning that as a man working with young children, the 'rules are different'. He said 'I think people are more used to women changing children, people are more used to women having close physical contact with children'. As a consequence of what people are used to, Trevor believes that men's behaviour with children is open to misinterpretation, despite his long years as a teacher and in his childcare centre. 'I put the rules on myself . . . I just feel it's . . . you have to be . . . I think as a man you have to be aware of [the rules]' he said.

As men and women are employed on the basis of equal opportunities, Trevor did not agree that the rules of employment could be overtly different, but rather that men have a responsibility to be cautious in their practice. For example, Trevor said:

> nobody should be in room like this on their own with a child on their knee with the door locked . . . [and] I would tell a person that I was changing a child, or if I was taking a child anywhere in the building . . . so that people know I'm away with a child.

These practices were not the result of management directives, but

> we're all kind of aware of it, and it's something we should all do anyway. I think probably female staff feel less . . . do it less often than I do, so they obviously feel the need to do it less often than I do, so I possibly feel more aware of it than they do . . . that's the conclusion I draw from it.

Trevor was aware that being cautious about his practice in the area of physical contact with children had consequences: he said he didn't think he comforted children who were upset as well as women staff did. In addition, men staff still had to negotiate how to be physically affectionate with children:

> It's not wrong to show affection for a child, it's not wrong to be physically close to a child, I think that's wholly appropriate, I think there are times when you have to do that, that's part of your job and that's part of your relationship and that's part of your being and working with small children.

Trevor's reflections on his practice clearly placed him as a conscious Other as a consequence of being not what people expected of those who care for children. He also revealed a lack of consciousness about these issues on the part of women colleagues, and an absence of debate among the staff group as a whole. He was isolated with his personal code of caution, a code which has probably worked well over time, but one that has still left him slightly anxious about the boundaries of touch.

Trevor's position was echoed by Stuart. Asked if he was extra cautious in his physical contact with children, Stuart gave the example of the supervision of children going to the toilet.

> I'm always . . . I would never . . . 'cos where the toilets are downstairs we've got a fire door between the toilets and two little toilets. I would never go in there on my own if a child was going to the toilet . . . I always keep the toilet door open and the fire door, and that's just for my protection I think . . . I don't know if the women would do that.

He continued to say that it hadn't been discussed by the staff as a group, and that he didn't think his cautionary practice had been noticed by his female colleagues. Despite this he felt aware that he shouldn't be hidden away in private places with children. Furthermore, he acknowledged that 'it's silly really 'cos I know that men aren't always the perpetrators and that's the assumption, that men are abusers . . . no one looks at women abusers.'

Nick acknowledged the vulnerability of staff to accusations, whatever gender they are. With young children where language is 'maybe not clearly developed and something can be misconstrued and . . . you know fingers can be pointed at people with maybe not a lot of evidence, then I think that can place somebody in real jeopardy that their whole career could feel sort of shattered'. But Nick went on to say that he thought team working in childcare meant the opportunities to be alone with children were rare, 'even if a man took children swimming, you know there's an attendant there, there are other people around . . . you know it's rare that there would be a completely unsupervised situation'. Nick thus subscribed to the view that organisational opportunism was central to sexual abuse occurring and the objective of management was to ensure that risk was minimised through organisational practices.

Women workers did not voice feelings of vulnerability about allegations of sexual abuse being levelled against them. Hannah summed up their position thus: 'I haven't been accused; parents trust us and we trust the parents'. This sense of security about women workers' situation on the issue of physical contact and touch was almost universally felt. Two mentioned imposed restrictions on their practice: one said she had been taught in college not to be 'over-physical' with children, such as lifting and swinging them in case they injured themselves or the worker slipped and injury was caused by the worker; the second said the institution had introduced a policy of workers not taking children into their own homes in response to an incident elsewhere. Michelle protested at the prospect of creeping restrictions on relationships with children. She said: 'who says who can't cuddle a child? You could get into a situation where you'd never pick up a child or do anything with them.' All of these restrictions relate to both men and women, and were imposed by the institution: the central difference from the constraints on men is that the latter tended to be self-imposed, and to operate without women staff necessarily being aware of them.

Strategies and Policies for Intimate Care

The area of nappy changing is one part of personal care of young children which has been marked out for policy attention. The assumption here is that nappy changing is a discrete area of childcare practice which potentially offers opportunities for intimacy and privacy with children, and so also opportunities for sexual abuse or misinterpretation of staff's behaviour during this time. It is also an area closely associated with women's domain in the family, and subject to cultural rules about women's responsibility for such intimate care. The institutions in this study had varying responses to the issue of nappy changing.

One response was to ignore nappy changing as an issue meriting policy attention, and not to develop policies that exclude or include men. Staff working in five of the ten institutions regarded the issue as one where all, parents and staff, were dependent on mutual trust to ensure children's safety. A balance had to be struck that enabled risk to be minimised without compromising men and women workers' equality. For example, Nick argued that although he was aware of policies that did not allow men to be on their own if a nappy was being changed, there had been a decision not to adopt such a policy in his institution. 'I think there is a feeling that because people are working in groups that, OK, you might not be able to see everything but you're not that far away, people are not completely isolated.' The protection for workers and children was as good as it could be 'without being over-zealous really'.

The policies that were in place varied. In one centre, nappy changing excluded students and temporary staff. In another, a family centre where mothers were normally nearby, staff did no nappy changing, parents were called out of their sessions to do this if necessary. In another family centre, nappy changing and toileting explicitly excluded men workers. This was called a personal care policy and was seen as being for men's protection. Oliver reported that when the men workers first started there had been a lot of discussion about personal care, and, with no clear policy from the parent voluntary organisation, the family centre agreed to exclude men from personal care. The reasoning for the policy was that many of the women who attended the centre had had difficult and painful experiences of men, and consequently found it difficult to trust them. Working in the same environment, Lloyd said 'the basic reason [for the policy] is about protecting men from the feelings of the parents who've been abused'.

Oliver expanded that 'we have had some families who've had fairly traumatic experiences particularly with men . . . and these women in turn have been fairly quick to make accusations against all sorts of people . . . and we've had it happen here, fortunately not against the men workers. I think there was a general feeling that it was a problem we could do without and the one way of preventing the problem occurring was to say "well, we've got a policy here that the men won't do these things" . . . to allay some of the mothers' fears.' Both Lloyd and Oliver disagreed with the policy, but said they could understand it. Lloyd thought he should be able to offer counselling to the women to deal with their anxieties about men caring for their children. Oliver thought it was part of the experience of being a man childcare worker: whereas 'everyone accepts a woman . . . an actual issue [is] made about having a man [worker]'.

The remaining nappy changing policy was to have two people change each nappy. Georgia reported that there was a local authority policy of two people changing nappies, but it was impractical to follow through, as the necessary number of staff to both change nappies and supervise the rest of the group was not always available. 'It's not so bad here because all the doors are open and it's quite open plan, there's always someone about', said Georgia, so the policy was managed rather than adhered to. Georgia reported that the man worker in this centre informed parents at the beginning that he was likely to be changing their children's nappies and thereby gained their permission for doing so.

At Sheffield Children's Centre, a clear 'witnessing policy' was in operation. This was a response to the concerns of male staff about how men workers would be perceived by wider society. It was part of a broad protective strategy for men and children, and involved a man and a woman at each nappy change, which took place in a nappy room. The problem of adequate staff supervision was said by Yusuf not to arise: 'there is never, ever a problem about staff. And if there is a problem about staff, we got lots of staff, you know, like floating ones, one base to another base.'

This was the only example of a formal policy on nappy changing that worked, seemed to have the support of workers, and, if we recall from the discussion of parents' views in Chapter 6, had their support as well. In addition, the policy was flexible enough to be subject to the cultural and religious wishes of parents after discussions among the staff group (Bateman, 1998). It might be argued that such a policy should not be necessary if men and women workers were seen as equals, and equally trusted, with children. It might also be argued that the luxury of plentiful staff to cover such an arrangement would not be available in many childcare centres, and that therefore it is pointless to advocate a witnessing policy. Furthermore the evidence of the centres in this study is that such policy is not really necessary if the layout of the nappy changing area is sufficiently public to permit witnessing in any case.

The approach adopted by Sheffield Children's Centre on the issue of protection is informed by the same principles of equality and being responsive to internal debates given to issues in other practice areas and documented in earlier chapters. In a sense, the centre is sensitive to the charge that the children are more vulnerable because they employ so many men. This charge is confronted by the centre, where children's safety is seen as a key issue. The co-ordinator argued that the witnessing policy was just one safeguard among other protection strategies used for the protection of everybody, not just men or children. The other strategies included an 'overall openness with service users' and encouraging (older) children's assertiveness and self-expression on issues of gender and child protection, and more broadly discussions were conducted on 'what's right and what's wrong with all age groups of children'. The witnessing policy, then, should not be seen in isolation, but as a product of a twin approach to meeting criticism of children's possible vulnerability and supporting gender equality in the workforce. It is a reflection of consensual policy-making and a part of a strategy of 'openness'. The principle of witnessing one anothers' work also extends beyond nappy changing to all other areas of childcare work.

Would it be appropriate for other childcare institutions to adopt a similar approach? There is no doubt that staffing levels in most childcare centres do not permit two members of staff to be away several times a day witnessing nappy changes. It is also apparent that policies without the resources to carry them out, as in the examples given earlier, do not work. Policies that exclude one gender from personal care also seem fundamentally unfair and divisive. There may also be an issue about children's privacy where nappy changing and toileting occur in public, or *en masse*. The Sheffield Centre claims that its approach to witnessing intimate care is subject to ongoing review and evaluation in which a central principle is children's right to privacy (Meleady, personal communication) (Article 16 of the UN Convention on the Rights of the Child makes reference to the child's right to privacy).

Fundamentally, as Fred argued, it is questionable whether having rules about such matters as toileting is worthwhile, and whether they can possibly be effective. Determined would-be child abusers can always evade rules as both the Hunt and the Barker enquiries showed (Hunt, 1994; Barker *et al.*, 1998). But the merits of the witnessing policy (in the particular context of Sheffield Children's Centre) was that, in contrast with the other policies and practices adopted by institutions in this study, the issue of possible abuse can be confronted at all levels. Honesty, openness and equity are seen as critical to the protection of all. When implemented following these principles, witnessing is a policy that encourages mutual trust through working together. This contrasts with other approaches respondents raised, such as ignoring the possibility of abuse and the consequent need for a protection policy. This can effectively bury the anxiety of men and physical intimacy with young children until such time as a parent might raise the matter, and possibly make a male worker feel exposed. It also contrasts with the approach based on a ruling that men workers do not do intimate care tasks, thus making the assumption that one gender cannot perform as well as the other, and ultimately passing on the iniquitous message to boys and girls that this is one job men don't do.

Incidents Involving Allegations about Abuse

As with Margolin's (1993) findings, there were no cases of sexual abuse in the childcare centres we visited. Most staff had not had any allegations made about their practice nor knew about any complaints about staff behaviour at their centres. However, six respondents described incidents that had occurred in five of the centres which we will report here. Two of these six involved allegations about a child being 'molested', one by a man worker, one by a child. One manager reported that while he had been a manager, a parent had made:

> an allegation against another male worker that a child had been molested whilst having a nappy change . . . and that was investigated and it was felt nothing could be proven . . . however the parent took the child out of the centre, I mean I think the parent felt 'OK, I accept your investigation but I still don't feel comfortable about leaving my child here.'
> [What was your hunch about what happened?]
>   I think my hunch was that the member of staff may have . . . he might have done something a bit silly in terms of maybe tickling a child or something while she was having a nappy change . . . but I don't . . . and something a bit naive . . . and I'd never had any occasion to feel uncomfortable before or after that . . . there was [never] any other concern and certainly from talking to him for a while afterwards I know how he felt about this accusation that he had molested this child and OK . . . he was not suspended but I think he felt that he could have done with some counselling and he'd suffered for a long time as a result of it.

In the second case, staff were not directly implicated. The manager recalled that:

> a mother rang to say that her daughter was saying a boy here had touched her in the toilets. I took the decision to involve social services, even though I felt it was a very small incident. That meant the girl had to have a medical examination, and there were social workers and police here, and it was very traumatic for all concerned. We had counselling as a staff group afterwards and I was surprised that [the man worker] said he felt he could possibly be suspected of some wrong doing. I was shocked he could take it so personally. The social services were thorough but it made me think twice about involving them again, certainly about that type of case.

Many issues arise from these two examples of allegations of molestation. First, the target in both cases was felt by men workers to be themselves, regardless of the allegation or the truth of the matter. Although we do not have these men's own stories, the reports of their response suggests that in both cases they felt acutely aware that they were answerable for the allegation primarily because of their gender, and then because of their actions. Would a woman be accused of molesting a child for tickling them during a nappy change? Or feel accused by a story of a child molesting another? We would suggest 'possibly' to the first, and 'unlikely' to the second of these questions.

Second, the authority of, and the disruption caused by, the investigation process was shattering to staff, again regardless of the truth of the matter. The effects of the investigation process itself were felt to be bruising to the staff group, and the institution, and doubts about further use of the investigation process were raised. As Anne put it, she would hesitate before involving outside agencies again because of the effects on staff; and Nick reported that his man worker 'suffered' even though he was not found to be at fault. Third, parents are not necessarily satisfied with the outcome of the investigation process. In the case Nick reported, the child was removed by the parents, despite the findings of the investigation process. Once a parent's trust in a childcare centre is doubted, it is hard to regain. This is central to the whole issue of men's employment in childcare in a climate of fear of abuse in centres where gender is invisible and unrecognised.

As we saw in Chapter 6, parents rely on trust in management and staff as their main means of assessing both the suitability of childcare centres and the happiness of their children in childcare centres. If there are areas of sensitivity, and the employment of men might be one, parents look to the institution as a whole to provide them with reassurances. The investigation process does not appear to help institutions provide reassurance in the case of suspected molestation of children. This is not to say that allegations should not be investigated, nor that abuse never occurs. In cases where there is clear evidence, the investigation process no doubt uncovers it. But in cases which rest on suspicion, the issue of 'truth' appears difficult to resolve through the investigation process, leaving lingering doubts for parents, and perhaps in some cases among the staff group. Critically for our discussion, it may be that men workers are marginalised among colleagues through their implicit sense of responsibility for those members of their gender who have abused children, whether in services or not. To speculate a comparison with women: perhaps women workers regard women who abuse children as representing an aberration in the human condition, whereas men workers feel an accusation about their practice could be next. Investigation, in other words, does not appear to contain anxiety on the part of parents or staff, and may even fuel it.

There were two allegations representing worries about staff practice at Sheffield Children's Centre. Fozia reported that a father of a new child repeatedly visited the centre and asked questions about who was changing and feeding his child, and eventually said 'I just feel my child is being abused here'. He was concerned about the number of men staff involved in looking after his child, and wanted her cared for 'in any other [part of the centre] where there's not male staff'. The response of the institution was to invite the manager and both parents and relevant staff to discuss the reasons for the father's concerns. Fozia's view was that as the child was quite young and attending very part time, she was taking some time to adjust to the centre. The mother explained the father's concerns by saying he was very close to the child and felt jealous of the men staff 'and (Fozia reported) the girl might be, you know, more close to them than him'. In the event, the allegation was retracted by the father. Fozia said 'they apologised to the male members of staff saying that it was negative feelings and negative thoughts that they had and that they're really sorry about it . . . they feel very embarrassed by it that they had their negative feelings.'

The second allegation was about men workers supervising children who were watching television. Yusuf explained that there were two adjoining rooms, one a rest and TV room, the other an activity room. Between the two rooms was a glass wall and the door was 'always open', providing a clear view between the two. A parent came in one day and saw what was going on and the following day questioned why two men were inside with the children while the women were outside tidying up. Yusuf felt the implication was that they did not like the men workers being inside the TV room with the children where both children and men workers were relatively unsupervised. Yusuf explained to the parents that the work had been divided according to a rota system, and that day the work just happened to be organised in that way. The parents accepted this and apologised to Yusuf and subsequently there were no problems in staff-parent relations.

Both these allegations were about misunderstanding the centre's way of organising their work. Both complaints were discussed internally, involving the parents in so doing and in both cases the allegations were retracted and the parent(s) apologised to the staff. The role of the institution in both cases was to investigate parental worries as matters of serious concern, and simultaneously to uphold the centre's principles about equitable mixed gender working. This contrasts with the potential effect of using external agencies in investigation, as in the cases reported above.

The third set of allegations was about physical abuse and neglect. In one case, a man worker was working with a mother where the baby was in local authority care, and she alleged that he hit her when he was at her house, so there were no witnesses to the alleged assault. Upon investigation by his seniors, the mother 'changed the story from me actually hitting her to scratching her arms and when they looked at the scratches' and asked her directly, she admitted it was a 'false allegation'. Kieran explained that the mother was 'livid and I don't blame her for being upset' because he had had to advise her of a change of plans with regard to her access to the child. There had been discussions about suspending Kieran prior to the investigation, but this had not happened. While he at first thought the allegation had occurred because he was a man, on reflection 'I truly believe today, that no matter who had picked that baby up, she'd have made that allegation . . . some sort of allegation . . . you know, it was convenient that I'm a fairly big fellow and an . . . allegation of actually hitting me did cause some to stir.'

The last case was the only one to involve a woman member of staff in a family centre. She was out walking with a family, two parents and a child. The child climbed up on a bench and fell off the back. The parents complained that the member of staff should have taken responsibility for the child, despite the parents being present, but as Vera said 'the parents were there, so it was actually their responsibility to look after their child, it wasn't mine'. The complaint was investigated by the centre but not upheld.

We have given some detail about these complaints and allegations because they give some idea of the climate in which childcare takes place. Although sexual abuse by men workers was not reported, half of our ten institutions had had some experience of allegations about staff practice of one kind or another. In one sense, the ability to complain is a mark of accountability, and a method of ensuring that the services children attend are as safe as they can be. On the other hand, the act of complaint involves the disruption of the bond of trust on which parents and institution depend for their mutual relationship (see Chapter 5).

Protection: Dilemmas and Solutions

The British discourses of risk and equality incorporate aspects of both the Scandinavian approach, where men are actively recruited into childcare work and the issue of abuse is minimised and separate from the recruitment issue, and the North American position, where the discourse of risk predominates and men are seen as the culpable gender. In the latter approach, the question of protection is for children, from workers; in the former approach, protection is either seen as not an issue, or it is seen as relevant for both children and workers. One result of this focus on processes and outcomes for children (Finkelhor et al., 1988; Faller, 1988; Kelley, 1994; Kelley et al., 1993; Booth and Horowitz, 1992; Margolin, 1993; Bybee and Mowbray, 1993) is that there is very little material examining the role, and gender composition, of the staff group in childcare centres in developing or carrying out protection (beyond Pringle, 1995). The common characteristics of the two centres which represent exceptions in Britain and are outlined above are a culture of open discussion, policy making and respect for, and incorporation of, the views of parents, staff and children.

This section will return to the title of this chapter and examine dilemmas and solutions posed by the parallel discourses of risk and gender equality in childcare work. The aim, as throughout this book, will be to examine how, when the issue of gender is invoked, childcare practice by workers, their assumptions and ideologies, become apparent: and what was previously buried becomes visible.

In the British context, gender is just below the surface in any discussion of risk in childcare practice. While estimated prevalence figures are not high, men were much more likely to be involved than women. There is no equivalent study to that of Finkelhor et al. (1988) in Britain: as reported earlier in the chapter, a search by Owen and Josephs for allegations of abuse that had reached the courts found only two cases in early childhood services. There is, nevertheless, a discourse of risk around men as childcare workers. This stems from men representing a disruption of normative patterns of childcare as mother-care, and childcare being constructed as like mothering; from evidence of men's abuse of their caring employment in services such as residential care; and from men being the focus of concern about risk in welfare services.

For example, in introducing a 'manager's perspective' to a conference on the 'Abuse of Children in Day Care Settings' (NSPCC, 1994), Walby drew attention to the issue of men workers and said 'the reality is that the prevalence of sexual abuse is widespread and that some very persuasive and apparently very credible men have gained access to, and acquired considerable trust in, situations of working with vulnerable children . . . I do, however, believe very strongly in the need to have mature caring men working in day care settings . . . For me the jury is still out' (NSPCC, 1994: p. 18). The welfare and men as risk viewpoint of the conference was again demonstrated by the Conclusion and Recommendations, one of which urged those working in childcare to 'share concerns and debate *difficult issues*, like, for example, *whether men should work in day care*' (NSPCC, 1994: p. 59) (emphasis added).

There is no doubt that abuse, particularly sexual abuse, and the risk of abuse are highly charged, sensitive areas for discussion among staff groups and at a policy level. As one contributor to the same NSPCC conference put it, the reality of an allegation of abuse against a colleague is devastating:

> deep rifts will develop between you and colleagues, colleagues and managers, and between your agency and others. You will question your beliefs and principles. You will feel incompetent and useless
>
> *(ibid.,* p. 23)

In addition, questions of truth are very complex and sometimes never unravelled due to factors such as the privacy in which abuse takes place, the young age of the children concerned, and the difficulties of using the judicial system. To take an example from the NSPCC conference report again, allegations of abuse against two members of staff involving a number of children attending a day care service were never brought to trial because the judge decided that the 'witnesses (all children) were too vulnerable, and he then declared the alleged perpetrators "not guilty" ' (*ibid.*, p. 55).

Cases that are not dealt with through the courts, and sometimes even where they are, leave unresolved doubts about the truth of the matter. In cases of sexual abuse in childcare services reported in the US, 'dropped charges' is a common outcome for investigations. Finkelhor *et al.* reported that 'in 44 per cent of cases resulting in an arrest, the charges were dropped' (Finkelhor *et al.*, 1988: 232). Commenting on the community response to child sexual abuse, they argued that it 'arouses contradictory responses: anger and fear about its occurrence and the danger it poses to children, but also denial that it can occur and that respectable citizens perpetrate the abuse' (*ibid.*: p. 232). As Bybee and Mowbray (1993) found, these doubts can translate into community divisions that endure. In a case where a US day care centre closed after allegations of abuse against the managers but where a conviction was obtained, 'local key informants estimated that the community was still evenly divided over whether sexual abuse had actually occurred' (Bybee and Mowbray, 1993: p. 279) up to three years later.

These examples illustrate just some of the difficulties of negotiating allegations, investigations and prosecutions for sexual abuse in early childhood services. Given these difficulties, and given the over-representation of men among known cases of sexual abuse in childcare, despite the overall rarity of abuse occurring, some key dilemmas suggest themselves. The two discourses we have identified, that of risk and that of gender equality, may have different responses to these dilemmas.

Dilemma: Should Men Work with Young Children?

From a risk discourse perspective, and as argued by Pringle (1995), men's employment in childcare should be restricted to those situations where children can express themselves clearly, and where they are not likely to have additional problems, such as a history of sexual abuse themselves. This would rule out men working in family centres, and in nurseries. However, the evidence of men's involvement in abuse through childcare services is far more widespread than employment, as Finkelhor et al. (1988) and Margolin (1993) found. In both these studies, men gained access to children as relatives of carers, as volunteers, drivers and in other ancillary positions to childcare. In addition, and as previously noted, men's abuse of children also takes place in the home, so this would rule out fathers, step-fathers, grandfathers, uncles and male family friends. Margolin (1993) also found male adolescents to be responsible for abuse, so these would have to be ruled out, too. The prospect of a male-free world for preschool age children on the grounds of eliminating the prospect of abuse does not seem credible. Moreover, the evidence against men does not seem sufficiently great to warrant it.

The gender equality discourse does not view the question as appropriate. The men and women in this study, both workers and parents, endorsed and welcomed men's contribution to childcare practice. Across the range of settings, some primarily educational, some primarily welfare oriented, the staff and parents did not seem to be preoccupied with issues of risk of abuse. Rather, the discourse sees the employment of men as 'natural', given that fathers (in theory) exist to help raise children. Further, it sees the employment of men as part of a larger project to demonstrate equality between men and women both at work and in the home, with the possibility of changing stereotyped views about what men and women do. As Smedley (1998) noted, invoking the 'natural' is problematic, and may inadvertently reinforce gender stereotypes rather than challenge them. This collision of expectations from the natural was illustrated by the parents and workers in our study (see Chapters 4–6), but use of the idea served to place men's employment as 'taken for granted' rather than exceptional. The evidence from this study, then, and the difficulties of implementing the conclusions of the risk discourse on this question, would appear to endorse men's employment in childcare.

Dilemma: How do we Optimise Protection?

The second dilemma is that given that we believe men should be employed in childcare, how do we optimise the protection of both children and staff? The risk discourse sees men workers as out of control of their sexuality and thus dangerous. The protection of children, and in some cases of mothers attending centres, thus requires men workers to be excluded from certain tasks which afford access to the intimate care of children, such as nappy changing and personal care. Men workers need to be constantly supervised during their working day to restrict their opportunities for abusing children. Bateman (1998) cites an example where a male worker was on loan to another institution and where, as a result of a request from a parent, 'the manager directed the other staff (female) to interpose themselves between the worker and the child so that no interaction could occur' (Bateman, 1998: 170). Another example of working within the risk discourse came from our study, where as Lloyd and Oliver reported earlier, men were excluded from the personal care of young children as a means of avoiding the possibility of allegations from their mothers. In Britain, the Hunt Report (1994), illustrated the need for, and the difficulties of, staff supervision, when it showed that it was possible to sexually abuse children even when in the same room as other adults.

The equality discourse would see these methods of protection as largely undermining the purpose of employing men in the first place. It is difficult for children, and staff, to see men as equal-but-different workers if their position within the workplace is so obviously circumscribed. Rather, attention should be focused on those features of the organisation which facilitate and inhibit abuse. The organisation is central, as the NSPCC conference heard, for the 'abuser will take advantage of conditions where their behaviour is least likely to be challenged' (NSPCC, 1994: 28). A critical factor appears to be the extent to which staff discussion, reflection on practice and debate is conducted and translated into policy. A second factor is the reliance on hierarchy to impose decisions on staff and the disempowering effect this might have (as reported by Barker *et al.*, 1998). Added together, lack of debate and over-reliance on hierarchy contribute to a 'culture of secrecy' in which abuse may flourish. Alternatively, a culture of openness, debate, attention to children's assertiveness skills, the involvement of parents, and developed and critical team working all appear to be factors which inhibit abuse. As will be apparent, none of these organisational features focuses on men. They depend on managerial style and an inclusive approach to protection.

Dilemma: How do we Ensure that Staff are Suitable and Trustworthy?

The risk discourse points to the Warner Report (1992) which concluded that it was not possible to screen out potential abusers using tests such as psychological profiles, as those of sex abusers were not 'significantly abnormal' (Pringle,

1995). Moreover, knowledge about the behaviour and methods of paedophiles suggests that some may take 'determined covert measures' to 'infiltrate', 'often under a cloak of friendliness, innocent charm or altruism' (Hunt, 1994: 185).

In Britain, police checks are available for those who work with children, but, as Local Authority Circular 93 (1) made clear, criminal record checks are limited in their application: they are not required for those working in the private and voluntary sector childcare facilities and 'checks should not be sought in relation to their staff unless special local agreements are in place' (para. 29). The Circular also said that such checks were limited in their scope as a tool of protection:

> It is unsafe to rely on criminal record checks on their own as a means of preventing children being exposed to the risk of abuse. They cannot detect first offenders or repeated offenders who have never been caught. Some of the worst offences of child abuse have been committed by people with no previous convictions.
>
> (LAC 93 (1), para 30).

However, despite these limitations, subsequent guidance has specified more precisely who should be checked: childminders, local authority social services staff with substantial access to children, senior crèche workers; play leaders and workers in play schemes, and staff of voluntary sector provided nurseries and similar facilities should all be considered for police checks. Parents, supervised helpers and ancillary staff should not normally be checked (Tanner, 1997).

It would appear that no means have yet been found to adequately screen the potential workforce to identify child abusers or would-be child abusers. Attention has been paid, however, to good practice in recruitment and selection. This was the focus of the Warner Report (1992) into residential care and the relevance of the recommendations of this report were discussed at the NSPCC conference. The report recommended that meticulous attention be given to every stage of recruitment, selection, appointment, managerial supervision, training and staff care to ensure that appropriate staff were appointed and children's safety maintained (NSPCC, 1994: 21).

Even so, the conference authors remind us that 'these procedures, however meticulous, cannot guarantee the process of screening for staff as potential abusers' (*ibid*: p. 22). As with LAC 93 (1), employers should obtain a full employment history, check references thoroughly and seek an explanation for unexplained gaps and inconsistencies. Further, new employees should not be left on their own with groups of children or an individual child for lengthy periods (LAC 93 (1) para 30). The relevance of these recommendations for recruitment of paid and volunteer staff to voluntary sector organisations was also set out in a code of practice in 1993 (Smith, 1993).

The perspective of the gender equality discourse would concur that all childcare centres recognise the need to have suitable and trustworthy staff, and recognise the importance of good selection procedures. For example, Sataøen (1998) reported on the introduction in Norway of legislation to require all childcare workers to have a Police Certificate with regard to previous offences of child abuse. However, some would argue that care must be taken to ensure that the objective of formal procedures focused on elimination of potential risk is not in conflict with gender recruitment policies. At the Sheffield Children's Centre, for example, where a priority was placed on recruiting men workers, suitable candidates were taken on with fatherhood experience, rather than formal childcare qualifications. On appointment they were given a 'professional and personal development programme', which included active and close support and mentoring from existing staff as well as external training. By this means the Centre has been able to recruit sufficient men to achieve a workforce evenly divided between men and women within three years, and now there is a waiting list for job applicants.

Dilemma: How do we Minimise the Trauma of Child Protection Investigations?

The final dilemma we consider here is this: how do we minimise the trauma of child protection investigations and deal with the issue of 'truth'? Bybee and Mowbray (1993) argued that most investigations are designed to deal with intra-familial abuse and single offenders. Cases of abuse in childcare centres, however, are usually on a larger scale, with more children and more perpetrators involved. 'The details are less predictable and the context is more volatile and more public' (Bybee and Mowbray, 1993: 269). An example of a case of abuse in a childcare centre that widened to encompass numerous adults and children before narrowing to the original suspect was that of the Bjugn case in Norway, referred to earlier. In this case, the inquiry began with an allegation against a male teaching assistant and widened to include concerns about the behaviour of 14 other adults (Satøen, 1998). Thirty-five children were suspected of being sexually abused, and the investigation further widened to include statements from 220 persons and 61 interrogations of 40 children. Then the focus narrowed to dropping all charges except those against the original suspect, who was charged with abuse of ten children but eventually acquitted (*ibid.*). Satøen concluded that 'this is a typical example of a case that has gone off the tracks and then it is impossible to put it straight again' (*ibid.*, 1998: 134).

Not only are external, statutory agency, child protection investigations in childcare services usually complex, they are traumatic for those involved, with differing impacts on differing institutional settings, according to the availability of staff support, established procedures, and preparatory training (NSPCC, 1994). In addition, child protection investigations in centres are likely to generate the attention of the community, sometimes divided, both among parents and further afield (Bybee and Mowbray, 1993). The risk discourse, with its emphasis on men as at risk for being abusers, would see the child protection investigation as a necessary and inevitable tool for uncovering the truth about events leading up to an allegation of sexual abuse. Childcare centres should be prepared in advance for such investigations with training, procedures and support services in place, presumably particularly where men are employed.

The gender equality discourse, on the other hand, would see the culture of the centre as critical to the course of allegations. For example, as noted above by Fozia and Yusuf, allegations can be resolved through internal meetings and discussion with all relevant parties, rather than involving external agencies. In the case of Anne, who called in external agencies even though she felt the allegation was 'minor', she found the experience of investigation so traumatic for all concerned that she would hesitate before doing so again. Allegations have to be taken seriously, evidently, but the authoritative weight of the current organisation of investigation would appear to be off-putting to managers, whose discretion is relied upon in these cases. There would appear to be a need to effect some more subtle investigative instruments to deal with so-called minor cases of suspicion in order that the consequences of the investigation are not so devastating for children as well as staff working in childcare centres.

Summary

In this chapter we have documented the evidence from the literature about the extent of risk to children from workers, both male and female, in early childhood services. Most of this evidence comes from the USA. We compared three perspectives used to address the problem of risk from workers in services for young children, before examining the findings of this study. Issues of physical contact were considered: workers generally saw physical contact such as reassurance of children as an essential part of their job, but some male workers felt they had to operate a personal code of caution to try to ensure their actions were not misinterpreted. Strategies and policies for intimate care of young children among the childcare institutions we visited were discussed; and some detail was given about allegations made against staff. There were no cases of allegations about sexual abuse by workers in the study, but a few cases of allegations about practice. Finally, we documented what we described as four dilemmas in reconciling the issues of gender equality and issues of risk of worker abuse.

As the discussion of sexual abuse progressed in this chapter, issues of gender have become less relevant. This is because it has become clear to us that the issues of gender in childcare practice and the issues of potential sexual abuse in early childhood services must be separated. Examination of the British evidential base for gender (or men) as central to the prevention of abuse do not appear to warrant linking these two features of childcare policy and practice. Both are important, and for both, the solutions may be similar. But we find it difficult to argue that men's place as childcare workers is invalidated because of the incidence of sexual abuse in these centres. There are common themes to both issues that have emerged in this chapter. Central among them, indeed central to the argument of this book, is that staff should engage in critical self-reflection to achieve both a 'gender-conscious' environment in which men's and women's respective contributions are valued, and an environment where the safety and protection of both staff and children are paramount.

Notes

1. Two points about this study are worth noting. 1. 'Substantiated' means that 'at least one of the local investigating agencies had decided that the abuse had occurred and that it had happened while the child was at a day-care facility' (Finkelhor *et al.*, 1988:13). The threshold for substantiation was thus set lower than a court conviction. 2. The authors believe the number of cases they uncovered to be incomplete due to under-reporting and problems with recording systems in certain states. They argued that a better estimate of the total number of substantiated cases would be between 500 and 550 for the three years in question (1983 – 1985).

8

Men in the Nursery: Throwing Light on Gender in Childcare Work

In this final chapter we draw together the findings of the study and the themes we have developed to provide a context for our analysis of gender and caring work with young children. We will first review the evidence presented in earlier chapters and examine the contribution of the study to the literature on men as workers in early childhood services and the wider debate about gender and work. We will then review the themes of the book and suggest ways in which the study has developed our thinking in this area. Finally, we will re-examine the case for and against men as workers in early childhood services and suggest some strategies that might be deployed in the development of a mixed-gender workforce.

A key premise of this book is that the study of men and women workers renders visible what was previously concealed – that work in centres for young children is underpinned by gendered understandings of the job. As we have seen throughout the book, the work of childcare is not only gendered by virtue of the distribution in the workforce, but the ideas on which the work is based are also infused with gendered understandings of roles. In other words, it is not just that the workers are nearly all women, but that through the experiences of men workers compared with those of women, we can see that the work is threaded with ideas about caring as substitute motherhood. This posed difficulties for men workers, whose role within childcare work is seen to be at odds with emulating motherhood, and much less clearly defined, if at all.

However, this study conceptualised gender difference not just as a binary division between men and women, but employed the idea of multiple gender identities in order to lend complexity to the gender categories 'men' and 'women'. This was because both the workers we spoke to, and indications from the literature (e.g., Connell, 1987), emphasised variations within genders as well as between genders. This means that drawing conclusions about 'what men do' and 'what women do' is inevitably a rather too broadly based distinction, and exceptions to general patterns are likely to be found.

Two further points about the study need to be reiterated here. First, there are limitations in the generalisability of the findings of a study of 21 workers:

158

instead we focused on the production of subjective accounts from a wide range of different types of childcare institution. The conclusions we draw are therefore tentative, but are related to the available literature on men and childcare work. Second, because men tend to be employed in childcare institutions as a minority of one or perhaps two, the study, like existing research, was largely limited to an analysis of this situation (only one centre had a workforce equally composed of men and women). The limitation is that this 'token' situation may produce different accounts than in centres where the workforce is more evenly gender balanced.

Reviewing the Evidence

Chapters 1 and 2 provided a context for the study. Chapter 1 set out the ideas, literature and debates we found helpful in developing our analysis and in Chapter 2 we gave a brief account of the extent and organisation of early childhood services compared with services in three other European countries. Chapters 3 to 7 documented the evidence from the study and in this section we review the findings from these chapters on gender in childcare work.

Chapter 3 discussed how men and women enter the childcare workforce and what factors led them to stay or leave the work. We found that there were some clear gender patterns.

Women entering childcare work:

- Most decide while at school/in higher education.
- Some decide while in related employment.
- A few decide while unemployed.
- Link family experience with children to career options while growing up.

Men entering childcare work:

- Many decide while unemployed.
- Formulate individual, philosophical and intellectual reasons for a change of career.
- Interpret wanting to work with children as teaching.
- Do not link family experience with children to career choices.
- See childcare as a second chance career.

Careers in childcare:

- More men's careers than women's were chequered rather than linear.
- Men had a wider range of previous employment experiences.
- Part-time courses attracting mature students may be particularly suitable for men.
- Role of career agencies and advisers and employment agencies critical in supporting changes in career choices.

Support from family and friends:

- Straightforward and committed for women.
- Reaction from some men's families and friends was surprise and incomprehension.
- Where family beliefs and models already supported caring professions, men's choices less exceptional.
- Effects of lack of support diminish with time, seniority in post and evolving peer friendships.
- Views of family and friends likely to be an effective inhibitor to recruiting men.

Ambition:

- Women more likely to stay put than plan to move sideways or up.
- Men, especially those in more junior posts, more likely to plan to move sideways or up than to stay put.
- Centres' ability to nurture skills and ambition has an effect on plans to stay or leave.

In Chapter 4 we discussed gender in the working environment, both among the staff group and working with children. Rather than divergent reporting along gender lines we found that men and women raised issues of gender in different ways. One recurring theme was the men's experience of feeling Other.

Staff conditions:

- Most workers in childcare centres were paid below the national average for women.
- Pay was lower in private day nurseries and in the workers' co-operative than in public and voluntary sector childcare centres.
- Few staff were members of trade unions or professional associations.

After work social life:

- Men did not participate as much as women.
- Encouraged in only two institutions.

Staff meetings:

- Few opportunities for critical reflections on practice issues such as gender or a man's role as a worker.

Staffrooms:

- Seen as a forum for women's talk.

- Men's styles of communication and subjects of conversation often marginalised.

Working with children:

- Sometimes women assume men are not competent.
- Required time to build up mutual trust between men and women.

Support from managers:

- Nearly all workers found managers supportive.
- Being able to solve problems more important than managers' gender identity.

Support from staff teams:

- Most workers felt supported by their staff teams.
- Both men and women saw support as a necessary part of the work.

Sources of satisfaction and dissatisfaction:

- Both men and women valued intrinsic reward derived from working with children.
- Both men and women find work low paid, devalued and at times stressful.
- A few could find nothing bad about their jobs at all.

Jobs and skills:

- Women believed jobs shared out equally.
- Men were asked to do different jobs from women.
- Men were sometimes expected to like particular types of play.
- Staff planning and discussion helped to raise awareness of gender patterns.

Children:

- Gender seen as rarely generalisable.
- Seen as having individual rather than gender based differences.

Men and women meeting children's needs:

- Some saw men's and women's practice as indistinguishable.
- Others saw employment of men as challenging gender stereotypes; replicating gender roles in families; compensating for father absence or father behaviour.

Role models:

- Women modelling a professional worker.
- Men modelling aspects of masculinity or personality.
- Posed dilemmas for men – how to reconcile expectations of others' with own gender identity.
- Very difficult for a sole male worker to realise varied objectives of role models.

Chapter 5 discussed practice with parents. We found that men and women workers did report different experiences of working with parents.

Building a relationship with parents:

- Straightforward for women, more difficult for men.
- Gender presence can be a barrier to success in the job of communicating with parents, e.g. parents can withold information about children from men.
- Men are not only not women, also not mothers.
- Some subjects of conversation seen as beyond men's remit.

Working with fathers:

- Fathers do not visit centres as often as mothers.
- Some fathers raised more objections to men workers than mothers, particularly on religious or cultural grounds.
- Employing one or two men on their own had not encouraged fathers; perhaps requires a more structural approach.

Parents' views about men workers were discussed more extensively in Chapter 6. The main points were:

- More than 80 per cent of both mothers and fathers were in favour of men workers.
- Men workers seen as useful role models for boys; for demonstrating gender equality to children; for children of lone mothers.
- Management entrusted to recruit and screen suitable workers.
- A few parents emphasised possibility of men abusing children in nurseries.
- Fathers were less likely to visit and be involved with centres than mothers.
- Men workers' skills noted as fun; physical; spontaneous; women's skills seen as in-depth caring and nurturing; planning and taking fewer risks.

In Chapter 7, the issue of risk to children's health and wellbeing from staff behaviour in childcare centres and its relationship to gender was discussed. Both men and women workers in this study:

- Saw physical contact with children as an essential part of providing emotional reassurance and security.

But:

- Some men had been told not to cuddle children.
- Some men felt they had to operate a personal code of caution.
- Some men felt open to accusations of misusing touch.

And:

- Some believed that managerial and supervision arrangements could facilitate or help inhibit the possibility of sexual abuse occurring: such arrangements were seen as critical to prevention strategies.

On the basis of the evidence presented by the workers, we argued that:

- Policies for witnessing intimate care such as nappy changing need to be part of a whole-centre approach including children's assertiveness and staff discussion and reflection on practice.
- In the two cases of child 'molestation' reported, men workers felt accused, regardless of the actual allegation.
- Investigation of allegations by child protection agencies was a shattering experience for whole staff groups.
- Issues of gender in childcare practice and issues of sexual abuse should be seen as separate and distinctive and each given attention.

On Men and Caring Work

How do these findings relate to the existing literature on men working in early childhood services? While our findings on men's routes into and through childcare centres are largely supported by other studies, some of the evidence on men working in centres does diverge. Two examples of this are role models and men workers encouraging fathers to visit centres. As we saw in Chapter 4, the literature on men employed in caring work with young children supports the idea of men workers as role models for children, but our investigation of the type and meaning of role models suggests a rather more confused picture. While the women saw themselves as professional role models, the men were seen as modelling aspects of their personality or perceived masculinity, and could be asked to be different kinds of role models in relation to children in differing circumstances (such as boys, or children living with lone mothers). A lack of clarity about what the men were to model, and when, may perhaps be related to a lack of a wider consensus about men's and fathers' roles with children. By contrast, there appears to be a clearer societal consensus about women's roles with children.

On the matter of men encouraging fathers, another point on which the literature has previously been agreed, the evidence in Chapters 5 and 6 suggested that employing a sole, or virtually sole, male worker was unlikely to make much impact on fathers visiting centres without a more structural and wide ranging approach to gender issues within the centre's practice, and including male and female workers. This brings us to a main theme and conclusion of the book: that opening up issues of gender in the workforce for critical discussion is related to wider centre-based issues of reflexive practice: making gender visible requires a consciousness of gender as a practice issue with consequences not only for the recruitment and retention of the workforce, but also for the achievement of objectives such as demonstrating diversity and equality to children, and, not least, ensuring that protective strategies are in place for children and workers.

We have situated this study in a British context on men in caring work which we defined as encompassing elements of both a Scandinavian-led discourse focusing on measures to achieve gender equality and a North American-led discourse emphasising men working with young children as a potential risk to children's well-being. The workers and parents in this study by and large supported the former discourse, although they were aware that, and felt the issues of, risk had to be seriously addressed.

Employment Trends May Encourage Men into Caring Work?

As we have seen, men workers in childcare remain very much in a minority, even in Scandinavian countries which have emphasised gender equality in employment and childrearing, although recruitment campaigns have recently raised the proportion of men students quite considerably. Despite the Scandinavian evidence, a question is raised about the extent to which it is feasible to encourage a mixed-gender childcare workforce. Crompton (1997) reviewed the evidence on changes in men's and women's work and suggested that the sexual division of both domestic and waged labour will be further eroded as more jobs are created in the service sector, thus paving the way for the recruitment of men into caring work of all kinds, including children.

Crompton (1997) made three main points to support her suggestion about gendered employment trends. First, she argued that more men are undertaking unpaid domestic work, particularly when women work full time. Second, increasing numbers of women are moving into full-time managerial and professional occupations and there are increasing numbers of two-earner households overall. More service sector jobs, such as caring work, will be created to support dual-earner households. The third point Crompton made was that men will move into these service sector jobs as they are created. A conclusion we can draw from these trends is that employment conditions are shifting in the direction of supporting men working in early childhood services.

Moreover, the social and political conditions may be more accepting of men as early childhood workers. Crompton cites evidence of attitude surveys that show a growing rejection of traditional stereotypes about men's and women's roles in the family and in employment (*ibid.*, 1997: 139). This would accord with the views of parents in this study who largely supported the practice of employing men workers, and of the views of childcare lecturers, many of whom saw the employment of men childcare workers as a measure to increase and demonstrate gender equality (Cameron, 1997b). The policy conditions for encouraging men workers can be seen in the government's White Paper on childcare which included an endorsement of the positive role male carers can offer children and childcare work (DfEE, 1998, and see Chapter 2).

Subjective Experiences May Inhibit Men as Workers in Childcare

While the objective conditions for the recruitment of mixed-gender workforces may be shaping up in favour of men workers, one of the findings of this study is that the experiences of men working within childcare centres where nearly all the staff are women differ from those of women. While the apparent disadvantage of being a minority gender is to some extent compensated for by their more complex and focused career goals, distinct features of men's subjective employment experience as a marginalised member of a staff group, or Other, are worth noting. This experience of being Other was reported by workers as spanning men's recruitment into childcare work, their initial reception by staff teams, their work with children and interaction with parents, and their response to allegations against staff practice. Length of experience in post and the approach adopted to issues of gender by the institution as a whole can ameliorate the negative effects of these subjective experiences, but we argue that such experiences may interact with men's career goals and affect their willingness to stay working with children.

The Themes of the Book

There were four main themes of the book: caring work constructed as mothering-work; an analysis of gender incorporating the self and multiple gender identities; gender visibility in childcare work and reflexive practice; and gender equality in caring work and resistance to men as caring workers. The process of analysis of evidence from workers and parents has helped our thinking on these themes and here we will briefly review what seem to us some central points.

Caring Work as Mothering Work

We have argued throughout the book that the predominant ideology of motherhood has informed and shaped understandings of how caring work in early childhood services is constituted. We noted in Chapter 1 that the ideology has contributed to limited policy measures with respect to the development of early childhood services, with an emphasis on parental responsibility, on part-time attendance in early education services and on mothers' availability to young children. Caring has been led by a nurturing model, nurturing itself being principally defined as like mothering. Early childhood services have to a greater or lesser extent been seen as offering mothering substitutes, and an obvious demonstration of this is the virtually all female workforce; women are the visible carers and women proxy mothers. The emphasis within a nurturing model of care is on adult expertise and interpretation of the world, and the dependence of young children on this knowledge in order for them to make sense of their world.

There are alternative constructions of care within childcare centres as we outlined in Chapters 1 and 5. It is possible to understand the worker not in relation to a mothering type role, but as either a pedagogue, focusing on young children's early learning, or as a gendered pedagogue, explicitly exploring the role of gender difference. In both these understandings, the child can be seen as a co-constructor of her or his environment, where their active participation in constructing knowledge and identity is seen as central, and where the role of the adult shifts from a nurturing model of adult expertise to engaging with the child in this process of construction. By rejecting the idea of mother-emulation or being a care technician, the link between the worker and the parent in understanding the purpose of the worker is uncoupled. Instead the worker can be seen as a researcher of young children's experiences and learning processes.

There may be a connection here between the working styles of men reported in this study and such a shift in the workers' role. For example, where differences between men and women workers were noted, men were described as 'playful', 'spontaneous' and 'fun'. These kinds of attributes could be meshed with theories of workers as co-constructors to develop new models of workers' methods with young children that are less reliant on a model of nurturance derived from, and informed by, ideologies of motherhood. Such an evolution of understandings of caring work is akin to the Norwegian debate on 'masculine caring' discussed by Nilsen and Manum (1998) (see also Cameron, 1997c), which could also be seen as moving away from an understanding of care as mother-care.

Another aspect of the ideology of caring as mother-caring is an emphasis on a one-to-one relationship between caring workers and particularly infants. We saw in Chapter 5 that this can have consequences for men workers' relations with parents. Men's relations with parents can take longer to build, and may be punctuated by regular challenges to their credibility as a worker or as a man, because their gender identity is so unexpected. For example, one strategy employed by parents to challenge the credibility of male workers may be to withhold essential or detailed information about a particular infant from a man and make it available only to a woman worker. But being able to relate confidently to, and be trusted by, parents is critical to workers' success in the job of childcare, and so such strategies may make the work more difficult for male workers. The one-to-one relationship can thus offer different experiences of work to men and women, with the potential for men workers to feel isolated or marginalised in the experience of caring work.

Incorporating the Self and Gender Identities

A second theme of the book was the self and identity. Throughout, we explored ideas of the salience of gender as a part of identity, both for children and for workers. We explored the idea of *difference* and showed how a tension exists for workers between being different from each other and being the same as each other. Difference implies apart from, Other, and distanced, not necessarily valued in a team approach to working; and sameness implies being as one, as in 'we treat them all the same'. Sameness implies eradicating difference, and, as difference is often considered on a par with discrimination, sameness is valued in a project of equality – or non-discrimination.

Such questions of sameness and difference apply to categories of 'children' or 'workers' and avoid the category of gender. More valuable is the elevation of the individual, particularly individual children, but also to some extent workers, as having needs which require itemisation and satisfaction. We argued that a focus on individuality was part of a larger project within childcare and endorsed in children's legislation on the idea of meeting the child's needs which ties in with theories of attachment and childcare as replacing the mother. So sameness and individuality are claimed by workers to be the salient ingredients of identity within the childcare workplace.

However, the experience of men workers showed that in many circumstances they feel themselves to be different from women workers, despite the rhetoric of sameness. We noted these circumstances above in the summary of findings. Differences occurred both in how men got into the work, how they interacted with staff, children and parents when in the work and differences were structured around the type of centre and particular career path of individual men. Other factors, such as the religious and cultural background of parents, also shaped how difference was experienced.

It is clear that workers' identities are not just dependent on gender, but gender in a context. We found the theories of Connell (1987; 1995) particularly helpful in providing this contextual, multiple perspective on gendered identities. The context of childcare work is structured by policy (both national, such as legislation and guidance, and local, such as internally devised ways of working), notions of 'tradition' and the 'natural', and underpinned by dominant ideologies of caring. Men workers' gender identities emerged in relation to this context: their difference or novelty set them apart from women workers in ways that were not clearly articulated but drew on notions of playing, friendship, affection, demonstrating values such as being decent, nice or trustworthy, and, pushed further, of challenging stereotypes about men's behaviour in the home and with children.

In contrast with the women, whose role in childcare was said to be both professional and 'natural', the men were not expected to emulate domestic, parental roles with children, to be substitute fathers. So while women's gendered identities within childcare are drawn from mothering and caring work, men's gendered identities in childcare work are evolving and as yet undefined in relation to dominant ideologies of fatherhood or parenting.

Policy measures could potentially be used to help shape men's gendered identities: our evidence showed that one childcare centre (Sheffield) had focused on gender as an issue and had included attention to differences between men as well as 'men' as a category (we also know of another centre, Pen Green, which has done this). National policy measures to date have recently encouraged the idea of men childcare workers (DfEE, 1998: 2.25), but not recognised any differences between men, or between men in the different settings in which childcare exists.

Our analytic task, then, sought to integrate three features of the interrelationship between work identity, sense of self and institutional practice. First, the importance workers placed on individuality and sameness in their construction of work identity; second, an understanding of ideological constructions of gendered roles (drawn from parenting); and third, the policies and practices of particular childcare institutions. The concept of multiple gendered identities seemed to us to hold the potential to integrate these three features, so that gender is seen as salient to work identity, but salient in terms of multiple sources of gendered identity, namely masculinities and femininities (Connell, 1987, 1995), and subject to ongoing review and change in particular work environments.

Discussions of sameness and difference led us to discuss individuality and identity; it also led to a discussion of the experience of being Other. The concept of Other was discussed in Chapter 1. As described above, the experience of being Other was seen as a distancing or isolation from the work group on account of gender or gender plus other factors, such as being new, or being a manager. Being Other was a male phenomenon in childcare work. No woman reported feeling on the outside of the staff group, or marginalised in day-to-day practice through her gender. Being Other seemed to be an effect of gender: it was more than being physically different from women, it was an assumption of different behaviour, of not fitting in with 'tradition', of being less predictable as a worker, of the unknown.

Bauman made the point that the 'usual fashion [is to use] a mirror to paint the image of the Other' (Bauman, 1997: 28). But the Other can be seen as an oppositional force, its effect being to reinforce the self, the 'normal' or 'natural', by the example of difference. The challenge of the Other is to avoid its assimilation and to respect heterogeneity (Levinas, cf. Dahlberg et al., 1999). In the context of childcare work, women workers' approach to men as Other took two forms: either assimilation of men, ignoring any differences; or confronting the Otherness and challenging, or undermining, their differences. The men's sense of Otherness helped define their subjectivity or identity of being a worker. Being Other was not, therefore, reciprocally reported by women workers, and being Other was an experience in being peripheral. Centres where there had been a conscious attempt to respect heterogeneity were also those where men were not constituted as, or constituted themselves as, Other, such as at Sheffield Children's Centre. The effect of interrogating gender was to release the men workers from the isolation felt by their colleagues in other centres.

A further aspect of the self which may become incorporated into the gender identity which workers bring to their childcare work is sexuality. Dunne (1997) argued that 'doing gender', or articulating gender differences, involves creating a tension between genders and this is at the heart of the construction of heterosexual relationships. Differences between genders can become translated into needs and dependencies and become eroticised. Doing gender, then, overlaps with doing heterosexuality. Furthermore, Dunne argued that negotiating gender equality by challenging gender relations challenges not only notions of 'fairness', but also one's sense of gender identity. Through the lens of sexuality, then, it is possible to gain deeper insight into the significance of gender difference. Dunne argued that in same sex settings there is less pressure to affirm gender difference and less awareness of gendered individuality (*ibid.*, 7). In this study, women workers in particular, in the gender majority at work, emphasised 'sameness'. But for men workers, the 'difference' (compared with the majority) is perhaps more evident.

Although none of the respondents in this study mentioned their sexual identity as relevant to their work identity, or others' perception of their sexuality-plus-work identity, work in the US has shown that men doing childcare work can represent a transcendence of gender appropriate categories. This is linked to an everyday perception of men's (hetero)sexuality as questionable (King, 1994). Men who work with young children, then, are sometimes seen by others, such as parents, as 'abnormal' which is translated, pejoratively, into 'homosexual' (*ibid.*).

There are two points, then, about sexuality as relevant to ideas about the self, gender and work identity. First, a focus on sexuality as a dimension of gender relations makes explicit that gender encourages difference, and, in so doing, heterosexuality. Second, transgressing gender appropriate categories can be seen as a comment on individual sexuality. In a sense, sexuality is a highly personal dimension of a work identity that can be negatively appropriated by others.

Gender Visibility and Reflexive Institutions

The third main theme linked the production of gender as a practice issue with the style of management and approach to reflexivity in childcare institutions. This was outlined in Chapter 1 and the opportunities gender issues afford for reflexive discussion of workers' roles and experiences were referred to throughout the chapters presenting evidence from our study. The importance of discussion in childcare work has been noted by others (Vernon and Smith, 1994; Penn, 1997).

What we have uncovered is the difficulty men and women workers have in realising their different approaches without adequate opportunity for discursive practice and, moreover, the contrast, in terms of the recognition of gender, in childcare institutions where reflexive discussion is inbuilt into the working week. Discursive practice might involve, on the model developed by early childhood institutions in Reggio Emilia, employing both staff time and tools to examine and problematise staff practice as a group. Dahlberg *et al.* (1999) outlined features of discursive early childhood work in Reggio Emilia as including a practice of documenting work with children, the support and training role of peripatetic specialist staff as well as regular opportunities for analysis and reflection on practice.

We have argued that discursive opportunities are the essential, but initial, starting point for the 'opening up' of gender. As important is the use made of these opportunities. Staff meetings were variously described by workers in this study as being sometimes unconstructive, insensitive, subject to being hijacked by minority interests, or plain boring. Reports from workers suggested that meetings were more or less exclusively used for business and administration purposes, with little or no time for extending understandings of what the work constituted, or subjective experiences of doing the work. On the other hand, meetings could be seen as enabling and supportive where the managerial style encouraged this and where the views of all were seen as important. In these circumstances masculinities and femininities have a chance to flourish, as do other sources of identity such as cultural backgrounds and practices. We argue, then, that the workers in this study provided evidence of too few opportunities to reflect on practice.

Critically, a constructively discursive environment stimulates consensus about local policy, and can act as a protector for the unusual or Other. An example from the study was the issue of parents' objections to male workers. A work setting where there is no culture of discussion leaves a man worker isolated when a parent objects to his employment, and very much dependent on the individual support of his manager. A man in the same situation working in a centre with an institutionalised means of resolving disputes between parents and the centre removes the focus from his individual performance onto staffing policy: debate is conducted at one remove from the man concerned, so offering him the support of the institution.

Lastly, making gender visible and subject to reflexive debate enables questions about the purpose and ethos of caring work to emerge. Questions such as what caring consists of, and whether it looks like care modelled on parental care or another form of caring, could be asked. Questions about the role of the institution and of the workers in upholding 'traditional' or 'alternative' models of caring could be addressed. Aspects of the reported benefits of male workers, such as 'role models', could be related to parental roles. Questions about how centres work with children relates to men's and women's roles with children in wider society could be identified. The scope exists, then, for the childcare centre to occupy a critical and central place in civic society, as we suggested in Chapter 1. It seems to us, though, that a necessary first step is for institutional practice to recognise the importance of considered debate and reflection in the working week of childcare.

Gender Equality and Resistance to Men

A fourth theme of the book has been about resolving the dilemmas of a discourse of equality and one of risk. In the search for gender equality in the workforce, women moving into 'men's work' and vice versa is one method of demonstrating equality. But, as Cockburn (1987) noted, there is an extra dimension of resistance to men moving into caring work. There is an issue of poorer pay and conditions generally being attached to women's work, but Scandinavian evidence, where pay and conditions for childcare work are broadly similar to less gendered work such as teaching, suggests that pay is but one aspect of a multi-facted problem of how to attract men into the field (Hauglund, 1999).

We have argued that resistance to men workers is, at least in part, a product of constructing the work as something women are 'naturally' good at, while men are 'unnaturally' suited to the work. Workers and parents in this study expressed the idea of resistance to men workers at varying points. For example, men workers reported surprise and incomprehension on the part of family and friends; and shock and curiosity on the part of parents to their presence. Another point of resistance to men can be seen in the interpretation of men's sexuality and sexual orientation towards children when they work in childcare. While the equation of male workers with homosexuality was not reported in this study, it has been in other studies (King, 1994; Tobin, 1996). Moreover, an assumption that men workers will be either sexually abusive or paedophiliac in tendency pervades public debate about men with children and as early childhood workers (Cameron and Moss, 1998) although the workers and parents in this study were not, on the whole, preoccupied by the possibility of sexual abuse in their childcare centres.

However, the issue of safety and risk is a potent one in Britain and requires a measured approach. Ensuring children's safety is the paramount purpose of the regulation of childcare services in Britain (DoH, 1991: 4.9). In Chapter 7 we considered the issue of men workers and sexual abuse and showed that although there is very little evidence of men's sexual abuse of children in childcare institutions, the fear of risk of abuse is widespread, and this fear was seen in various incidences of allegations reported in the childcare institutions we visited. In particular, men workers' practice altered in response to this perception of risk. They reported being extra cautious in their physical contact with children, and in their use of communication strategies with colleagues to try to ensure they were not left unsupervised with young children.

We concluded, however, that it is important to separate out the two issues of men workers' recruitment and the protection of workers and children. Joining them inevitably views males as *the* risk to children and this both overlooks potential female abuse of children and exaggerates the evidence that men as a whole pose a risk. In fact, as the allegations itemised to us showed, complaints were made against women workers and children as well as men workers. It seems to us that both children and workers need policies and working practices that offer both protection from untrue allegations and sensitive methods of investigating complaints. We argue then, that the issue of safety and risk should not prohibit men workers' employment in childcare. Instead, the issue of safety and risk should be the driving force behind scrupulous and stringent recruitment strategies and well thought out supervision practices (both peer and managerial) for all childcare staff, underpinned by a democratic and discursive environment.

The Case for Men Early Childhood Workers: Strategies for a Mixed-Gender Workforce

We argued in Chapter 1 that our objective was not necessarily advocacy of a particular policy route, but to investigate how and in what ways gender is embedded in childcare practice through the gender identities of the workforce and the reflections on practice of workers and parents. Nevertheless, we feel there is merit, in our conclusion, in setting out the case for a mixed-gender workforce and some strategies for achieving this.

The main reasons for recruiting men into early childhood services were set out, mostly from a Scandinavian perspective, by Jensen (1996). She argued that the benefits of men were: to children by demonstrating gender equality and encouraging recognition of gender differences; to improved staff communication, through recognition and discussion of different, gendered ways of talking and being; to parents, particularly fathers, who should be encouraged into centres through the presence of men workers; to men in general, for whom opportunities to develop their caring side are limited, and who, as workers, could contribute to the gradual eradication of cultural gender stereotypes about roles; and to the labour market, through helping to ensure equal opportunities in employment. Two main arguments against men childcare workers are the possibility of men taking the senior positions – cited by childcare lecturers (Cameron, 1997b) and which to some extent they are doing in private nurseries (LGMB, 1999) – and the possibility of an increased risk of cases of sexual abuse, particularly through the inadvertent recruitment of men with paedophilia to work in childcare centres (Barker *et al.*, 1998).

This study has provided some complexity and depth to the arguments both for and against men in early childhood services. We have argued that in the childcare centres we visited, some of the benefits of men workers outlined above were endorsed by workers and parents, while some were more problematic to achieve and others were not endorsed as we have seen in the discussion in this chapter. Similarly, the case against men workers is not straightforward. The link between gender and sexual abuse of young children, for example, is not clear cut. But it seems to us that while gender as an issue could lead to polarisation of 'men' on the one hand and 'women' on the other, this is not the objective of employing a mixed gender workforce. More men employed in caring work could have consequences for the way caring responsibilities in families are distributed. Finally, we believe demonstrating diversity in the workforce to children through the visibility of men and women both as categories and in their infinite variety, alongside the visibility of people of colour, is an important goal for enhancing the quality of childcare, and could lead, as we argued above, to re-examining how, and for what purpose, caring work is conducted.

It seems to us that if change is wanted in the gender composition of the childcare workforce, a number of steps are possible.

The work:

- A public debate about the purpose(s) of caring work and the pay and conditions for all workers could help positively evaluate the skills required and the importance of childcare work.
- Setting targets for the national recruitment of male students and workers could help make gender a visible issue for colleges and employers. For example, the Norwegian government has a recruitment target of 20 per cent men workers by 2001.
- Develop recruitment strategies that recognise differing career paths into childcare. Careers advice and subject selection in school is important, but some centres have shown how it is possible to recruit adult men with aptitude and commitment and provide them with a training and mentoring programme.
- Focus attention on recruiting men into centres that include 'play' and 'education', and span after-school care as well as preschool age care.
- It may be that recruiting men into a few mixed-gender centres of excellence could provide inspiration for other centres of what can be achieved and avoid the sole or 'token' man situation.

Practice:

- Make gender in childcare visible within institutions. Encourage discussion of men's and women's subjective differences about caring, working together and working with parents. Incorporate men and people of colour into visual displays about caring for children.
- Develop protection strategies for all. Uncouple the perceived link between men childcare workers and sexual abuse of children in young children's childcare institutions. This may exist or have existed in other institutions, such as residential care, and it does exist in families, but the evidence within childcare centres is limited.
- Rethink the nature of the work. Debate the purpose of childcare institutions and examine who is included and excluded, whose needs are served and whose are not. Perhaps there is a case for renaming nurseries 'early childhood institutions' with a focus on childhood rather than parental care needs.
- Develop reflexive practice and consensual policies. This is at the heart of the matter and underpins the rethinking and debating about childcare we have argued for here.

The experience of doing this study and writing this book has shown us that starting from the rather specific theme of men in the nursery leads to broader themes: women in the nursery and men in the home. For it proves impossible, or at least unproductive, to extract one aspect of the gendered nature of caring and consider it in isolation. But looking at men in the nursery does prove productive as a means of exploring gender and care, helping to make the invisible visible and throwing light on the implications of gendered working.

We suggested in Chapter 1 that childcare centres could be understood as 'forums in civil society where children and adults can engage together in projects of social, cultural, economic and political significance'. One of those projects could be to problematise and reconstruct gender roles and relationships, in particular in relation to caring, a project involving children, parents and staff, but also others including policy-makers, politicians and other interested members of the wider community. This does not require that men work in the nursery – although it may well help. It does require a commitment to document, discuss and reflect upon practice, and how it is both the effect, and source, of discourses and constructions around gender. It seems to us that this has been how a few institutions, such as Sheffield Children's Centre, have already chosen to work, with the consequences that they have both men in the nursery and gender as an important subject of reflective practice – in short, making a reality of the childcare centre as a forum for the project of questioning and understanding gender.

Appendix 1

Further details of the male and female workers interviewed:

Table 1: *Duration in post and gender of childcare workers*

N = 21	Male	Female	Total
Under two years in present post	4	4	8
Between two and five years	2	2	4
Over five years	5	4	9
Total	11	10	21

Table 2: *Job titles of men and women childcare workers in rough order of seniority*

N = 21	Male	Female	Total
Nursery Assistants/Nurse	1	2	3
Nursery Officers	2	3	5
Family Aide/Family Centre Support Worker	1	1	2
Day Care Worker/Project Worker/Family Care Worker	3	2	5
Teacher+Coordinator/Nursery Teacher+ Supervisor	2	-	2
Deputy Head of Centre	-	1	1
Head of Centre/ Headmaster/Owner+Head	2	1	3
Total	11	10	21

Table 3: *Gender, marital and parenting status*

N = 21	Male	Female	Total
Single	4	5	9
Cohabiting/married	7	5	12
Own children/step children	6	4	10

Table 4: *Childcare workers' household arrangements*

N = 21	Male and Female
Married/cohabiting with own children	8
Married/cohabiting with step-children	1
Married/cohabiting with no children	3
Single parent with child	1
Single, divorced, own children + step-children	1
Single, living with parents/family	3
Single, living independently	4
Total	21

Table 5: *Childcare workers by gender, age and seniority*

Average age (years) for group of posts	Men (n = 11)	Women (n = 10)
'Basic'	37	28
Senior posts	38	34

'Basic' included the following job titles: nursery officer, nurse and assistant, project and support worker, family aide and family care worker.
'Senior' included the following job titles: senior teacher, teacher plus supervisor, manager, deputy, owner, headteacher.

Appendix 2

Details of the Centres Visited

The criteria for the inclusion of centres in the study were:

- Half the sample to be in London, half to be from outside.
- A mix of types of institution.
- Half the sample of men to be 'new recruits', in post for around two years; half to be 'old hands', in post five years or more.
- A woman member of staff who had been in post a comparable length of time to the man/men.

Using professional contacts in local authorities and the private and voluntary sector, the following centres were found with at least one male employee. They reflect the diversity of England's group childcare provision, although they over-represent the public sector.

- Private sector: two day nurseries that were part of a chain; one in the City, one on the northern fringe of London. One Montessori nursery school in west London.
- Public sector: three local authority day nurseries, one run by the social services department, two run by the education department, all in London. One family centre run by the social services department of an eastern county.
- Voluntary sector: two family centres run by a national children's charity, one to the west of London, the other to the north. One children's centre workers' co-operative, in a northern city.

All the centres were visited between March and August 1997.

Appendix 3

Some Characteristics of the Parent Sample

Household Organisation

Seventy-seven parents took part in the survey of parents' views. This represented 52 mothers/co-mothers and 25 fathers from 51 households. Thirty-five were from couple households, and 16 from lone mother households. In all the lone mother households, the father was not pursued for interview, because of the possibility of encroaching on sensitive post-marital issues or disputes. In nine couple households, the fathers did not make themselves available for interview.

Employment

Table A2.1: *Mothers and fathers and employment status*

	Employed	Unemployed	Student	Other (sick, disabled, voluntary work)	Totals
Mothers N = 52	25	20	4	3	52
Fathers N =25	22	2	1	-	25

Mothers' employment: of 52 mothers/co-mothers, 27 were not earning their own income: of these two were sick or disabled; one was doing voluntary work; four were students; and 20 were unemployed.

Of the 25 mothers who were employed, 19 of whom worked full-time, these job titles were given:

1. high status: consul-general; money market dealer; assistant director of fund management company; personnel officer; legal negotiator; principal officer (social services department); tutor in law; bookshop business manager; charity business manager; photographer/lecturer; administrator; neonatal nurse; coordinator of social work education (university); teacher; social worker; nursing lecturer; nursery teacher; manager of theatre company.

2. low status: medical receptionist; care assistant; supermarket display assistant; supermarket provisions assistant; administrator (social work).

Fathers' employment: of 25 fathers, only three were not earning an income; one was a student, the others were unemployed. The remaining 22 gave the following job titles, 21 of whom worked full time:

1. high status: senior software engineer; head of structured finance in an international bank; global business manager; chartered surveyor; project manager; supermarket deputy manager; quantity surveyor; youth and community worker; development officer for ethnic minorities; assistant psychologist; photographer; personal tax manager; community worker; day centre manager; artist; principal officer (SSD); freelance tutor and translator; maintenance manager.

2. low status: carer; electronics panel wiring; agricultural worker.

Women were much more likely to be not earning a living themselves, and more likely to be in low status occupations. Some of the women not earning were part of a household with a high earner; and some families had no earners. Of the 16 lone mothers, ten were unemployed.

Access to Centres

Household composition was broadly related to the type of centre their children attended. Children of lone mothers were much more likely to be attending public and/or priority access centres such as family centres or local authority day nurseries than to be attending private centres.

Table A2.2: *Household composition and access to childcare centres*

N = 51	Lone mothers	Couples	Totals
Public, priority access (4 centres)	9	10	19
Private access (3 centres)	2	12	14
Mixed access (3 centres)	5	13	18
Totals	16	35	51 households

In summary, the families came from across the range of employment status and household types. There were couple families whose job titles and whose access to private centres suggested an affluent lifestyle; there were lone mothers who were unemployed and whose attendance at priority access centres suggested they were at a material disadvantage. There were also couple families and lone parents whose job title suggested a broad middle range income. Most striking, though, was the concentration of disadvantage, of income and household status, among those attending the family centres and public day nursery with priority access.

Table A2:3 *Age of parent respondents*

N = 77	Mothers	Fathers	Total
under 20	3	1	4
20 – 30	20	5	25
31 – 40	22	11	33
41 – 50+	6	8	14
55+	1	-	1
Total	52	25	77

Children of Parent Respondents

Altogether, the parents interviewed had 97 children between them: three-quarters of the 51 households had one or two children; and only 13, or one quarter, had three or more children. As would be expected, most of the children were under school age: this was the case for two-thirds of the households, although a small minority did have children of over 17 years of age. Of the total of 97 children, 57 were boys, and 40 were girls.

Table A2:4 *Ages of children and proportion of the total who were preschool age*

Age of children	Number	Proportion under 5
Under 1	4	
1 – 2 year olds	27	
3 – 4 year olds	33	64 (66%)
5 – 16 years old	27	
17+	6	
Total	97	97

37% parents had used the centre for one year or less; 25 or 49% had used it for one or two years, and 7 or 14% had used the centre for three or more years.

References

Acker, K. (1991). Hierarchies, jobs, bodies: A theory of gendered organizations. In S. Lorber and J. Farrell (Eds), *The Social Construction of Gender*. Thousands Oaks, CA: Sage Inc.

Acker, S. (1994) *Gendered Education: Sociological reflections on women, teaching and feminism*. Buckingham: Open University Press.

Ærø, L. (1998). Training and recruiting men to work in services for young children: Is it possible to move towards a more mixed-gender workforce? In Owen *et al.* (Eds). *op.cit.*

Arnot, M. (1983). A cloud over co-education: An analysis of the forms of transmission of class and gender relations. In S. Walker and L. Barton, *Gender, Class and Education*. London: Falmer Press.

Arnot, M. (1987). Political lip service or radical reform? Central government response to sex equality as a policy issue. In M. Arnot and G. Weiner (Eds), *Gender and the Politics of Schooling*. London: Hutchinson.

Baldwin, S. and Twigg, J. (1991). Women and community care – reflections on a debate. In M. Maclean and D. Groves, *Women's Issues in Social Policy*. London: Routledge.

Banks, M. *et al.*, (1992). Careers and Identities, Buckingham. Open University Press.

Barker, R., Jones, J., Saradjian, J. and Wardell, R. (1998). *Abuse in Early Years: Report of the Independent Inquiry into Shieldfield Nursery and Related Events*, Newcastle Upon Tyne: Newcastle City Council.

Bateman, A. (1998). Child protection, risk and allegations. In Owen *et al.* (*op.cit*).

Bauman, Z. (1993). *Postmodern Ethics*. Oxford: Blackwell.

Bauman, Z. (1997). *Postmodernity and its Discontents*. Cambridge: Polity Press.

Beauvoir, S. du (1983). *The Second Sex*. Harmondsworth: Penguin (original edition, 1949).

Booth, S. and Horowitz, A. (1992). Child abuse in care settings, paper given at 9th International Congress on Child Abuse and Neglect. Chicago: August/September.

Bowlby, J. (1952). *Maternal Care and Mental Health*. Geneva: World Health Organization.

Brannen, J. and Moss, P. (1988). *New Mothers at Work: Employment and childcare*. London: Unwin Paperbacks.

Brannen, J. (1997). replace with Holterman, *et al.* (1998).

Brannen, J. and Moss, P. (1991). *Managing Mothers: Dual earner households after maternity leave*. London: Unwin Hyman.

Brophy, J. (1994). Parent management committees and pre-school playgroups: The partnership model and future management policy, *Journal of Social Policy*, Vol 23, No 2, 161–194.

Brophy, J., Statham, J. and Moss, P. (1992). *Playgroups in Practice: Self help and public policy*. London: HMSO.

Budge, D. (1995). The stunted careers of the carer sex. *Times Educational Supplement*, 5 May.

Burgess, A, and Ruxton, S. (1996). *Men and their Children: Proposals for public policy*. London: Institute for Public Policy Research.

Bybee D. and Mowbray, C. (1993). Community response to child sexual abuse in day care settings, *Families in Society: The Journal of Contemporary Human Services*, May, 268–281.

Cameron, C. (1997a). A review of staffing in childcare centres in Six Countries, *Early Child Development and Care*, Vol 137, 47–67.

Cameron, C. (1997b). Men Wanted, *Nursery World*, 15 May.

Cameron, C. (1997c). A Man's Place? *Nursery World*, 22 May.

Cameron, C. and Moss, P. (1995). The Children Act 1989 and early childhood services, *Journal of Social Welfare and Family Law*, Vol 17, No 4, 417–429.

Cameron, C. and Moss, P. (1998). Men as carers for children: An Introduction, in Owen *et al.*, (*op.cit.*).

Chandler, T. and Dennison, M. (1995) Should men work with young children? In NSPCC Conference Report, *op.cit.*

Chandler, T. and Dennison, M. (1995). Should men work with young children? In *The Abuse of Children in Day Care Settings*, Leicester: NSPCC National Training Centre.

Christianson, L. (1994). Head Start Male Role Model Child Development Associate Credentialing Curriculum Project, Community and Economic Association of Cook County, Chicago, ED 374 901.

Clarke, S., and Popay, J. (1998). I'm just a bloke who's had kids: Men and women on parenthood. In J. Popay, J. Hearn and J. Edwards (Eds). *Men, Gender Divisions and Welfare*. London: Routledge.

Clyde, M. (1989). Who is the odd man out: Men in early childhood settings, *Early Child Development and Care*, Vol 52, 93–99.

Clyde, M. (1994). *The Attitude of Female Early Childhood Workers in Australia to Male Colleagues*, paper presented to the AERA Conference, New Orleans, April.

Cockburn, C. (1987). *Two-Track Training: Sex inequalities and the YTS*. Basingstoke: Macmillan Education.

Collier, R. (1995). *Masculinity, Law and the Family*. London: Routledge.

Colton, M., and Vanstone, M. (1996). *Betrayal of Trust: Sexual abuse by men who work with children in their own words*. London: Free Association Books.

Connell, R.W. (1987). *Gender and Power: Society, power and sexual politics*. Cambridge: Polity Press.

Connell, R.W. (1995). *Masculinities*, Cambridge: Polity Press.

Crompton, R. (1997). *Women and Work in Modern Britain*. Oxford: Oxford University Press.

Dahlberg, G., (1997). Images of the Child, Knowledge and Learning, lecture given at a Summer Institute of the School of Child and Youth Care, University of Victoria, BC, July.

Dahlberg, G., Moss, P., and Pence, A. (1999). *Beyond Quality in Early Childhood Education and Care: Postmodern perspectives*. London: Falmer Press.

Davin, A. (1978). Imperialism and Motherhood, *History Workshop Journal 5*.

Department for Education and Employment (1998). *Meeting the Childcare Challenge: A framework and consultation document* (Cm 3959). London: DfEE.

Department for Education and Employment (1997). Pupils Under Five Years of Age in Schools in England – January 1996 (Statistical Bulletin, 2/97). London: DfEE.

Department of Education and Science (1972). *Education: A framework for expansion*. London: HMSO.

Department of Education and Science (1967). *Children and their Primary Schools* (the Plowden Report). London: HMSO.

Department of Health (1991). *The Children Act 1989, Guidance and Regulations Volume 2; Family Support, Day Care and Educational Provision for Young Children*, HMSO.

Department of Health (1995). *Child Protection: Messages from Research*. London: HMSO.

Department of Health (1997). *Children's Day Care Facilities at 31 March 1996, England* (AF96/6). London: DoH.

Department of Health and Social Security (1980). *The Needs of the Under Fives in the Family* (the Brimblecombe Report). London: HMSO.

Deven, F., Inglis, S., Moss, P and Petrie, P. (1998). *State of the Art Review on the Reconciliation of Work and Family Life and the Quality of Care Services*. London: Department for Education and Employment, Research Report 44.

Dunne, G. A. (1997). What Difference Does Difference Make? Sexuality and Gender Accountability, Sociological Research Group, Social and Political Sciences, University of Cambridge.

Edwards, R. (1989). Pre-school home visiting projects: A case study of mothers' expectations and experiences, *Gender and Education*, Vol 1, No 2, 165–181.

Elfer, P. (1994). *Parental Views on the Development of Day Care and Education Services for Children Under Eight in England*. London: National Children's Bureau.

Elfer, P., and Beasley, G. (1997). *A Law unto Themselves? A survey of appeals and prosecutions under Part X of the Children Act 1989, concerning childminding and day care provision*. London: National Children's Bureau.

Equal Opportunities Commission (1998). *Facts About Women and Men in Great Britain 1998*. Manchester: Equal Opportunities Commission.

Esping-Anderson (1990). *The Three Worlds of Welfare Capitalism*. Cambridge: Polity Press.

Evans, M. (1998). At all costs, *Nursery World*, 29 October.

Faller, K. (1988). The spectrum of sexual abuse in daycare: An exploratory study, *Journal of Family Violence*, Vol 3, No 4, 283–298.

Finkelhor, D., Williams, N., with Burns, N. (1988). *Nursery Crimes: Sexual abuse in day care*, Newbury Park: Sage.

Foucault, M. (1988). *Politics, Philosophy, Culture: Interviews and other writings, 1977 – 1984*. (L. Kritzman, ed.), New York: Routledge.

Ghedini, P., Chandler, T., Whalley, M., and Moss, P. (1995). *Fathers, Nurseries and Childcare*. European Commission Equal Opportunities Unit/EC Childcare Network.

Gold, D. and Reis, M. (1982). Male Teacher Effects on Young Children: A Theoretical and Empirical Consideration. *Sex Roles*, Vol 8, No 5, 493-513.

Graham, H. (1983). A labour of love. In J. Finch and D. Groves (Eds). *A Labour of Love: Women, Work and Caring*. London: Routledge and Kegan Paul.

Hakim, C. (1996). *Key Issues in Women's Work*. London: Athlone Press.

Hall, S. (1996). Introduction: Who needs identity? In S. Hall and P. du Gay (Eds), *Questions of Cultural Identity*. London: Sage.

Hartmann, H. (1982). Capitalism, patriarchy and job segregation by sex. In A. Giddens and D. Held (Eds), *Classes, Power and Conflict: Classical and contemporary debates*. Basingstoke: Macmillan Press.

Hauglund, E. (1998). *A Norwegian Perspective*, paper presented to a fringe event at the ENSAC Conference, October.

Hauglund, E. (1999). A Norwegian Perspective. In Men and Childcare Scotland, unpublished working paper, January.

Hearn, J., and Parkin, W. (1992). Gender and organizations: A selective review and a critique of a neglected area in A. J. Mills and P. Tancred (Eds). *Gendering Organizational Analysis*. Newbury: Sage.

Hetherington, P. (1998). Nursery staff ran paedophile ring, *The Guardian*, 13 November.

Hill, R. (1990). Involving men in the caring and educational services, *Local Government Policy Making*, Vol 17, No 3, 36–39.

Hilton, G. (1991). Boys will be boys – won't they?: The attitudes of playgroup workers to gender and play experiences, *Gender and Education*, Vol 3, No 3, 311–313.

Holtermann, S., Brannen, J., Moss, P., and Owen, C. (1998). *Lone Parents and the Labour Market: Results from the 1997 labour force survey and review of research*. Report prepared for the Employment Service – draft.

Hubberstey, S. (1993). Should men care?, *Co-ordinate*, May, 5–6.

Hunt, P. (1994). Report of the Independent Inquiry into Multiple Abuse in Nursery Classes in Newcastle Upon Tyne. Newcastle Upon Tyne: City Council of Newcastle Upon Tyne.

Jensen, J.J. (1996). *Men as Workers in Childcare Services: A discussion paper*. European Commission Network on Childcare and other measures to reconcile Employment and Family Responsibilities for Women and Men. Brussels: European Equal Opportunities Unit.

Jowell, R., Brook, L., Taylor, B. and Prior, G. (1991). *British Social Attitudes – the 8th report*. London: Social and Community Planning Research.

Kanter, M., (1977) *Men and Women of the Corporation*. New York, Basic Books.

Kelley, S. (1994). Abuse of children in day care centres: Characteristics and consequences, *Child Abuse Review*, Vol 3, 15–25.

Kelley, S. (1998). Men as childcare workers: Are the risks worth the benefits? In Owen *et al.*, (*op.cit.*).

Kelley, S., Brant, R. and Waterman, J. (1993). Sexual abuse of children in day care centres, *Child Abuse and Neglect*, Vol 17, 71–89.

King, J. (1994). Uncommon Caring: Primary Males and Implicit Judgements, conference paper, ED 375 086.

Kirkwood, A. (1993). *The Leicestershire Inquiry 1992*. Leicester: Leicestershire County Council.

Lather, P. (1991). *Getting Smart: Feminist research and pedagogy with/in the postmodern*. London: Routledge.

Lepkowska, D. (1998). Minister promises to act on boys' failure, *Times Educational Supplement*, 9 January.

Local Government Management Board (1999). *Independent Day Nursery Workforce Survey 1998 England*. London: Local Government Management Board.

Lorber, J. and Farrell, S. (1991). The Social Construction of Gender. Newbury Park, CA, Sage Publications.

MacNaughton, G. (1998). Improving our gender equity 'tools'. In N. Yelland (Ed), *Gender in Early Childhood*. Sydney: Routledge.

Malaguzzi (1993). For an education based on relationships, *Young Children*, No 11, 9–13.

Margolin, L. (1993). In their parents' absence, *Violence Update*, Vol 3, No 9, 1–8.

Maxwell, I. (1995). A man's job?, *Scottish Child*, November/December, 12–13.

Mayall, B. (1996). *Children, Health and the Social Order*. Buckingham: Open University Press.

McQuail, S. (1997). Why is childcare women's work? *Co-ordinate*, November, 4–5.

Meltzer, H. (1994). *Day Care Services for Children*. London: HMSO.

Mooney, A. and Munton, A. (1997). *Research and Policy in Early Childhood Services: Time for a new agenda*. Institute of Education: University of London.

Moss, P., Owen, C., Statham, J., Bull, J., Cameron, C. and Candappa, M. (1995). Survey of day care providers in England and Wales, a working paper from the TCRU Children Act Project. Institute of Education: University of London.

Moss, P., and Penn, H. (1996). *Transforming Nursery Education*. London: Paul Chapman Publishing.

Murray, S. (1996) 'We all love Charles', Men in child care and the construction of gender, *Gender and Society*, Vol 10, No 4, 368–385.

National Society for the Prevention of Cruelty to Children (1995). The abuse of children in day care settings, conference report. Leicester: NSPCC Training.

National Society for the Prevention of Cruelty to Children (1997). Protecting children from sexual abuse in the community: A guide for parents and carers. London: NSPCC.

Nilsen, T., and Manum, L. (1998). Masculine care: The nursery school as a man's workplace. In Owen *et al.* (Eds) (*op.cit.*).

Nobes, G. and Smith, M. (1997). Physical punishment of childrem in two-parent families, *Clinical Child Psychology and Psychiatry*, Vol 2, No 2, 271–281.

Oakley, A. and Rigby, A. S. (1998). Are men good for the welfare of women and children? In J. Hearn *et al.* (Eds) (*op. cit.*).

O'Grady, C. (1998). Please Sir! Where are you?, *Times Educational Supplement*, 1 May.

Owen, C. (1997). Parents' Perspectives. In M. Candappa (Ed), *Policy into Practice: Day care services for children under eight*. London: The Stationery Office.

Owen, C. and Josephs, M. (1996). *Newspaper Evidence of Sexual Abuse in Day Care* (in preparation).

Owen, C., Cameron, C. and Moss, P. (Eds) (1998). *Men as Workers in Services for Young Children: Issues of a mixed gender workforce*. Bedford Way Papers, Institute of Education: University of London.

Owen, S. and McQuail, S., (1997). *Learning from Vouchers. An evaluation of the four year old vouchers scheme, 1996/7, a Summary*. ECU Occasional Papers series.

Penn, H. (1995). The relationship of private daycare and nursery education in the UK, *European Early Childhood Education Research Journal*, Vol 3, No 2, 29–41.

Penn, H. (1996), Three men and a baby, *Nursery World*, 19 September.

Penn, H., and McQuail, S. (1996). *Childcare as a Gendered Occupation*, report for the DfEE/OECD.

Penn, H. (1997). *Comparing Nurseries: Staff and children in Italy, Spain and the UK*. London: Paul Chapman Publishing.

Penn, H. (1998). Summary: Men as workers in services for young children. In Owen *et al. (op. cit.)*.

Preschool Learning Alliance (1998). Minimum wage, under five contact, October, 14.

Pringle, K. (1995). *Men, Masculinities and Social Welfare*. London: UCL Press Ltd.

Pringle, K. (1998). Men and childcare: Policy and practice. In J. Hearn *et al*. (Eds) *(op. cit.)*.

Pugh, G. (1985). Parents and professionals in partnership: Issues and implications. In G. Pugh and E. De'Ath (Eds), *Parent Involvement: What does it mean and how do we achieve it?* Partnership Paper 2, London: National Children's Bureau.

Pugh, G. (1996). A policy for early childhood services. In G. Pugh (Ed.), *Contemporary Issues in the Early Years*. London: National Children's Bureau.

Rawstrone, A. (1998). Flexing their muscles, *Nursery World*, 15 October, 12–13.

Rennie, J. (1996). Working with Parents. In G. Pugh (Ed.) *(op. cit.)*.

Rinaldi, C. (1993). The emergent curriculum and social constructivism. In C. Edwards, L. Gandini and G. Forman (Eds), *The Hundred Languages of Children*. Norwood, New Jersey: Ablex.

Ritchie, J. and Spencer, L. (1995). Qualitiative data analysis for applied policy research. In A. Bryman and R. Burgess, *Analyzing Qualitative Data*. London: Routledge.

Ruxton, S. (1992). *What's He Doing at the Family Centre?: The dilemmas of men who care for children*. London: National Children's Homes.

Saradjan, J. (1996). *Women who Sexually Abuse Children*. Chichester: Wiley.

Sataøen, S.O. (1998). Men as workers in services for young children. In Owen *et al. (op. cit.)*.

Seifert, K. (1974). Some problems of men in child care center work. In S. Pleck and J. Sawyer (Eds), *Men and Masculinity*. New Jersey: Prentice Hall.

Seifert, K. (1984). Career Experiences of Men who Teach Young Children, AERA Conference, New Orleans.

Shephard, G. (1995/6). Putting purchasing power into parents' hands, *Child Care Now*, Vol 3, 3.

Sherriff, C. (1995/6). Vouchers – What they mean for Preschool Education, *ChildCare Now*, 3.

Singer, E. (1993). Shared care for children, *Theory and Psychology*, Vol 3, No 4, 429–449.

Siraj-Blatchford, I. (1996). Why understanding cultural differences is not enough. In G. Pugh (Ed.) *(op. cit.)*.

Skelton, C. (1991). A study of the career perspectives of male teachers of young children, *Gender and Education*, Vol 3, No 3, 279–288.

Smedley, S. (1997). Men on the margins: Male student primary teachers, *Changing English*, Vol 4, No 2, 217–227.

Smedley, S. (1998). Men Working with young children: A natural development? In Owen *et al.* (*op.cit.*).

Smith, D. (1993). *Safe from Harm – A Code of Practice for Safeguarding the Welfare of Children in Voluntary Organisations in England and Wales*. London: Home Office.

Smith, T. (1980). *Parents and Preschool*. London: Grant McIntyre.

Smith, T. (1996). *Family Centres*. London: HMSO.

Suffolk County Council (1998). HERA 2 Interim Report: Child care training in the United Kingdom. Suffolk County Council.

Sundqvist, E. (1998). What happens when men move into female-dominated occupations. In Owen *et al.* (Eds) (*op.cit.*).

Tanner, P. (1997). Vetting workers: Selecting volunteers and paid staff to work with children, *Childright*, No 141, November.

Thoburn, J., Lewis, A. and Shemmings, D. (1995). *Paternalism or Partnership: Family involvement in the child protection process*. London: HMSO.

Thorne, B. (1993). *Gender and Play: girls and boys in school*. New Brunswick: Rutgers University Press.

Tizard, B. (1981). *Involving Parents in Nursery and Infant Schools*. London: Grant McIntyre.

Tobin J. (Ed.) (1996). *Making a Place for Pleasure in Early Childhood Education*. New Haven: Yale University Press.

Vernon, J., and Smith, C. (1994). *Day Nurseries at a Crossroads: Meeting the challenge of childcare in the nineties*. London: National Children's Bureau.

Wallace, W. (1995). A man about the place, *Times Educational Supplement 2*, 13 October.

Whalley, M. (1996). Working as a team. In G. Pugh (Ed.) (*op.cit.*).

Whalley, M. (Ed.) (1997). *Working with Parents*. London: Hodder and Stoughton.

Wharton, A., and Baron, J. (1987). So happy together? The impact of gender segregation on men at work, *American Sociological Review*, Vol. 52, 574–587.

Whelan, A. (1993). *Paying the Price: An analysis of staff turnover in long day care and preschool services in NSW – 1990*. Community Child Care Co-operative Ltd.

Whitebook, M., Howes, C., and Phillips, D. (1989). *Who Cares? Child care teachers and the quality of care in America*. Oakland, CA: National Child Care Staffing Study, Final Report.

Whitebook, M., Howes, C. and Phillips, D. (1993) *National Childcare Staffing Study Revisited. Four Years in the Life of Center-Based Child Care*, Child Care Employee Project, Oakland, CA.

Whitebook, M., Howes, C. and Phillips, D. (1998). *Worthy Work, Unlivable Wages: The National Child Care Staffing Study 1988 – 1997*. Washington: Center for the Child Care Workforce.

Williams, C. (1992). The glass escalator: Hidden advantages for men in the 'female' professions, *Social Problems*, Vol. 39, No 3, 253–267.

Williams, C. (1995). *Still a Man's World: Men who do 'women's work'*. Berkeley: UC Press.

Williams, F. (1998). Troubled masculinities in social policy discourses: Fatherhood. In J. Popay, J. Hearn and J. Edwards (Eds), *Men, Gender Divisions and Welfare*. London: Routledge.

Yates, L. (1997). Gender equity and the boys debate: What sort of challenge is it? *British Sociology of Education*, Vol 18, No 3, 337–347.

Young, R. (1990). *White Mythologies: Writing history and the West*. London: Routledge.

Index